VOICES AND VISIONS

An Integrated Approach to Reading and Writing

Russell J. Meyer

Emporia State University

Sheryl A. Mylan

Stephen F. Austin State University

St. Martin's Press
New York

Senior editor: Karen J. Allanson
Development editor: Mark Gallaher
Managing editor: Patricia Mansfield Phelan
Associate project editor: Nicholas Webb
Production manager: Patricia Ollague
Art director and cover design: Sheree Goodman
Text design: Amy Rosen
Text illustrations: Debra Solomon
Cover art: Steve Barbaria

For information, write:
St. Martin's Press, Inc.
175 Fifth Avenue
New York, NY 10010

ISBN: 0-312-08385-8

Acknowledgments
Acknowledgments and copyrights can be found at the back of the book on page 369, which constitutes an extension of the copyright page.

To our parents:
they taught us to learn.

PREFACE

Voices and Visions is designed to help basic writers develop their individual voices within a familiar social and cultural context. At the heart of our vision is a respect for the abilities of basic writers and a belief that research in the collaborative and social nature of learning, in the stages of cognitive development, and in rhetoric offers effective tools to help them develop their potential.

Critical thinking is best developed by a community of learners making meaning together rather than by individual writers working in isolation. For this reason, we emphasize peer work from the earliest stages of the writing process rather than waiting to introduce students to collaborative activities at the later revising or editing stages. From the outset, students discuss their ideas, their reactions to readings, and their own writing—both their short responses and longer works-in-progress. These activities help them develop the critical and analytical skills they need when examining their own and others' writing. Working collaboratively at every stage also helps students both better understand their own working style as writers and appreciate that there is no single "correct" approach to writing. By examining the work-in-progress of others, students come to realize that there are a variety of successful ways to analyze and respond to a writing situation.

Our goal is to help students communicate successfully regardless of the rhetorical context. By integrating critical thinking, reading, writing, and discussion, and by moving from more familiar worlds of discourse, including magazines and talk shows, to the less familiar world of academic discourse, we can help writers skillfully negotiate these worlds.

OVERVIEW

Voices and Visions is a rhetoric, a reader, and a brief handbook in a single text. The chapters cover skills that every writer needs, including techniques for getting started, ways to distinguish fact from opinion, practices for using evidence from a broad variety of written and oral sources, and methods of audience analysis. Although the chapters are sequenced to move from personal recollection to academic writing, and from coverage of common but serious errors to less troubling ones, we have designed the book so instructors can easily choose among assignments and have easy access to those parts of chapters that best meet the needs of their students.

So that such access is both easy and clear, for students as well as instructors, each chapter is organized consistently around the same set of features:

- *Goals* We start by highlighting the main points covered in the chapter to give the reader a brief overview of the material.

- *Writing Preview* By previewing the major writing assignment for the chapter, we encourage students to have the assignment in mind as they work their way through the chapter. Chapter exercises, readings, and examples are all geared toward the assignment so students have plenty of ideas and material once they begin drafting.

- *Before We Start . . .* This activity gets students writing and discussing their ideas on the main topic of the chapter; here students learn that they already have some ideas on the topic, and they have the opportunity to explore their own ideas and hear the ideas of their classmates.

- *Writing Skills Instruction* Each chapter begins by focusing on a different general writing issue: techniques for getting started, distinguishing fact from opinion, using evidence to support ideas, and so forth. While the discussions are sequenced to introduce these issues in a logical order, instructors can also dip into them as they wish, rearranging the presentation to best suit their own students' needs.

- *Readings* Most chapters include three readings, along with pre- and postreading exercises to help students develop their abilities not just as writers, but also as analytical readers. Critical reading strategies are introduced in Chapter 4 and are presented in exercises throughout the text.

- *Writing Skills Instruction* Following the readings are further discussions of specific writing issues, focusing on such basic skills as paragraphing, writing openings and conclusions, and using appropriate vocabulary.

- *Writing Assignment* Finally, the main writing assignment in each chapter is described in detail, following a standard sequence.

    Summary of Steps provides a checklist that guides students through the drafting process for the chapter's writing assignment.

Student Sample offers a student essay in response to the chapter's writing assignment.

Peer Review encourages students to analyze and comment on each other's discovery drafts with easy-to-use forms provided at the end of each chapter that include specific questions to answer and suggest areas to focus on. A further form,

Writer's Response to Peer Review, asks students to reflect on the reviews they receive and decide how they will revise based on those reviews; this form also allows students to give their reviewers feedback on what was helpful in the reviews.

Revising Your Discovery Draft offers guidelines designed to help students analyze their drafts based on peer reviews and their own rereading in order to make substantial changes as necessary.

Editing Your Draft offers specific editing advice focusing in early chapters on common grammatical problems, such as subject-verb agreement and sentence fragments, and in later chapters on correct punctuation and effective transitions; various methods of sentence combining are also covered in these sections. Practice exercises are included in the text, but, more important, students are encouraged to practice editing skills in the context of their own papers. These sections serve as an integrated handbook, incrementally providing students with instruction in grammar and punctuation while working on their own writing.

Additionally, each assignment sequence concludes with a suggestion for writing a "metaessay" in which students examine the process of completing that assignment, assess their strengths and any areas in need of improvement, and reflect on the conscious choices they made—in effect taking charge of their own development as writers. A concluding self-evaluation form is also provided for students to submit with their final draft.

Throughout each chapter are examples of student writing at various stages of development and a variety of additional individual and group activities for both writing and discussion.

The appendix, "A Survivor's Guide to English," is not meant to be a comprehensive handbook, but a supplement to the integrated handbook. It is a concise guide to help students eliminate common errors without overwhelming them with unfamiliar and arcane rules. We believe that as students develop as writers, they will benefit from more advanced studies of grammar and mechanics; our goal here, however, is to help them write clearly and thoughtfully, free from serious errors that impede communication.

NOTABLE FEATURES

A Conscious Attempt to Engage Students at Their Own Level   Regardless of their writing skills, students respond to and analyze the world in ways that we recognize and respect in this text. We capitalize on the analytical skills they already have, building on those abilities as the students are initiated into the less-familiar community of academic discourse. Most important, we meet students at a familiar level and with a friendly, informal voice. Early chapters focus on popular culture and are marked by many illustrations, bulleted lists, boxes, and sidebars—all designed to appeal to students' visual senses and help put them at ease in using the text. Later chapters are increasingly text-based and focused on more academic issues.

Integration of Talking, Critical Reading, and Informal Writing into the Writing Process   In each chapter students are given the opportunity to discuss, read about, and write informally about that chapter's central topic. Consequently, when they begin to draft, they will already have many ideas and notes to work with.

Full Support for a Collaborative Workshop Approach   Instructors often remark on the difficulties of having students perform peer analysis of one another's writing. Students, they say, sometimes feel uncomfortable participating in such analysis, and the feedback they produce is frequently not especially helpful to the writer. We meet this problem by encouraging group work *throughout* the development of an essay, beginning with the "Before We Start" activity that opens every chapter. We have found that, given the opportunity, students establish a rapport and trust that helps them produce more effective peer analyses. Further, in addition to peer-review guidelines tailored to each assignment, we also offer response guidelines to help students reflect on the review process and the commentary they have received so that both writer and reviewer can improve their analytical skills.

Integrated Handbook   Rather than being treated in isolation from students' writing, most of the text's coverage of grammar and punctuation is integrated into the "Editing Your Draft" section of the Writing Assignment. Each chapter focuses on a different problem or solution so that students can master sentence basics incrementally as they work through the text.

Alternate Table of Contents   An alternate table of contents for the writing skills and the grammar and punctuation issues covered in the text makes it easy for instructors to have access to material as it best suits their classes and for students to find the information they need when it's important to them.

We've both had a great deal of ongoing dialogue while writing this text, and we'd like the opportunity to expand that conversation to include you—both teachers and students—the actual users of the text. We are both available on E-mail for tips on using the book in class or to hear your comments about the text and what is working (or not working) for you. You can reach Russ Meyer at meyerrus@esuvm1.emporia.edu and Sheryl Mylan at fmylansa@titan.sfasu.edu. We would both enjoy hearing from you.

ACKNOWLEDGMENTS

Voices and Visions has truly been an exercise in collaboration, not just by the two of us whose names appear on the title page, but also by dozens of others: reviewers, editors, and students. They all have our gratitude, especially those students in our classes, who cheerfully joined in our experiment and taught us what was wrong with our ideas as well as what was right. We also thank the following reviewers for their insights and suggestions, nearly all of which were incorporated into this text in one way or another: Paul Beran, McClennan Community College; Jo Ann Buck, Guilford Technical Community College; Lillie Fenderson, Seminole Community College; Karen Houck, Bellevue Community College; Sharon Jaffe, Santa Monica College; Jane Maher, Nassau Community College; Nell Ann Pickett, Hinds Community College; Bob Roth, Middlesex County College; Julie Warmke-Robitaille, Sante Fe Community College; and Mark Wiley, California State University, Long Beach.

We also want to thank Karen Allanson at St. Martin's Press for encouraging us from the outset of this project; Nick Webb for his unflaggingly cheerful attention to the many details involved in turning a manuscript into a book; and Christine Kline for her swift and tireless efforts to secure permissions agreements. Mostly, though, we want to express our gratitude and indebtedness to Mark Gallaher, an extraordinary editor, who always managed to come up with just the right question or just the right answer. If there were true justice in the world, Mark's name would appear on the cover of this and a great many other books.

Finally, we want to thank Helga, Hillary, Geoff, and Michael, who have really proven the saying that they also serve who are forced to stand and wait . . . and wait . . . and wait.

Russ Meyer
Sheryl Mylan

CONTENTS

CONTENTS

3 Recognizing Facts and Opinions: *Expressing Your Views*   87

CONTENTS

5   Using Evidence Effectively: *An Essay on Language*   175

CONTENTS

CONTENTS

ALTERNATE CONTENTS

Integrated Handbook

ALTERNATE CONTENTS

VOICES AND VISIONS

An Integrated Approach to Reading and Writing

WORKING TOGETHER

Collaboration

GOALS

In this opening section we'll focus on the following goals:

- Introducing the concept of collaboration—working with others—as part of the process of writing

- Understanding different working styles so that you can collaborate more effectively in your writing

Facing a writing assignment, students react in a variety of ways. Some are concerned about how quickly they can get it over with—how many words or pages will meet the minimum requirement. Some will get started right away; others will put off writing until the last minute because they can't stand staring at a blank piece of paper. This latter group usually includes students who can't seem to think of what to say unless they are given a specific topic and a way to organize it. Others, though, don't want to be given any specific topic; they would rather express themselves freely on a topic of their own choice.

BEFORE WE START . . .

How do you react when you are asked to write a paper for a class? Take a few minutes to write down some of the first things that come into your mind about writing. Don't worry about using complete sentences, correct spelling, or even connected ideas. Just write whatever you think of.

Then talk over your reactions to writing with a small group or your whole class. Do many of you have the same reactions? Are you surprised at how similar or different other people's reactions are?

If you can't think of anything to say, just keep writing something like "how I react to a writing assignment" over and over until some ideas pop into your mind.

COLLABORATIVE WRITING

Many people who may have difficulty writing their ideas down have no trouble talking with others about their views. In fact, most people would probably say that

Talking and Writing

Do you prefer to write or talk about ideas? Why?

What differences between talking and writing make one harder or easier for you?

Would you rather go on a TV talk show and express your ideas or write an editorial for a newspaper?

they'd rather talk about ideas than write about them. It's usually more pleasant to talk through an idea with others than to work alone. Working with others allows us to recognize different viewpoints and to refine our ideas and our expression of those ideas based on the disagreement, support, and advice of others.

In this book we will encourage you to work closely with other students as an essential part of your writing process. Such working together is called collaborative writing, and many writing experts believe that this kind of collaboration is a better way of improving your writing skills than working in isolation.

You're probably more familiar with collaboration than you realize. Nearly everyone has to collaborate with others on the job or even at home when co-workers or family members or roommates work together to solve a problem, make a decision, or get a job done.

Collaborative writing *is:*

- Discussing ideas with others to clarify your viewpoints
- Asking a fellow writing student to read a draft of a paper to note how well it's organized and developed, how clear and forceful it is, what information should be added or deleted, and so forth
- Having a classmate read a revision to see how effective a new version of a paper is and to suggest further areas for improvement
- Having a classmate identify areas in your draft where grammar and sentence structure errors obscure your meaning

Collaborative writing is *not:*

- Telling your ideas to a friend who tells you what to write or who writes part of your essay for you
- Having a friend rewrite the sections that your evaluators suggest that you change
- Having a friend correct your mistakes in grammar and sentence structure

DIFFERENT WORKING STYLES

Collaboration usually involves some negotiation because we all have different working styles.

- Some people need to go off by themselves to think ideas through before they discuss them with a group.
- Some people think best while they're talking to others.
- Some people are good at organizing a job into a series of smaller tasks.
- Some people have trouble organizing a job but can carry out the tasks when someone else has done the organizing.
- Some people have trouble giving advice, while others are able to offer advice freely.
- Some people are able to accept advice easily, while others take offense at any advice and regard it as a criticism.
- Some people talk a lot; others prefer to listen and speak only when they feel they have something really important to say.

All of these factors come into play as you collaborate when you write—whether you're talking over ideas, completing a group task, or making suggestions to each other about your writing.

Before you begin the serious work of collaboration in this course, you might want to think about your own habits and preferences when working with others as well as about what you most admire and find most difficult about the habits and personalities of others when they work with you.

GROUP ACTIVITY

First, take ten minutes or so working alone to list some of the ways you work best.

Then compare your list with the lists of other members of your group. Discuss how your differences in working style might be used to complement one another in your group.

GROUP ACTIVITY

As a group, consider the following situations:

Situation A   You are a member of a group in which another member tends to dominate all discussions, assert his or her own ideas and opinions very forcefully, and ignore the ideas and opinions of others. The other members of the group are intimidated and uncomfortable speaking their mind.

Situation B   You are a member of a group in which most members talk freely but one seems to have trouble speaking up—because of shyness, lack of understanding, or some other reason. Your group tends to ignore this person.

Situation C   You are a member of a group in which a couple of other members don't take the tasks of the group seriously—they don't do the work they are supposed to, spend their time joking about the class or talking about other things, and make it difficult for you to get your work done.

As you and your group or class discuss these three situations, try to come up with some ways that individual members of the group might be able to improve each situation. You might do some role-playing, having one student play, for example, the dominating student in situation A or the quiet student in situation B while others assume roles as other members of the group.

When you have finished your group discussion, take fifteen minutes or so on your own to write out your ideas about the role you generally assume in groups and how you might have the most positive effect on any group you are a part of.

CHAPTER ONE

GETTING STARTED

A Writer's Autobiography

GOALS

To help you write a writer's autobiography, we'll concentrate on the following goals in this chapter:

- Using prewriting strategies to generate ideas and details for your writer's autobiography or for any other writing assignment. These strategies include

    brainstorming

    clustering

    freewriting

    making tree diagrams

    keeping a notebook of ideas

- Being specific and making your writing more effective by using relevant details

Writing Preview

Using what you learn in this chapter, you'll write a brief paper about a personal experience that influenced your attitude toward writing, using specific examples so that your reader can clearly understand what the experience was like.

Handwriting

At the grade school I went to, students learned to print in the first grade and then began to learn cursive writing in the last half of the second grade. But my second-grade teacher got sick over the Christmas break, so we had a substitute for about two months. She was old and crabby and made us start writing cursive all at once, without any practice. I hated it. I had so much trouble forming my letters that that's all I could think about, not about ideas. Even now, years later, I think my handwriting is awful, and I get stuck for ideas whenever I try to write, just like I did then.

Rochelle Thomas

BEFORE WE START . . .

What memories do you have about your early experiences as a writer? Take ten minutes or so to jot down your earliest or most striking memories of writing.

In a group or with your class, share your experiences. Do different students seem to have had any similar experiences? Are most people's early experiences with writing basically positive or negative? Why do you think this is so?

If you can't think of anything to write, you might want to read the strategies for getting started now.

A Chore

I remember writing as a chore because every time I got presents, I had to write thank-you notes. Since our family was so large, I got a lot of presents from my aunts and uncles and grandparents. It seemed to take forever to write the notes. But we had to write them before we could use any of our gifts. That's fairly easy when I get presents I really like, for example, money or a tape that I've wanted for a long time. It's a lot harder, though, to say something interesting about socks or new underwear.

Even now I still see writing more as something I have to do rather than something I do just for fun. I have to write research papers and reports for school, and, of course, I still have to write those thank-you notes.

Geoff Allen

STRATEGIES FOR GETTING STARTED

Just about every writer finds that one of the hardest things about writing is getting started. Some people think that you have to have everything you want to say in mind before you start writing. But that doesn't allow you to expand new ideas and change directions if you wish. And if you think you have to have everything planned out before you write the first word or if you wait for inspiration before you start, you may just give up when nothing occurs to you.

Getting started is difficult, even for people who've been writing for years. But experienced writers have some tricks to help them get started, whether they're working in a group or by themselves. Here are five of those tricks:

- brainstorming
- clustering
- making tree diagrams
- freewriting
- keeping a notebook of ideas

All of these processes can help you when you've been assigned a topic and don't think you have a thing to say about it. These techniques will help you see that you probably have a lot more to say than you think you do.

They will help you look at a topic from new angles and get more ideas than you actually need, so you can select the best from among them, arrange them in the order that you prefer, and use them in your essay.

Brainstorming

When you brainstorm, you just write down things as they pop into your head. (Because you list these ideas and thoughts, brainstorming is sometimes called list-making.) Some of the things you write down may be only vaguely related to your topic; others may be precisely what you'll end up writing about in your paper. As its name implies, though, brainstorming should be a period in which you just let ideas explode, without any attention at all to where they came from, how they're related, or whether they're going to help you write your paper. All you're trying to do is get ideas down on the page so that you can consider them later.

Don't bother writing out full sentences; if you do that, some of the ideas will get away while you're writing down others. Just use key words or very short phrases.

Once you have your brainstorming list, you can go back over it and eliminate some items, add others as they occur to you, and number the list to indicate the order in which you initially think you'd like to use them.

Here are the results of Rochelle Thomas's brainstorming list of memories about writing:

high school papers

learning to print

playing school with friends

bad handwriting

cursive writing in 2nd grade

my sister's a good writer

passing notes in class

boyfriends

love poems

diary

no ideas

Some of these ideas and details were used in Rochelle's paragraph, but many weren't. Rochelle wrote them down as they occurred to her, in no particular order.

Brainstorming with Your Group

*Y*ou can brainstorm by yourself, of course, but sometimes it helps to do it with a group. When you brainstorm as a group, make sure that at least one

Continued

Continued

member is writing every idea down.
Here are some other things you need to
remember:

■ Accept every idea that's offered.

■ Don't try to evaluate your own ideas

or anyone else's; just write them all
down.

■ Feel free to combine or modify ideas.

■ Allow the ideas to keep coming until
no one has anything left to offer.

You can keep adding to your list until you get an idea to write about and enough
details to develop it.

Clustering

Clustering is a way of organizing ideas. In clustering, you try to show the relationships among ideas by linking them with lines. In effect, you draw your ideas on
the page. Start by putting your main idea in the middle of the page, and circle it. (If
you aren't sure what your main idea is, start by putting some key words from the

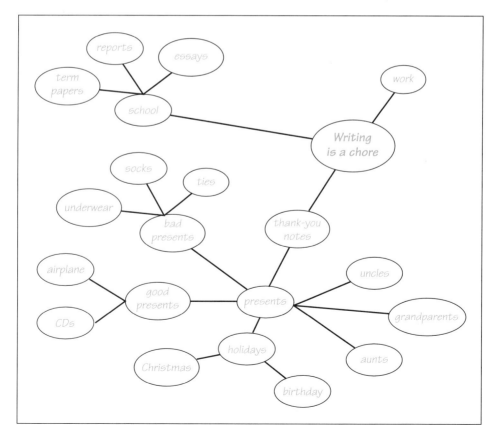

Clustering with Your Group

Sometimes you can cluster with your group to help you come up with more ideas or to see ideas in a new way. There are several methods of group clustering, but the easiest way is to use "sticky notes" (such as Post-it Notes). Working alone, each member of the group writes ideas on the sticky notes, one idea on each note. After each of you has written down all the ideas you can think of, one member of the group puts his or her notes on the board. Here is some group clustering on Geoff's idea of writing as a chore.

Then another group member puts notes up, sticking ones that seem similar together and starting new groups with those that don't seem to fit elsewhere.

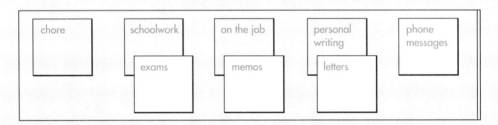

Then another group member does the same.

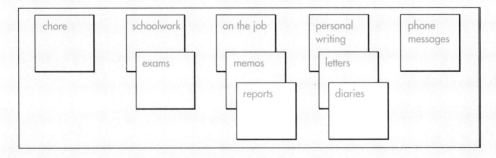

Once everyone in the group has put up all of his or her notes, members work together to see how the various notes fit together.

assignment in the middle of the page.) Then write down related ideas, also inside circles, and draw lines connecting them.

Geoff Allen did some clustering about his memories of writing. Since his first memory was that writing was a chore, he began with it near the center of his cluster.

Notice that Geoff's cluster had the most related details about thank-you notes, not about writing for school or work, so this was the idea he decided to write about. When you cluster your ideas in this way, you can more clearly see the relationships among them. In fact, you might even try clustering the ideas you come up with from your initial brainstorming. That might help you come up with some new ideas and see more easily how the ideas are related.

Making Tree Diagrams

Tree diagrams are also visual representations showing how items are related. To make a tree diagram, start with your main idea halfway down the left side of the paper; next to it, list details to explain or support that main idea, leaving plenty of room on the right side. Next to these details, list more specific details or examples, drawing lines to show the connections. If these more specific details have further examples, list these too. See the tree diagram that Alesia Plata did on writing for school.

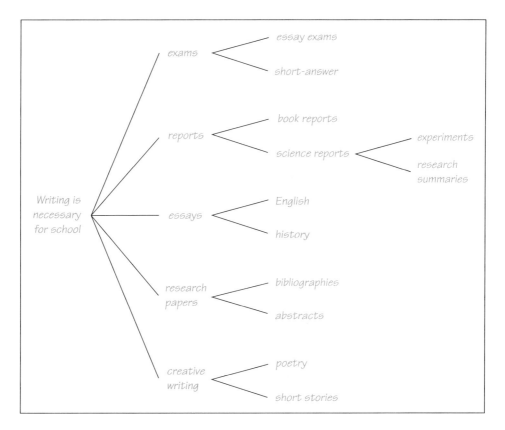

Sometimes you'll work from a brainstorming list or a cluster to develop a tree diagram; sometimes you'll just start with a tree diagram. Starting with a cluster or a tree diagram works especially well if you already have a good sense of the connections among items and just want to clarify them before you start to write.

Freewriting

Freewriting means pretty much what it implies: writing without any attention to details or connections. You don't even worry about how the ideas get into your head. Freewriting is something like brainstorming, but you keep writing continuously. There are two main tricks to freewriting:

- Always give yourself a set amount of time (usually ten minutes or so—longer isn't often very helpful).
- Continue writing for the full period, even if you can't think of anything to say. If you're completely stuck, just write over and over "I don't know what to say," write down rhymes for words you've already written, or just rewrite your last word. Eventually something will jump into your mind.

After you've finished your freewriting, you may be surprised at how much you've had to say. Use your pen or a highlighter to mark the ideas you might want to work with in your paper.

Here's an example of freewriting about memories of writing:

I'm supposed to write about my memories of writing. That seems like a silly thing to do. Writing about writing. Well I remember the time I wrote a play for my church youth group. It was for Mother's Day and it was supposed to be about relationships between mothers and children. I think people were surprised because I wrote about conflicts instead of sappy stuff. I used to write letters to my parents trying to explain how I felt about things, like when I felt like I couldn't talk to them or we'd had a fight. I can't think of anything else to say. Fight. Night. I used to write a lot late at night alone in my bedroom. But I can't really remember what kind of stuff. Poems I guess and papers for school. School writing was always boring. They made us write everything in five paragraphs, beginning, middle, and end. Send letters. I don't write letters much now. I don't really write anything except when I have to.

Keeping a Notebook of Ideas

You might find it useful to jot down your ideas about a specific subject or assigned topic in a notebook at various times of the day, when they occur to you. If

Sometimes Inspiration Strikes, and Sometimes It Doesn't.

other things occur to you while you're writing down those ideas, by all means feel free to write them down, too. But the main function of the notebook (it might actually be a few pages in a notebook you're using for this or some other class) is to give you a place to record your thoughts on a particular subject or topic. This will help you keep your thoughts focused on the subject for at least a few minutes each day. And it will help you avoid putting off all of your writing until the very last minute.

Some people find it useful to keep a daily journal to record their thoughts; a journal can give you practice in writing as well as preserve ideas that you can later develop into essays. Whether you keep a daily journal or a notebook of ideas for a specific assignment, the main point is to allow your ideas time to form. But you can't just wait for inspiration to strike. You have to be thinking about your topic if you're going to say anything worthwhile about it. That's what keeping a journal or a notebook of ideas on the topic will help you do.

READINGS

In the following essays, three very different writers recall times when writing was important to them. As you read these essays, pay particular attention to the details that the writers include.

LEARNING TO READ AND WRITE
Malcolm X (with Alex Haley)

In this selection from his autobiography, Malcolm X tells about his early attempts to write letters to his friends from prison. Because he was unable to express himself, Malcolm came to see the importance of learning how to be a better writer and reader. Perhaps more important, he came to appreciate the power of words to help him further his own causes.

1   I've never been one for inaction. Everything I've ever felt strongly about, I've done something about. I guess that's why, unable to do anything else, I soon began writing to people I had known in the hustling world, such as Sammy the Pimp, John Hughes, the gambling house owner, the thief Jumpsteady, and several dope peddlers. I wrote them all about Allah and Islam and Mr. Elijah Muhammad. I had no idea where most of them lived. I addressed their letters in care of the Harlem or Roxbury bars and clubs where I'd known them.

2   I never got a single reply. The average hustler and criminal was too uneducated to write a letter. I have known many slick sharp-looking hustlers, who would have you think they had an interest in Wall Street; privately, they would get someone else to read a letter if they received one. Besides, neither would I have replied to anyone writing me something as wild as "the white man is the devil." . . .

3   It was because of my letters that I happened to stumble upon starting to acquire some kind of a homemade education.

4   I became increasingly frustrated at not being able to express what I wanted to convey in letters that I wrote, especially those to Mr. Elijah Muhammad. In the street, I had been the most articulate hustler out there—I had commanded attention when I said something. But now, trying to write simple English, I not only wasn't articulate, I wasn't even functional. How would I sound writing in slang, the way I would *say* it, something such as, "Look, daddy, let me pull your coat about a cat. Elijah Muhammad—"

5   Many who today hear me somewhere in person, or on television, or those who read something I've said, will think I went to school far beyond the eighth grade. This impression is due entirely to my prison studies.

6   It had really begun back in the Charlestown Prison, when Bimbi first made me feel envy of his stock of knowledge. Bimbi had always taken charge of any conversation he was in, and I had tried to emulate him. But every book I picked up had few sentences which didn't contain anywhere from one to nearly all of the words that might as well have been in Chinese. When I just skipped those words, of course, I really ended up with little idea of what the book said. So I had come to the Norfolk Prison Colony still going through only book-reading motions. Pretty soon, I would have quit even these motions, unless I had received the motivation that I did.

7   I saw that the best thing I could do was get hold of a dictionary—to study, to learn some words. I was lucky enough to reason also that I should try to improve my penmanship. It was sad. I couldn't even write in a straight line. It was both ideas together that moved me to request a dictionary along with some tablets and pencils from the Norfolk Prison Colony school.

8   I spent two days just rifling uncertainly through the dictionary's pages. I'd never realized so many words existed! I didn't know *which* words I needed to learn. Finally, just to start some kind of action, I began copying.

9   In my slow, painstaking, ragged handwriting, I copied into my tablet everything printed on that first page, down to the punctuation marks.

10   I believe it took me a day. Then, aloud, I read back, to myself, everything I'd written on the tablet. Over and over, aloud, to myself, I read my own handwriting.

11   I woke up the next morning, thinking about those words—immensely proud to realize that not only had I written so much at one time, but I'd written words that I never knew were in the world. Moreover, with a little effort, I also could remember what many of these words meant. I reviewed the words whose meanings I didn't remember. Funny thing, from the dictionary's first page right now, that "aardvark" springs to my mind. The dictionary had a picture of it, a long-tailed, long-eared, burrowing African mammal, which lives off termites caught by sticking out its tongue as an anteater does for ants.

12   I was so fascinated that I went on—I copied the dictionary's next page. And the same experience came when I studied that. With every succeeding page, I also learned of people and places and events from history. Actually the dictionary is like a miniature encyclopedia. Finally the dictionary's A section had filled a whole tablet—and I went on into the B's. That was the way I started copying what eventually became the entire dictionary. It went a lot faster after so much practice helped me pick up handwriting speed. Between what I wrote in my tablet, and writing letters, during the rest of my time in prison I would guess I wrote a million words.

1. Malcolm X says that trying to write letters made him want to learn more about how to express himself. What reasons do you have for wanting to express yourself better?

2. What other ways could Malcolm X have used to acquire his "homemade education"?

3. Besides reading a dictionary, how else can a person improve his or her vocabulary, reading, and writing skills?

A HOUSE IS NOT A HOME
Hillary King

Hillary King is the daughter of a writing instructor, so it's probably not surprising that she likes to write. She didn't get her appreciation for writing from her father, though, but from another writer whose name she forgot a long time ago. She remembers what that writer told her, however, and in this essay she recalls that significant experience.

1   I became interested in writing at a very young age. I was quiet and shy and never had much to say to anyone, but my feelings and ideas were expressed through pen and paper. My favorite kind of writing as a child was creative writing. I took this as my chance to tell the world my dreams and fears through pseudonyms and fictional characters.

2   When I was nine, I trusted my fourth-grade teacher with a few pieces I had been working on. She said she was entertained with my overrun imagination. She also told me about a young writer's conference where students my age could get together and hear published writers talk about writing. I thanked her but thought I could find a better way to spend a Saturday morning. I just enjoyed making up stories—not sitting in an uncomfortable chair listening to some old guy grumble about subject-verb agreement and parallel structure.

3   On my way home from school, I began thinking about the authors of the books I enjoyed reading—Judy Blume, Beverly Cleary, Shel Silverstein. I thought about how much I enjoyed their stories and how, when I read them, it didn't seem like work. I wondered if those were the kind of authors that would be at this convention. If they know how to make their stories that interesting, I thought, surely they could make a lecture interesting, too. I decided to go.

4   Well, come the convention day I was a little disappointed. Judy Blume was not there, and neither was Beverly Cleary or Shel Silverstein. But since I was already there and had met a lot of kids who enjoyed writing almost as much as I did, I stayed and listened to what the authors had to say.

5   The convention was very well organized, and every half hour our group would move on to hear a new writer speak. The last period of the

day, I was moved with my group into a small room. In it stood a slender man with a beard and moustache, making last-minute adjustments to his speech.

6   "Hello, boys and girls," he greeted us.

7   He introduced himself and gave the same little speech we had heard half a dozen times since this morning about how wonderful writing can be. Then he threw in a twist.

8   "Stories are more than just words thrown together," he said. "Words are more than just letters thrown together. You must also consider the tone or the mood of your ideas."

9   He let that idea sink in and then asked the class, "Can anyone tell me the difference between a house and a home?"

10   We all looked around at each other, thinking that was a silly question.

11   "They're spelled differently."

12   "They have a different number of letters."

13   "They sound different."

14   "One has two vowels and the other has three."

15   Everyone guessed at the difference, but no one could seem to find the correct answer. Finally, we gave up.

16   "Class," he explained, "the difference between a house and a home is in the mood or the tone. A house is the structure—the wood, the bricks, the lighting fixtures, the refrigerator. A home is the love and warmth and comfort you feel as you walk through the door."

17   I've kept that statement in my memory ever since that day. Writing is more than just filling up a blank piece of paper with words; it's about expressing your ideas with clarity and the appropriate mood. And that's why I like it.

POSTREADING EXERCISE

1. Hillary King's favorite kind of writing as a child was "creative writing." Did you like to write as a child? If so, what kind of writing did you enjoy? If not, do you know why?

2. How would you define creative writing as opposed to other kinds of writing?

3. Try to list several other combinations like "house" and "home" that mean almost the same thing but are really quite different.

MY MOTHER'S STEAMER TRUNK IN THE ATTIC
Dorothy Regner

In this essay, Dorothy Regner writes about her childhood some fifty years earlier and a very private and special place that she lost when she was young. Because of the pain she associated with this loss, she also lost all enjoyment in writing for many years.

1   My mother's steamer trunk was a treasure to me, and I cherished it. It was filled with the things my mom brought from Europe: a feather quilt her mother-in-law gave her as a wedding gift, her wedding dress, even the shoes and a beautiful lace scarf she wore over her hair when she was married. She had all the pictures of her family there, and of my father, too, who died when I was very young. I'd give anything to have the pictures and all of her treasures today, but they're all gone now.

2   I made the attic where my mom kept her steamer trunk my personal domain; I wouldn't even allow my sister to come up there with me. She was not as sentimental as I was, and she didn't even care about the trunk and all the things in it. She was too young to remember our father, too, so I guess those things weren't as important to her as they were to me. I asked my mother many times to tell me all about her and my father, how they met and fell in love. She told me all about him and about all the things in the trunk, but she warned me not to talk about him or the steamer trunk when my stepfather was home. It was some time before I found out why.

3   I always loved school and hated vacations, even short holidays, because being home was no pleasure for me. I liked to help my mother with work, but when I was home from school I spent most of my time upstairs in the attic with that old steamer trunk and all its memories. That's what made me happy. I even kept the dress there that I made for myself when I graduated from grade school, and sometimes I'd take it out and look at it and remember how hard it was to sew and how proud I was to wear it on that special day.

4   I did a lot of writing and reading then, and a lot of fantasizing. We were poor, and real life was dull for me. I did a lot of dreaming and wondering about the world. I used to write about the trains that went along the tracks near our house, making up places that they went to and imagining what it would be like to be there. I wrote about everything that came into my head, and I kept all my stories with my mother's memories in her steamer trunk.

5   One day my little stepbrother Johnny was upstairs in the attic with me; I was trying to help him with his arithmetic, but he was not trying very hard. He got angry at me and told me that his father—my stepfather—had told him he didn't have to listen to me. When I argued with him and tried to get him to work harder, he swore at me, using the same words we heard his father use so often. I slapped him across the mouth, and he started to cry.

6   His father came up the stairs to see what caused all the commotion. When he got mad at me and started shouting and swearing, I told him that he was a rotten excuse for a father and that he should clean up his language so his son wouldn't imitate him. He shouted some more and took Johnny and went downstairs, leaving me alone in the attic. I just stayed there looking through that old steamer trunk and crying and wishing my real father were alive.

7   The next day, before I got home from school, my stepfather took everything from my mother's trunk outside and burned it. All my writing and my graduation dress and my mom's wedding dress and even the beautiful quilt. They were all gone.

8   My mother was devastated, and so was I. With all my writing gone, I lost my desire to write. I didn't write after that except when I had to, and I never enjoyed it again. Frankly, I think my mother died of a broken heart because she never seemed to get over losing all those things that meant so much to her. And neither did I.

POSTREADING EXERCISE

1. Her mother's steamer trunk of treasured possessions made Dorothy Regner want to learn more about her family's past. Do you have any objects that connect you to your family's past? What are they, and how do you feel about them?

2. Why do you suppose the destruction of the steamer trunk caused Dorothy Regner to stop writing?

BEING SPECIFIC

It's OK when you're talking to say something like "Turn that thing this way about this much." After all, you can point to the "thing" and even use gestures to indicate how it should be turned. But when you're writing, you need to be more specific: "Turn the handle clockwise a quarter revolution." Writing needs to be more detailed than face-to-face conversation.

Details actually show your readers what you mean rather than making them guess or fill in the blanks on their own. Look at the following paragraph, for example:

I work and go to school, so I'm always really busy. It always seems like I'm trying to do two things at once. When I'm at work I'm thinking about things I have to do for school. And I never have any time to just relax or even sleep much.

The writer here gives us some information, but it isn't very specific or detailed. What does he mean by "work" or "go to school"? How many hours does he work? Does he go to school part time or full time? What does he mean when he says that he doesn't have time to relax or that he doesn't "even sleep much"? These are all the kinds of questions you might ask the writer if you were speaking with him, and they ask for information readers have a right to expect.

Here's a more detailed version of the same paragraph. The added details are indicated in italics.

I work *forty hours a week as a grocery clerk,* and I go to school *full time,* so I'm always busy. It always seems that I'm trying to do two things at once, *like memorize battle dates of the Civil War while I make my dinner or try to figure out a calculus problem while I bag groceries.* And I never have time *to go to a movie or a party with my friends* or even to get more than *five hours* of sleep a night.

Details help make writing clearer and more interesting because they give read-

Details Make a Difference.

ers specific information to help explain general points. Here's another paragraph without enough details:

> I began receiving writing assignments in my classes and was very proud of the work I handed in. When I got my papers back, however, I was appalled. My precious work was all marked up.

What does the writer mean by "all marked up"? We can guess, but will we guess that the teacher suggested changes in the wording, the content, the grammar, or a combination of all three? There's no way to tell. Cassandra Storz, the writer of this paragraph, later revised it to include more details so that her readers could tell exactly what she meant.

> I began receiving writing assignments in my classes and was very proud of the work I handed in. When I got my papers back, however, I was appalled. My precious work was *covered with red marks—criticisms and suggestions. My nouns and verbs didn't agree; I wasn't using enough specific details; I had used run-on sentences and fragments.*

The italicized words make clear precisely what the marks on Cassandra's paper were. By adding these details, Cassandra keeps her readers from guessing, perhaps incorrectly, what she means—and makes her paper more effective.

GROUP ACTIVITY

Look back at one of the readings appearing earlier in this chapter. Underline the specific details the writer uses that make general statements clearer and that contribute to your understanding of the writer's experience. Then write a sentence or two explaining why these details are effective. Finally, discuss your responses with your group or class.

You can add details to almost anything you write, but you have to be careful that the details you add actually fit with your topic and are important enough to justify including them. No matter what you're writing about, keep in mind that you need to *focus closely on the details that are important for your purposes.*

Let's look at the use of detail in the following two paragraphs.

> When I start to write, the worst part is staring at a blank piece of white paper. It's eight-and-a-half inches wide and eleven inches long and has thirty-five blue lines on it. And I know I need to fill every one of those lines. The paper is smooth to the touch, except if I run my finger along the edge. But I really feel

bad if I can't write what I mean on the paper. When I get especially frustrated, I take that piece of paper and crumple it into a ball about one inch across. It makes a rustling sound when I crumple it but not much sound at all when I throw it in the trash. Last week I got really frustrated with an essay and ripped the paper into thirty-two pieces.

Here's another version of the same paragraph.

When I start to write, the worst part is staring at a blank piece of white paper. My mind just goes blank when I see that blank paper. Sometimes I get so frustrated with the few words I've written on the page, or more likely with what I haven't been able to write on the page, that I rip the paper out of my notebook, crumple it up, and toss it in the trash. If I'm really upset, I rip it into tiny pieces and throw them on the floor.

Both of these paragraphs have a lot of detail. In fact, the first paragraph has more than the second. But not all of it seems important to the idea that the writer is trying to develop—her frustration with writing. It really wouldn't matter if the lines on the paper were green instead of blue, and in her frustration she might rip the paper into twenty pieces or forty. The point is that she has trouble filling the pages and is frustrated about it. The size of the paper, the color of the lines, how many of them there are, and how many pieces the writer tears the paper into aren't the kinds of details that help us understand the writer's frustration. So when you're writing, keep in mind that what's important is not just adding details but adding *relevant* details.

GROUP ACTIVITY

Read the following paragraph; then consider what kinds of details you could add to make the italicized words more specific. Together with your group or class, make a list of the details; then decide which of them would be relevant to the paragraph.

Everybody in my family writes *a lot*. My younger sister writes *regularly* in her diary about her *feelings*. My brother writes about *various activities* for his high school newspaper. My mother writes to *some of her family members* about our family's *important events* and *accomplishments*. Both my parents have *reports* and *letters* to write for their *jobs*.

INDIVIDUAL ACTIVITY

Look at what you wrote earlier about your memories of writing. Pick out a spot where including more details would help readers understand that experience more clearly. Then brainstorm to make a list of additional details, as many as you can. Finally, review your list to decide which of the additional details are most relevant and which are not really important.

DISCOVERY DRAFTS

As we said when we discussed strategies for getting started, beginning writers often assume that they need to know exactly what they're going to say before they start writing. This is what causes some people to sit staring at a blank page, unable to write the first word. If I don't know everything I'm going to say, their thinking goes, then I can't say anything.

There may be some people who begin by knowing exactly what they want to say. But for most of us, the only way to get started writing is to write, and sometimes you need to write to find out what you have to say. You write to discover. And that's what a discovery draft is all about.

For each writing assignment in this book, we're going to ask you to begin by writing a discovery draft for your essay. In this first draft, you should not worry about correctness; just try to get your ideas down on paper. You'll revise it later to take care of getting just the right words each time, making your sentences as clear as possible, checking for spelling errors, and so forth—but not in the discovery draft.

We also provide an opportunity for you to share your draft with peer reviewers in your class who can suggest ways you might improve the draft to convey your ideas more effectively. And, of course, you'll act as a peer reviewer for other writers' drafts, too. When you complete the peer review forms, answer each of the questions as thoroughly as possible so the writer can understand exactly what you have in mind. Try to avoid one-word or short-phrase answers—and don't just praise the writer. Try to provide information that will actually help him or her improve the paper.

Student Sample

Here's a discovery draft written by one of our students, Cassandra Storz. Read this draft; then complete the practice peer evaluation on pages 27–28. What advice would you give Cassandra about her discovery draft?

DISCOVERY DRAFT 1
Cassandra Storz

1   I use writing to work through my emotions. I have spilled out my deepest fears, my highest aspirations, and my biggest crushes to my notebooks. Writing has always held many purposes for me, but the biggest reason I write is to vent my feelings. I enjoy having this "friend" to "listen" to me. I also like to imagine characters and events and write about them. When I was little, I used to dream about becoming a professional writer, someone whose work would never be forgotten, like Mark Twain or John Steinbeck.

2   I began receiving writing assignments in my
classes and was very proud of the work I handed in.
When I got my papers back, however, I was appalled.
My precious work was covered with red marks—suggestions for improvement and criticisms. I recovered
from that slap in the face and learned that this
sort of constructive criticism, although intimidating, was necessary to help me become a stronger
writer.

GROUP ACTIVITY

Share your practice peer review with your group or class. Discuss the suggestions that you and other members of your group or class made. What changes should Cassandra make to improve her paper? Remember, the purpose of a peer review is to help the writer produce a more successful essay, so don't hesitate to suggest changes that will make the paper clearer and more detailed.

WRITING ASSIGNMENT: A WRITER'S AUTOBIOGRAPHY

Write a paper about an experience with writing that has influenced your attitude toward writing. Take just one experience and use as much pertinent detail as you can to show your reader what this experience was like.

Summary of Steps

Here's a summary of the steps to take in completing this assignment. Check them off as you finish each one.

_____ In a few words, list as many experiences as you can remember that influenced your attitudes about writing. Consider such things as learning to write the alphabet, a school writing assignment, a teacher's praise or discouragement, writing or receiving letters, or writing on the job.

_____ Note as many details as you can about one of these experiences, using one (or more) of the prewriting strategies on pages 9–15.

_____ In your draft, describe the scene, the action, and the people involved as fully as necessary, as well as your thoughts and feelings. Be sure to use specific details in your description.

PRACTICE PEER REVIEW: A WRITER'S AUTOBIOGRAPHY

Writer's Name: _____*Cassandra Storz*_____

Reviewer's Name: _____

First number the paragraphs of the work you are reviewing. Then write out your answer to each of the following questions. Use the paragraph numbers for reference.

1. What single experience does the writer focus on in this paper? (If there is more than one experience, tell the writer which experience might prove most interesting, judging from the information in the discovery draft.)

_____

_____

_____

_____

_____

2. What words or phrases gave you the impression that this experience is the focus? (If there is no central focus, are there words or phrases that suggest an experience the writer could focus on?) List two or three of them here.

_____

_____

_____

_____

_____

3. What additional details would help you understand more clearly the experience that the writer is writing about?

_____

_____

_____

_____

_____

4. Point out any sentences that give information or details that do not seem to fit in the paper.

_____

_____

_____

_____

5. How many paragraphs are there? Does each one deal with just one topic?

_____

_____

_____

_____

Student Sample

Here's another example of a writer's autobiography by one of our students, Marte Gomez. Notice how Marte focuses on one kind of writing experience, writing letters to friends and family.

JUST PRETENDING
Marte Gomez

1   When I was little, I couldn't wait to learn how to write. It seemed like so much fun to write letters and receive them from friends. My mom used to write a lot of letters to her family and friends in Mexico. When she sat down at the kitchen table to write her letters, I'd sit there too and pretend to write. She'd give me a page of her stationery, which always had pretty flowers on it. I'd make circles or jagged lines across the page and make believe that I was writing. I'd pretend I was writing to my grandmother, my cousins, and my friends who had moved away. After I scribbled my letter, I'd "read" it to my mother. She always praised me and sometimes she'd even include my letter to my grandmother in the one she wrote to her.

2   Later, after I actually learned how to write, I wrote real letters to my friends and family. I bought my own boxes of pretty stationery and continued to write letters at the kitchen table with my mother. Now that I've started college and have a job too, I don't seem to have as much time to write. I tend to call my friends who live away, although occasionally I still write to them, especially about my most personal feelings. Even though it's fun to talk to my friends by phone, nothing beats getting a letter.

Peer Review

Once you have your complete discovery draft, you're ready to start peer reviews. Here's a recap of what you need to do.

- Exchange papers with a classmate.
- Be alert to what the writer both succeeds at doing and is having trouble doing.
- Write your peer review, using one of the forms on pages 31–32 and 33–34.
- Talk over your review with the writer for a few minutes.
- Go through the whole process with another classmate.
- After reading the peer reviews of your own draft, complete the Writer's Response to Peer Review forms that follow the Peer Review forms. These will help you decide how to follow any good suggestions from reviewers when you revise your discovery draft and will help your reviewers understand how they can provide the most effective information for you.

Revising Your Discovery Draft

By now you should have a small stack of paper: your notes, your completed discovery draft, and peer reviews written by two of your classmates. With these, you can start revising the discovery draft into the final version of your paper—the one you're actually going to turn in. Here's the process for revising.

- Reread your draft.
- Reread your peer reviews, noting what the reviewers found effective and what they suggested to improve the draft.
- Decide which of the comments you agree with and which you disagree with.

(Remember, you don't have to agree with or make the changes they suggest; you have the final responsibility for your essay.)

- Add information in the places noted by your reviewers (but be sure that the information relates to the focus of the autobiography). Do these additions make the essay seem fuller and more interesting?

- Note the places where the reviewers suggested that you delete information because it is off the focus of the essay. Take out these words and phrases. Does the draft seem more focused on a main impression now?

- After you have written a second draft, reread your revised version. Do you find it more focused, more interesting, and more detailed? If you are still not completely satisfied, you might wish to have another class member read it and do another peer review for you.

- Once you are satisfied with the organization and detail of your essay, read it carefully to be sure that you've used enough details and that all of them are actually relevant to your topic.

- Finally, complete the self-evaluation form that concludes this chapter and turn it in with the final version of your essay.

PEER REVIEW FORM 1: A WRITER'S AUTOBIOGRAPHY

*Writer's Name:*_____

*Reviewer's Name:*_____

First number the paragraphs of the work you are reviewing. Then write out your answer to each of the following questions. Use the paragraph numbers for reference. When you have completed this review, tear out this page and give it to the writer.

1. What single experience does the writer focus on in this paper? (If there is more than one experience, tell the writer which experience might prove most interesting, judging from the information in the discovery draft.)

_____

_____

_____

_____

_____

2. What words or phrases gave you the impression that this experience is the focus? List two or three of them here.

_____

_____

_____

_____

_____

3. What additional details would help you understand more clearly the experience that the writer is writing about?

_____

_____

_____

_____

_____

4. Point out any sentences that give information or details that do not seem to fit in the paper.

_____

_____

_____

_____

_____

5. How many paragraphs are there? Does each one deal with just one topic?

_____

_____

_____

_____

_____

PEER REVIEW FORM 2: A WRITER'S AUTOBIOGRAPHY

Writer's Name: _____

Reviewer's Name: _____

First number the paragraphs of the work you are reviewing. Then write out your answer to each of the following questions. Use the paragraph numbers for reference. When you have completed this review, tear out this page and give it to the writer.

1. What single experience does the writer focus on in this paper? (If there is more than one experience, tell the writer which experience might prove most interesting, judging from the information in the discovery draft.)

_____

_____

_____

_____

_____

2. What words or phrases gave you the impression that this experience is the focus? List two or three of them here.

_____

_____

_____

_____

_____

3. What additional details would help you understand more clearly the experience that the writer is writing about?

_____

_____

_____

_____

_____

4. Point out any sentences that give information or details that do not seem to fit in the paper.

_____

_____

_____

_____

_____

5. How many paragraphs are there? Does each one deal with just one topic?

_____

_____

_____

_____

_____

WRITER'S RESPONSE TO PEER REVIEW 1

> *Read the peer reviews you received from the members of your group; then fill out one of these forms for each one. (This exercise will help you decide how you want to follow your reviewers' suggestions when you revise your discovery draft. It will also help your reviewers understand how they can provide the most effective information for you.)*

Writer's Name: _____

Reviewer's Name: _____

1. Did this reviewer's comments help you see the strengths and weaknesses of your discovery draft? If they were not helpful, what kind of information and suggestions were you hoping to get?

_____

_____

_____

_____

_____

2. Based on this review, in what ways do you plan to revise your discovery draft?

_____

_____

_____

_____

_____

3. Which of the reviewer's comments and suggestions did you find most helpful? Why?

_____

_____

_____

_____

_____

4. Which of the reviewer's comments and suggestions do you disagree with? Why?

_____

_____

_____

_____

_____

WRITER'S RESPONSE TO PEER REVIEW 2

> *Read the peer reviews you received from the members of your group; then fill out one of these forms for each one. (This exercise will help you decide how you want to follow your reviewers' suggestions when you revise your discovery draft. It will also help your reviewers understand how they can provide the most effective information for you.)*

Writer's Name: _____

Reviewer's Name: _____

1. Did this reviewer's comments help you see the strengths and weaknesses of your discovery draft? If they were not helpful, what kind of information and suggestions were you hoping to get?

_____

_____

_____

_____

_____

2. Based on this review, in what ways do you plan to revise your discovery draft?

_____

_____

_____

_____

_____

3. Which of the reviewer's comments and suggestions did you find most helpful? Why?

_____

_____

_____

_____

_____

4. Which of the reviewer's comments and suggestions do you disagree with? Why?

_____

_____

_____

_____

_____

SELF-EVALUATION FORM: A WRITER'S AUTOBIOGRAPHY

Name: _____

Essay Title: _____

Date: _____

Complete this evaluation and turn it in with your essay.

1. How much time did you spend on this paper? What did you spend most of your time on (getting started, drafting, revising, something else)? Do you think you needed to spend more time or less time on some of these parts of the writing process?

_____

_____

_____

_____

_____

2. What do you like best about your paper?

_____

_____

_____

_____

_____

3. What changes have you made in your paper since the peer review?

_____

_____

_____

_____

_____

4. If you had an additional day to work on your paper, what other changes would you make?

_____

_____

_____

_____

_____

5. What things would you like your instructor to give you special help with when reading and commenting on this paper?

_____

_____

_____

_____

_____

CHAPTER TWO

GATHERING INFORMATION

A Character Sketch

GOALS

To help you write a character sketch, we'll concentrate on the following goals in this chapter:

- Writing effective introductions: how to begin your character sketch in a way that will make your readers want to read on

- Using successful interviewing techniques: how to ask the kinds of questions to get the information for an interesting character sketch

- Finding a focus: how to maintain the focus of your character sketch

- Developing paragraphs: how to organize your information into a paragraph using a "focusing sentence"

- Maintaining subject-verb agreement: how to edit to avoid one of the most common "mechanical" errors

Writing Preview

Using what you've learned in this and the preceding chapter, you'll write a character sketch of a classmate, friend, or relative. You'll focus on just one interesting quality to show your readers why that person would be interesting to know. (If you'd like more specific details about the writing assignment, see page 66.)

BEFORE WE START . . .

When you start reading a newspaper or magazine article about a person, what kinds of things make you want to read on? What kinds of things make you want to stop reading the essay? Take five minutes to write down some of the things that attract your attention or make you stop.

> **S**tumped? Don't know what to say? See Chapter 1 for some hints on brainstorming, freewriting, and other ways to get started.

Once you've written some notes on the kinds of things that make you want to read on or stop, talk about your ideas with the members of your class or writing group. Did many of you come up with the same ideas? How do your ideas differ?

INTRODUCTIONS

The best character sketches don't tell the reader everything about the person being described. The writer picks especially interesting details and lets those create a main impression. This careful choice of details must begin in the introduction because the introduction is your first contact with your readers. It's your chance to get your readers' attention and to give them some preview of what's to come. A good introduction will make your readers want to read on. Look at the following two paragraphs. Which one makes you want to read more about Oprah Winfrey?

Paragraph A

Oprah Winfrey has a very successful talk show. She was very poor as a child. She lived with her grandmother in Kosciusko, Mississippi, until she was six, then with her mother in Milwaukee, Wisconsin, and then, when she was fourteen, with her father in Nashville, Tennessee. She went to Tennessee State University to study communications. In addition to her talk show, she likes to act. She appeared in *The Color Purple* and received an Oscar nomination as Best Supporting Actress. Oprah Winfrey is a very determined and successful person.

Paragraph B

From the time she was a small child, it was clear that Oprah Winfrey had the talent and the determination to be a great communicator. At three, for example, when most children hid shyly behind their parents, she gave her first speech on Easter Sunday at her Baptist church. She spoke so clearly and forcefully about the Resurrection that she amazed the congregation. But it was her determination throughout her youth to develop this talent that has led to her astonishing success.

Paragraph A gives us facts about Oprah Winfrey, but there's really nothing especially striking about them, and the paragraph really doesn't lead anywhere—it's just a list of details about her early life. Paragraph B, though, probably makes you want to read more to see what else the writer will show us about Winfrey's determination. It makes clear that the writer is going to focus the rest of the essay on her determination to succeed and what she did. Even though there are many other interesting things to say about her, the writer of Paragraph B focuses on just Winfrey's early talent and determination, and that gets the reader's attention.

A good introduction creates interest and sets up expectations about what will follow—especially what the writer is going to focus the essay on. As a writer, you have to capture your readers' attention and make them want to read on.

INDIVIDUAL ACTIVITY

The following three paragraphs form an introduction to a lengthy article on basketball champion Sheryl Swoopes. What do the details presented in the introduction tell us about her? What do you think would be the focus of the character sketch? Does this introduction make you want to read on?

Where Does Sheryl Swoopes Go from Here?

Basketball legends usually are big, strong, and skyscraper kind of men. They play in America's biggest cities and live in a speeded-up world of fast contracts, fast cars and fabulous women.

Then there is Sheryl Swoopes, who breaks the mold.

Swoopes is the girl/woman star forward who rose from the plains of West Texas to national prominence last spring. She's a willowy 22-year-old who favors red nail polish and hair bows. She does not look like a skyscraper, and she is not especially muscular and she doesn't cuss or even raise her voice.

Claudia Feldman, in *Texas: The Houston Chronicle Magazine*

Writing a good introduction is a lot like introducing people. Suppose you're at a party and you want to introduce a new friend to one of your longtime friends. You have a couple of options. You can say, "Kimberly, this is Brian. Brian, this is Kim." Then you can wander off, leaving them shuffling their feet and clearing their throats, stumbling from topic to topic as they try to find some common point of interest.

Or you can try this:

"Brian, this is Kim. She just took a course called Ecology and Politics and is thinking of majoring in Environmental Science. Kim, Brian worked at a recycling plant all last summer." Then you can leave as Brian and Kim focus their conversation around environmental issues and talk in more detail about these concerns.

Good introductions work much like this second example:

- They introduce one idea or point that you plan to focus your essay on.
- They use details that will interest your audience—the people reading your essay.

Note that the longer the essay, the longer the introduction a writer may need. For a short essay of two to three pages, an introductory paragraph or two is usually fine. Research papers may have several paragraphs of introduction. And you've probably noticed that many books have an entire introductory chapter.

READINGS

As you read the following character sketches, look especially at how the introductions prepare you as a reader for what is to come.

PREREADING EXERCISE

Often you can get an idea of what an essay is about by reading just the introduction and considering what hints the writer is giving you. Try this prereading exercise with each of the following character sketches: Read the first paragraph of each; then write a few sentences telling what you expect and what details in the paragraph lead you to expect this.

DALLAS MALLOY: A CONTENDER, REGARDLESS OF GENDER

Katherine Dunn

This character sketch originally appeared in Interview *magazine in 1993.* Interview *specializes in interesting profiles of individuals currently in the news.*

1   Dallas Malloy is a fighter. She was fifteen years old the day she saw the Marlon Brando classic *On the Waterfront* and decided to learn how to box. A year older now, the intense and articulate, five-foot-six, 132-pound

high school sophomore from Bellingham, Washington, packs a lethal left hook. Malloy composes music and writes novels, and eventually wants to act in and produce movies. But right now, her aim is to box against other women in the 1996 Olympics.

2   She sees the sport of busted beaks as a worthy challenge. "It's as strategic as chess," she says. "I could train all my life and still have more to learn." The guys who laughed at her when she first walked into the 12th Street Boxing Gym now call her "Angel Face" and are all business when they enter the ring to spar with her.

3   Malloy was ready for formal competition months ago, but there was a glitch: according to United States Amateur Boxing Inc., which governs the sport, women weren't permitted to fight in the amateur ranks. The rule applied to every state except Massachusetts, where a lawsuit forced the issue last year.

4   Malloy changed all that. Backed by the American Civil Liberties Union, she sued for gender discrimination, and in May a federal judge ruled in her favor. The temporary injunction, which is expected to become permanent later this year, allows women to train and compete against each other with the same status as men. Malloy's courtroom victory was a technical knockout for all American women who are fistically inclined. Her next fight will be in the ring.

POSTREADING EXERCISE

Without looking back at the character sketch, list three things that stand out in your mind about Dallas Malloy.

1.
2.
3.

JIM BELLANCA
David Hoag

This character sketch, which first appeared in Los Angeles Magazine, *is one of several such sketches about people who were voted Most Likely to Succeed when they were in high school and how they turned out as adults.*

1963: Palisades High
1991: Vice President, American International Bank

1   For the first few years after he graduated, the Pali High student body president and captain of the baseball and basketball teams lived up to

expectations right on schedule. His senior thesis at Harvard—written at the height of the Vietnam War—explored the then-novel concept of an all-volunteer army. He spent a year as a Vista volunteer in Honolulu, tutoring and coaching disadvantaged teenage boys, then graduated from USC Law School. But during the bar exam, he walked out at the lunch break and didn't return. Instead, he got a job in a pizza parlor.

2   "I think it was some kind of rebellion against doing what I thought would please other people," Bellanca says, his voice halting as if he were actually again getting out of that classroom chair. "There was also some fear of finally passing into 'manhood' and having to go out in the world and face the sort of bosses I didn't like."

3   The son of a CPA with his own Brentwood firm, Bellanca slung pizzas for a year before taking a job as a trainee with a Brentwood mortgage-banking company, where he learned the ropes of real estate, mortgages and appraisals and soon grew to like the business. A half-dozen banks and 18 years later, he's still at it, now a vice president and loan officer with American International Bank in L.A. Banking, he says, is "calmer, more reflective" than law. "I think I was looking for security," he admits.

4   Now 46, Bellanca lives in Granada Hills with his wife, Kathy, a bilingual teacher's aide for the L.A. Unified School District, and their two sons. "Back in high school, I never thought of a family in terms of success, but I do now," he says. "My family life couldn't be better—that's what matters to me today."

5   Bellanca holds no stock in the Most Likely to Succeed title. "It was a popularity contest. I was flattered because I was so much in need of approval. Whether or not I knew what to do with it, I wanted to win it. I was nice to everybody—I was too much the pleasing child, if you will, trying to remember everyone's name and say hi to them."

6   Did his classmates make the wrong choice? One of them, Scott "Most Outspoken" Tepper, who once tried to impeach Bellanca as student body president and confesses he was once envious of him, says the perception of success in the early '60s was not what it is today. "Jim was a wonderful generalist and could do everything well, and that's why he was voted Most Likely to Succeed," says Tepper, now a Century City attorney. "But now we live in a society that's very specialized. Good generalists are judged differently today than they once may have been."

7   Maybe nice guys don't always finish last. But some, like Bellanca, don't even want to enter the race. "I'm still grappling with the expectations of people from almost 30 years ago that are not entirely resolved," Bellanca says in a gentle voice. "I'm still wondering where my ambition is. Some of it seems to have gone out of me. There's sort of a voice still saying, 'You've got to make it'—whatever that means."

POSTREADING EXERCISE

Without looking back at the character sketch, list three things that stand out in your mind about Jim Bellanca.

1.
2.
3.

MY OLD MAN
Dick Wingerson

For this character sketch, which originally appeared in Pittsburgh *magazine, Dick Wingerson focuses on someone well known to him: his father. Notice how his memories cast his father as fun-loving and high-spirited, even in the most ordinary of circumstances.*

1   My old man never let me call him that. He thought it was a sign of disrespect. I felt it was a term of endearment.

2   Clair Andrew Wingerson was born in Lawrenceville in 1907. He was named Clair after his mother's ancestral home, County Clare, Ireland. He was named Andrew after his father's brother Andy, who shortened the family name from "Wingertszahn" to Wingerson because it was too long to fit over the stoop above his bakery at 235 Beaver Avenue in Marshall-Shadeland.

3   When Dad was a teenager, his mom and pop and six of their seven kids moved to what was then "the country" in Shaler Township on Anderson Road. They called the place "Hell's Half Acre," in honor of my feisty grandmother. It was once a halfway house for alcoholic priests. Today it's a centennial home in a subdivision.

4   My dad and mother, Dorothy McLaughlin Wingerson, went together for 11 years before they married—almost as long as Dick Tracy and Tess Trueheart. Those were Depression years, but that never kept my parents down. They sang a lot in the car. Their favorite was: "Oh, we ain't got a barrel of money, maybe we're ragged and funny, but we'll travel along, singin' a song, side by side."

5   We never even had a car radio until Dad got his 1957 company Pontiac. Until then, he'd keep us entertained with obscure songs as: "It ain't gonna rain no more, no more, it ain't gonna rain no more. How in the heck can you wash your neck if it ain't gonna rain no more?" And this World War I ditty: "Goodbye Ma, goodbye Pa, goodbye mule with your old hee-haw. I may not know what the war's about, but you bet, by gosh, I'll soon find out."

6   My old man read me *The Pittsburgh Press* comics on Sundays and taught me to swim the Australian crawl at the North Park pool. He also

taught me to love fireworks in Aspinwall, the Highland Park Zoo, the Police Circus at Forbes Field, the roller coasters at Kennywood, stock car racing at Heidelberg Raceway and South Park Speedway, Lionel electric trains from Conklin Radio on Lincoln Avenue and all kinds of antique cars.

7   Sometimes he'd fly with a friend in a biplane to Erie to pick up fresh lake pike to sell at Donahoe's, the grocery he then managed. Donahoe's ads in *The Press* and *Sun Telly* would say: "Fish So Fresh They Swam in Lake Erie This Morning." One weekend, Dad convinced my mother to take a ride in the biplane. She prayed the rosary the whole trip. The next week the biplane was on the front page: Dad's buddy had crash-landed into a tree. My mother never flew again until their silver wedding anniversary.

8   Dad loved to travel. As a sales manager for Westinghouse Appliance Sales, he'd win sales award trips and go to New Orleans (twice), pre-Castro Havana (twice) and the Kentucky Derby (twice). But he didn't just win trips. He won every appliance his company ever made, and doubles and triples of some. In fact, our whole house became a Westinghouse.

9   Once he made a "talking record" postcard from the observation deck of the Empire State Building and mailed it home. His last words— "I'll be home . . . I'll be home . . . I'll be home"—got stuck in the groove and kept repeating.

10   My old man loved sports. My parents followed the Pittsburgh Steelers ever since they really were steelworkers who played Sundays under the Bloomfield Bridge and passed the hat at halftime for their pay.

11   Dad sat ringside with my mother at Golden Gloves bouts. She once got blood on her dress and got miffed. In Lawrenceville, he showed us fighting Fritzie Zivic's bar on Butler Street. In Morningside, he showed us the house where former world middleweight champion Harry "The Pittsburgh Windmill" Greb once lived, on Jancey Street, near Saint Raphael's convent. My dad's big boxing claim to fame was that he witnessed the shortest bout in history—11 seconds—at the old Motor Square Gardens in East Liberty. We never believed the story, so he wrote a letter to *True Magazine* and had it verified.

12   Ice skating was another big kick. He and my mother would skate, arm in arm, on the Highland Park Pond and the North Park Lake. But what he really loved was being anchorman on "crack-the-whip." He'd lead the line of skaters at breakneck speed, then go into a power skid and let centrifugal force whip the skaters. The last one in line usually went airborne.

13   He played golf, too, but my mother was "Queen of the Links," Pittsburgh's Public Golf Course Women's Champion at Schenley Park in 1937 and '38, and she usually beat him. So he excelled at everything else.

14   Bowling was a big athletic and social deal. Ten couples had a league: "The Friday Knights and Their Ladies." They'd compete at East Liberty's Enright Bowling Alleys, just up Penn Avenue from the Enright Theatre where East Liberty's Gene Kelly got his start. The best parts of this league for us kids were picnics at Kernan's Allegheny River cottage in Oakmont and the Friday Knighters' Halloween parties.

15   How my dad loved those original Halloween costumes! One time he was Mammy Yokum with a live chicken. Another time he was a huge "wallflower," wrapped like a mummy in wallpaper and blending right in. One time he dressed up like a man on one side and a woman on the other, and spent the entire evening dancing with himself. My favorite costume was when he was a big Westinghouse console television set. He sat inside it in a corner for an hour with hand puppets and rubber masks and did the news, sports, weather and an entire Punch and Judy show.

16   Dad always said: "If I die tomorrow, I'll have no regrets. I've done everything I've ever wanted to do." At 57, he had a mild heart attack. Then he had another major one in the hospital as the doctor examined him. He went into cardiac arrest and died for 10 or 20 minutes, but they jump-started him and he lived another year.

17   At 58, he cut a long-stemmed rose for my mother and put it in a pil-sner glass in her kitchen. Then he went back outside to his garden and died for the last time. He was such a doer, he even had to die twice. At his funeral, more than one person said to me: "He may have only been 58, but he lived 85 years." Dad's mouth opened right before they closed the cas-ket. My mother said: "He never could keep it shut."

POSTREADING EXERCISE

Without looking back at the character sketch, list three things that stand out in your mind about "My Old Man."

1.
2.
3.

SHOOTING FOR THE MOON: MAE JEMISON

Nikki Giovanni

Nikki Giovanni is a popular, widely read American poet. The following is her character sketch of Mae Jemison, the country's first black female astronaut, which originally appeared in Essence *magazine.*

1   I am at breakfast with Mae Jemison. I am, naturally, nervous. I am a middle-aged, cigarette-smoking, unhealthy and uninterested-in-health

poet who has just snagged the opportunity of a lifetime. I get to interview Mae Jemison.

2   I would have liked her even if she hadn't said my smoking wouldn't bother her; I would have liked her even if she hadn't said, "Oh, I didn't get straight A's in school like my sister," with a devilish smile, "because I took subjects I was interested in." I would have liked her had she been arrogant and impatient with a poet whose view of space is metaphysical, not physical, but she was not only patient but kind.

3   "Aren't you bored a lot?" I was compelled to ask. I mean, she sits talking to people who haven't a hoot in hell what she actually does or can do. "A friend once told me: 'If you are bored, you're not paying attention.' I think he's right."

4   Over breakfast, Mae told me this story: "When I came home for Christmas, my first year at Stanford University, I had brought my calculus with me. My mother said, 'Why don't you ask your father to help you?' I thought she couldn't be serious. My father is a high school graduate, and I was this, well, hotshot at Stanford. But I did ask him for help, and he made it so clear to me. That one thing changed the way I thought about my father and myself."

5   There is something about Alabama men and numbers. My father, like hers, was a mathematical whiz, and like hers, was from a little city outside Mobile. My mother, like Mae's, also taught school. But I grew up in Cincinnati, and Mae's hometown is Chicago.

6   "You know what my mother told me one day?" Mae asked. "I was feeling really good about some project I had finished, and she just sort of looked at me and said, 'But you're illiterate.' I was crushed. How could my mother consider me illiterate?" Mae laughs and shakes her head. She was so upset that she set out to learn more about Black literature and history. Her undergraduate double degree at Stanford was in chemical engineering and African and African-American studies. "But what made you decide to go to medical school after undergraduate?" I asked her. "Well," she ponders, "I could have gone into dance, which I love, or I could have gone to medical school. I just chose medical school." There is something wonderful about the way Mae phrases her choices. They are, well, logical. She doesn't feel special, just prepared to control her options.

7   Opting against a traditional career in medicine, Mae joined the U.S. Peace Corps as a medical officer in Sierra Leone and Liberia. I asked her if this has had any effect on her desire to serve others. Intriguingly enough, she bristled: "I don't believe in altruism. I've gotten much more out of what I have done than the people I was supposed to be helping. When I was in a refugee camp in Thailand, I learned more about medicine there

than I could have in a lifetime somewhere else. I refuse to think those people owe me any thanks. I got a lot out of it."

8   After leaving the Peace Corps, she was a general practitioner and attended graduate engineering classes in Los Angeles when she was tapped by NASA in 1985. There have been four other Black women astronauts in training with her, but now she is the only one. Until her next flight, which is unscheduled, Mae spends her work days earthbound at NASA in Houston doing scientific experiments.

9   I'm the original little girl who wouldn't take biology because you had to cut up the frog. "Tell me," I bravely asked, "about your frog experiment." "We wanted to know," Jemison said, "how the tadpoles would develop in space, with no gravity. I hatched the eggs and developed the tadpoles. They showed no ill effects, and since frogs, like other life forms, take so much of their basic knowledge from their environment, we were curious if they would hear well, if they would turn out to be . . . well, normal frogs. When we got back to earth, the tadpoles were right on track and they have turned into frogs. . . ."

10   "What are your thoughts when you're whirling in space?"

11   "The first thing I saw was Chicago. I looked out the window and there it was," she says, and adds that she also saw all of earth. "I looked over at one point and there was Somalia." She was in space while others were in the last throes of starvation.

12   "Space is so meaningful to earth," Jemison says. "The third world will be the ultimate beneficiary of space technology because we're moving away from infrastructures. You don't need to lay telephone wire to have phones anymore; that's what cellular is all about. We don't need old-fashioned generators for electrical connections anymore. The third world will be able to jump over the industrial age into the space age." It surprises Jemison that there aren't more Afrocentric people excited about space and its technology.

13   "You know what I took up with me when I went up?" I did know, but I let her say it. "An Alvin Ailey American Dance Theater company poster, an Alpha Kappa Alpha banner, a flag that had flown over the Organization of African Unity, and proclamations from Chicago's Du Sable Museum of African-American History and the Chicago public school system. I wanted everyone to know that space belongs to all of us. There is science in dance, and art in science. It belongs to everyone. I'm not the first or the only African-American woman who had the skills and talent to become an astronaut. I had the opportunity. All people have produced scientists and astronomers." And though she bristles at altruisms, clearly all her interests are of service to humankind.

14   Was she afraid? "You are aware that you're on a controlled explosion; but I have confidence in NASA." Plus, you have to think whatever Mae Jemison knows about fear was left in her mother's kitchen.

15   Mae Jemison is a mind in motion. If that devilish grin and those piercing eyes could be stripped away, I think you would find pure energy in constant motion. We use *genius* very lightly. In the movie *Sneakers,* the geek had a license plate that said 180IQ; I knew Debi Thomas would not prevail when I saw that her license plate said SKATING FOR GOLD. It was too much pressure. Mae Jemison is enjoying her life and its opportunities. Single, thirty-six, and living in the home she bought in suburban Houston, she loves the music of Etta James, and she talks as easily to children as to scientists. She's comfortable with herself.

16   What's next? If she could design her ideal space trip, what would it be? Her answer: "Me in a clear bubble floating through the galaxy . . . shooting for the moon." Who would she want to go with her? "Sneeze, my cat. I think I'd like to have Sneeze. He came with me from Africa, so he's used to flying. Then," that grin again, "if some aliens came by and invited me to another galaxy—well, look for me on *Unsolved Mysteries.* I'm gone."

POSTREADING EXERCISE

Without looking back at the character sketch, list three things that stand out in your mind about Mae Jemison.

1.
2.
3.

GROUP ACTIVITY

Spend some time discussing these character sketches with your class or the members of your writing group, looking at them closely and critically. To respond critically to readings doesn't necessarily mean to criticize them in a negative way. It means to analyze, to find the essential or critical points they make so that you can apply these insights to your own writing.

Working with your class or group, consider the following questions:

1. Do the introductions you've read so far look like the kind you've been taught to write in the past? If they're different, how are they different?

2. After looking at the variety of introductions in this chapter, what do you think a good introduction does?

3. One of the marks of good writing is to make the ordinary seem unusual and interesting and to make the unusual seem within the grasp of all of us. How do the essays we've looked at in this chapter do this? Discuss the details you listed and how those details help give you an impression of what the subjects of each sketch would be like.

INTERVIEWING

By now you've seen the broad range of subjects possible for a character sketch. Sometimes a character sketch can be based on the writer's direct knowledge of the person; in "My Old Man," for example, Dick Wingerson wrote about his father, using his memories as his main source of information.

More often, though, the writer of a character sketch gets information about the person through research and interviews. That's what David Hoag did for his sketch of Jim Bellanca, first identifying people who were voted Most Likely to Succeed in high school and then locating and interviewing them. Similarly, Katherine Dunn researched and interviewed Dallas Malloy, and Nikki Giovanni conducted a long interview with Mae Jemison.

Although it's fine to use your memories and direct observations if you write about someone you know, we'd like you to do some interviewing as well, even if you choose to write about a close friend or relative. Interviewing will give you some practice in developing questions and selecting details, skills you can use in later papers and in other courses.

INDIVIDUAL ACTIVITY

Spend about five minutes listing people you might like to write a character sketch about. Here are a few you might consider:

- a classmate
- your parent or guardian
- one of your grandparents
- a brother or sister
- your closest friend
- a neighbor

- a member of an organization you belong to
- your boss or a co-worker

Choose a possibility from your list, and write down ten or twelve questions that you might ask when interviewing that person. Don't worry if some of the questions seem silly or obvious; they're just to get the interview started or to get it moving if the conversation should falter.

Here's a little bit of an interview of Whoopi Goldberg by Barbara Walters; note how Walters first gets Goldberg to answer a specific question, then has a follow-up ("Was that awful?") to get her to say more:

Walters: At age seventeen, trying to kick a drug habit, you go into rehab. . . . You meet a guy, get married, have a baby, get divorced. How did you support this baby?

Continued

Conducting an interview
is like carrying on a
conversation. You can't
just ask questions
without paying attention
to the answers:

It should be pretty obvious that this interview isn't going anywhere.

But look what happens
when you follow up on
your lead questions:

This is the kind of interview that can actually
get you somewhere.

Conducting an Interview

Continued

Goldberg: I'm a licensed beautician. . . . I was a cosmetologist. . . . And I worked in a morgue.

Walters: Was that awful?

Goldberg: Well, not for them, because they were dead. You could give 'em Joan Crawford lips and comb their hair. Sometimes they moved, because if you've not been embalmed, you have all these muscles contract and do strange things. And so you'd be doin' somebody's hair and their hand would move. It's like "Okay, get up. I'm going to the corner of the room. If you're not dead and you just runnin' a scam, I will not look. I will tell them that the body just disappeared. Just get out."

As we've said, even if you're going to write about someone you know well, it's still best to interview the person; you may learn some surprising things, and an interview will also help you focus your ideas. Having made notes about your subject's answers to the questions you've asked, you can look over your notes and ask yourself, What one thing about the person is the most outstanding?

This doesn't have to be something great the person has done, but just some facet of that person's life or personality that stands out—for example, Jim Bellanca's rebellion against the expectations others had of him or Dallas Malloy's unusual interest in boxing. Once you've decided on this focus, you can select the details to develop that idea.

For example, a writer might focus on a friend's interest in horror stories. She could begin with a statement like "Ralph likes to read horror stories, the creepier and gorier the better." Then she could include some details about her subject's childhood to show that his interest in horror began when he was frightened by the wind blowing through the trees near his house and he thought that the house was haunted.

Tips for a Successful Interview

You can use a tape recorder for your interview, but many people tend to clam up when a tape recorder is running. For that reason, reporters often take notes when they're interviewing a person one-on-one. If you take notes, here are some hints that will help you:

- When you start your interview, keep in mind that you probably won't need to ask all the questions you list. One might be enough to get the conversation going and lead you to the information you'll need for your sketch.

Continued

Continued

- Ask the question and listen carefully to the answer. Does the answer suggest any other related questions? Keep following these leads until you've found something that really strikes you about this person and enough details to write your character sketch.

- Use a notebook rather than loose sheets of paper.

- Jot down key words and phrases to jog your memory later.

- If you want to write down a complete quotation, feel free to ask the person you're interviewing to repeat the statement so that you're sure you get it right.

- After the interview is over, organize your notes, and write them out in more detail.

- If you have more questions or need more details, go back to the person you interviewed for a follow-up interview.

Remember: Don't trust your memory.

MAINTAINING THE FOCUS OF YOUR ESSAY

If your interview has been successful, you probably have a great deal of information. Some of the information will fit together in obvious ways; other things won't. Don't think that you have to use all of it, though; in fact, the most successful character sketches focus tightly on just one aspect of the person rather than trying to say everything.

To see the difference between a character sketch that tries to use everything and one that's tightly focused, let's look at two sketches of Oprah Winfrey. (You saw the introductions to these two sketches on pages 42–43.)

Character Sketch A

Oprah Winfrey has a very successful talk show. She was very poor as a child. She lived with her grandmother in Kosciusko, Mississippi, until she was six, then with her mother in Milwaukee, Wisconsin, and then, when she was fourteen, with her father in Nashville, Tennessee. She went to Tennessee State University to study communications. In addition to her talk show, she likes to act. She appeared in *The Color Purple* and received an Oscar nomination as Best Supporting Actress. Oprah Winfrey is a very determined and successful person.

She got her start by working at WVOL in Nashville. She didn't exactly plan to get a job there. Actually, she was trying to get money for the March of Dimes, so she stopped by the station to ask for contributions. The manager liked her voice and manner, so he gave her a job.

Oprah has had a lot of problems with her weight over the years. So most people would be surprised to know that she won Miss Black Nashville of 1972 and also the Miss Black Tennessee pageant. For the Miss Black America pageant, she performed a dramatic monologue and sang "Sometimes I Feel like a Motherless Child."

She moved to Chicago in 1983 and hosted the show *A.M. Chicago*. At first she was lonely. To help people and get rid of her loneliness, she worked in a soup kitchen the first day she was there, which was just a few days before Christmas. The show was a big success. Her talk show also broadcasts from Chicago, and she really enjoys living there.

Oprah almost won the Oscar as Best Supporting Actress for *The Color Purple* in 1986. She really liked the story when she read the book by Alice Walker. So she gave copies of it to all her friends as gifts. At first, she felt very nervous about acting, but she really enjoyed working with Steven Spielberg on this movie. Since then she has also acted in movies for television.

Oprah really made a lot of her life. She is a good role model for everyone. People like her because she seems warm and caring. I think more people should have these qualities.

Oprah Winfrey: One Determined Woman

From the time she was a small child, it was clear that Oprah Winfrey had the talent and the determination to be a great communicator. At three, for example, when most children hide shyly behind their parents, she gave her first speech on Easter Sunday at her Baptist church. She spoke so clearly and force-fully about the Resurrection that she amazed the congregation. But it was her determination throughout her youth to develop this talent that has led to her astonishing success.

While most other children are playing with blocks and other toys, Oprah was developing her skills as a communicator. By the age of three, she had already learned how to read and write. Because she had developed these abilities so early and because she was so bright, her first-grade teacher let her skip a grade. Throughout school, she was always an excellent student who worked hard, read a lot, and got good grades.

She combined her interests in reading and drama when she began to per-form dramatic readings in high school. Her performances were based on the lives of important black women throughout history, such as Sojourner Truth and Harriet Tubman. She continued to develop her abilities at Tennessee State University, where she majored in drama and speech, performing in *Jubilee, God's Trombones,* and *The Martin Luther King Story,* in which she played Coretta Scott King.

While she was at Tennessee State, she continued to work at WVOL as a newscaster, a job she had begun while in high school. Soliciting contributions for the March of Dimes, Oprah had impressed the station manager so much with her voice and her poise that he hired her and encouraged her to pursue a career in broadcasting.

Because she worked so hard during her youth to develop her talent for communication, it is no wonder that Oprah Winfrey is such a big success today.

Although character sketch A provides a lot of details about Oprah Winfrey, they're scattered about and don't focus on a central point. Character sketch B, on the other hand, keeps the focus on her determination. We certainly know what point the writer is trying to make—the title, the introduction, and the details all help convey the idea of her ambition and drive.

Focus is the key. Here's one way to get your notes into focus. First write down each of the major points you got from your interview; then try to group them so that similar ideas are together. You can do this by numbering each idea, by drawing arrows, or even by using sticky notes or bits of paper, as we suggested in Chapter 1 for group clustering.

Let's say that after your interview, you have a list like this:

1. Wayne was born in Alabama.
2. He's a vegetarian.
3. He's majoring in music, but his father wants him to be a business major.
4. Wayne dreams of being a jazz pianist.
5. He's played piano since he was three.
6. Wayne's mother says all musicians are poor.
7. Wayne isn't sure what he should do.
8. He thinks he could join the army.
9. His boss says he can work full time as a piano salesman.
10. Wayne practices the piano at least three hours a day.
11. He loves jazz.
12. His music teachers all encouraged him.

Before you can begin writing, you need to decide which items go together and which ones can be dropped. Most of the items on this list deal with Wayne's love of music and the choices he'll have to make about his future. Not everything on the list fits that theme, though, so some items will pretty clearly have to be dropped. No matter how interesting Wayne's being born in Alabama or his vegetarianism might be, for example, they just don't fit with the rest of the list. Remember, you don't have to tell everything you learn about the person you interview; even very interesting information may have to be eliminated if it doesn't fit the focus.

When you've decided on your focus, you must find an order for the main ideas. There's no hard-and-fast rule for ordering ideas. In fact, you may even find that as you write, you will rearrange your ideas as the essay starts to come into focus for you.

Don't think of your list as a rigid outline. It's only a plan, not an absolute commitment. You've probably made plans with your friends to do something specific only to have everyone decide in the middle of the evening to do something else, and the evening ends up being even better than you had planned. The same holds true for writing. Sometimes the original plan will work well; sometimes you may need to rearrange it several times while you're writing. It's just meant to serve as a general guide.

As you write, keep your focus in mind. You may even find it helpful to keep a note card bearing the main idea or focus of your essay in front of you as a reminder. This may help you as you're planning what to include and writing the discovery draft. And it will certainly help during revision, when you eliminate parts that are off the focus of your essay and add other details or examples that do relate to the focus.

1. ~~Ralph was born in France.~~
2. ~~He's a vegetarian.~~
3 ~~2~~ ~~3.~~ He's majoring in music, but his father wants him to be a lawyer.
2 ~~1~~ ~~4.~~ Ralph dreams of being a concert pianist.
5. He's played piano since he was three.
4 ~~3~~ ~~6.~~ Ralph's mother says all musicians are poor.
1 ~~4~~ ~~7.~~ Ralph isn't sure what he should do.
8. ~~He thinks he could join the army.~~
9. ~~His boss says he can work full time as a piano salesman.~~
7 ~~10.~~ Ralph practices the piano five hours a day.
5 ~~11.~~ He loves classical music.
6 ~~12.~~ His first piano teacher always encouraged him.

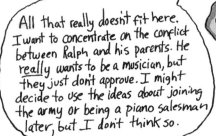

INDIVIDUAL ACTIVITY

After you've completed your interview and any brainstorming or other preliminary activities, write out the main points you want to cover in your character sketch. Be sure to write just one on each line, and number them.

Go back over these points and decide which ones you'll use and which you'll drop. Cross out the points you won't be able to use. Next, reorder the remaining points by renumbering them.

INDIVIDUAL ACTIVITY

Once you've finished your interviewing and ordered your list of items, you should have several useful details about your subject, so you can write a draft of the first paragraph of your character sketch. You don't have to write the entire sketch right now, just an introduction. Don't try to include everything you learned about the person. Look again at the first paragraphs of the sketches earlier in this chapter. Notice how the writers give you just a bit of detail—enough to make you want to read on, but not everything they have to say. That's the kind of introduction you should write. Give the one most striking detail about your subject in the introduction; later you'll have a chance to provide additional related details. What is that one most striking detail? Write it down before you start to write your introduction.

GROUP ACTIVITY

Bring your introduction to class with you, and read it aloud to your class or group. Listen carefully as each person reads his or her introduction.

After each writer has read his or her introduction, take a few moments to discuss how effective it is; does the introduction make you want to know more about the subject? If not, what suggestions do you have for the writer to improve it? Try to be as specific as possible in your suggestions, paying particular attention to whether the introduction is tightly focused on one central feature of the subject.

PARAGRAPHING

Let's start by making an admission: There's no one right way to write a paragraph. You may have been told that every paragraph must have a topic sentence to provide focus and several sentences to provide support. Although many paragraphs do have these characteristics, not all of them do. There are, in fact, many different ways to structure paragraphs, more than we could list here.

Did You Know That Writers Use Paragraphs That Reflect Their Culture?

Using a Focusing Sentence

That said, however, in many writing situations—particularly academic writing—you will find it useful to develop paragraphs with a topic or focusing sentence and support. The focusing sentence makes a general statement; the rest of the paragraph fleshes out that statement by adding supporting details and examples. A paragraph with a focusing sentence helps guide your readers so that they can tell exactly what each paragraph is about.

PARAGRAPHS

A group of sentences working together *as a single unit makes up a paragraph. One paragraph is made to stand out from other paragraphs by beginning on a new line (usually with an indenta-* tion). As a general rule, an effective paragraph will be unified, coherent, and developed.

In a unified *paragraph, all sentences deal with the same general topic. If*

Continued

Continued

*there's one sentence in the paragraph that doesn't fit with all of the others, chances are that it needs to be moved to another paragraph or deleted. In a co-*herent *paragraph, the sentences follow in an order that is clear and meaningful for the reader. Finally, a fully* developed *paragraph will usually be more than just one or two sentences long. Although there are some good uses for very short paragraphs that we'll discuss later, as a general rule writers of college papers should try to avoid paragraphs that have only one or two sentences.*

These kinds of paragraphs generally have the focusing sentence at the beginning, followed by several sentences that support the focusing sentence by adding specific information—details or examples. There's no set number of details or examples you need; that varies from paragraph to paragraph. But if you find that you have no supporting details, then perhaps your focusing sentence should really just be part of another paragraph.

Keep in mind these basic rules:

- If you have enough support for a point, it can have its own paragraph.
- If you don't have enough support, you have to combine that point with another in a way that relates both of them or drop it.
- When you shift to a different point, you should start a new paragraph.

Ways of Supporting a Focusing Sentence

Look at these focusing sentences from four paragraphs of Dick Wingerson's essay on his father (pages 47–49). Each opening sentence announces the main topic of the paragraph so that you can tell what it's going to be about:

Ice skating was another big kick. (paragraph 12)

He played golf, too. . . . (paragraph 13)

Bowling was a big athletic and social deal. (paragraph 14)

How my dad loved those original Halloween costumes! (paragraph 15)

Let's look at just one of these paragraphs, paragraph 12, to see how Wingerson has used the focusing sentence and supporting details.

(1) Ice skating was another big kick. (2) He and my mother would skate, arm in arm, on the Highland Park Pond and the North Park Lake. (3) But what he really loved was being anchorman on "crack-the-whip." (4) He'd lead the line of

skaters at breakneck speed, then go into a power skid and let centrifugal force whip the skaters. (5) The last one in line usually went airborne.

The first sentence provides the focus—on ice skating—and the rest of the sentences add the supporting details and examples. They tell us whom Wingerson's father skated with (sentence 2), describe what he liked to do (sentence 3), and provide an example and details to help explain sentence 3 (sentences 4 and 5).

We could illustrate what happens in this paragraph:

> Focusing sentence (1)
> > Detail (2)
> > Detail (3)
> > > Example (4)
> > Detail (5)

This isn't the only way of developing a paragraph with a focusing sentence, of course. In the following paragraph (paragraph 15), notice that Wingerson begins with a focusing sentence, follows it with four examples, and then supplies some details illustrating the fourth example:

(1) How my dad loved those original Halloween costumes! (2) One time he was Mammy Yokum with a live chicken. (3) Another time he was a huge "wallflower," wrapped like a mummy in wallpaper and blending right in. (4) One time he dressed up like a man on one side and a woman on the other and spent the entire evening dancing with himself. (5) My favorite costume was when he was a big Westinghouse console television set. (6) He sat inside it in a corner for an hour with hand puppets and rubber masks and did the news, sports, weather and an entire Punch and Judy show.

An illustration of paragraph 15 looks quite different from the one for paragraph 12:

> Focusing sentence (1)
> > Example (2)
> > Example (3)
> > Example (4)
> > Example (5)
> > > Details (6)

There are lots of different ways to use details and examples, so don't think that you have to produce precisely these two kinds of paragraphs. You should, however, try

Supporting Your Focusing Sentence

to use some paragraphs with focusing sentences when you write your character sketch. We'll be talking about other ways to organize paragraphs in later chapters, so before we're through, you'll have lots of ways of developing paragraphs at your disposal.

WRITING ASSIGNMENT: A CHARACTER SKETCH

After revising your introduction based on suggestions made by your classmates or group members, write a discovery draft for a complete character sketch.

Tips for a Successful Character Sketch

- *Introduction* Select a striking or memorable detail that characterizes the person and makes the reader want to read on.

- *Focus* The whole character sketch should be focused on elements related to this striking characteristic.

- *Paragraphs* Each paragraph should maintain the focus and help develop it in some way by adding more details or examples. Start a new paragraph when you start a new point.

Remember, you don't have to tell everything you know about the person you interviewed. Leave out any details that don't fit with your focus.

Summary of Steps

Here's a summary of steps to take in completing this assignment. Check off each step after you've completed it.

_____ Make a list of the main points you want to cover.

_____ Reorder your list so that you have the points in the order you want to present them.

_____ Decide which of the main points can be in their own paragraphs, should be combined with other main points, or should be dropped.

Student Sample

The following character sketch was written by one of our students, Allen Gerson. Allen brainstormed to come up with a list of questions, interviewed one of his classmates, wrote his introductory paragraph, drafted his character sketch, and then revised his discovery draft on the basis of suggestions he got from his classmates. His final essay appears here. Though it still needs some work, especially editing for mechanical errors, it is nonetheless a well-focused and clear character sketch.

RAZA HUSSAIN, HOSPITAL GROUPIE
Allen Gerson

1   The inner circle of friends that know Raza Hussain call him the Hospital Groupie of Houston. If he is not at Baytown General, Hermann Hospital, Ben Taub General, St. Joseph Hospital, or M.D. Anderson, then he must be at home sleeping. He just can't seem to stay away from the hospital scene. When at one of the many hospitals here he is either checking out the emergency rooms, patient waiting areas, just walking down the many halls getting used to all that goes on, or visiting with some of the doctors. Ask Raza why he wants to become one and he will tell you, "It just feels right. I've always wanted to be a doctor."

2   Raza has had this dream to become a doctor ever since he can remember. As a child he suffered from yellow fever and some other serious medical problems, which put him in contact with many doctors and hospitals. He would watch in awe at what the doctors could do. Ever since his earliest contact with doctors he knew that this is what he wanted to do for the rest of his life. It would be his life's work, his dream.

3   It has not been an easy road to follow the desire of becoming a doctor, for a lot has happened to Raza on his way. He had almost completed his third year of college in his native country of Pakistan when his entire family decided to move to Houston, Texas. School was out of the question because he had to get a job to help support his family. He applied at the hospitals but because of the language barrier it was impossible to get a good-paying job or any job at all there. He ended up in fast-food establishments until he became familiar

with English, then got a job with Walgreens as
assistant manager, and finally as a used-car salesman. The money was great but it was still not a hospital. He put most of his money away so that one day
he could realize his dream.

4   Now he and his family have saved enough money to
start him back on track. After being out of school
for eight years, he is back in school starting again
on his dream, knowing that he now faces another ten
to twelve years of schooling, an internship, and
advanced training before he can really practice as a
doctor. Now that he speaks the language like a
native and is not needed to help support his family,
he has applied for employment at the local hospitals. He's hoping to work there part time while
going to school.

5   His friends already call him Dr. Raza. In a way
this makes sense. In his language, "Raza" means
happy. And we know that someday Raza will be very
happy to be a doctor.

Although Allen has many details in this character sketch, there's still quite a bit
more that he learned from interviewing Raza. Here are Allen's interview notes. Notice
what information he left out of his draft.

Raza—born in Pakistan.

28 years old.

Name means Happy.

Moved here 8 years ago with his family.

Didn't know much English then, knows a lot now.

Wants to be a doctor.

Hangs around hospitals a lot during his free time (just to imagine what it would
be like to be a doctor).

Goes there most days after school.

Had yellow fever when he was a kid.

Good in math—used to be an algebra tutor in Pakistan.

Happy to be back in school.

Worked for McDonald's and Whataburger, then learned enough English to work for Walgreens. Became an assistant manager there. Didn't like it. Too much weekend work. No time for girls.

Has a girlfriend now. Parents don't know about his girlfriend, though. They expect to pick his wife for him. Conflict for him because they're pretty old-fashioned. Doesn't know if he'll do what they want.

Worked as a used-car salesman. Funniest experience there—sold a car to some guy for his 12-year-old kid. Didn't care that 12-year-olds aren't allowed to drive. Wouldn't listen to Raza or his boss.

Saved lots of money at this job to go back to school and just to work part time, hopefully in a hospital.

Likes to travel. Went back to Pakistan 2 times. Likes Europe too. Favorite city is Paris.

Likes to travel in the USA (New York, New Orleans, and lots of cities in Texas). Could probably have some fun traveling together.

Likes different cuisines; eats out a lot—especially at Pakistani restaurants.

Watches movies on TV (black and white—can't afford color TV or cable yet).

GROUP ACTIVITY

Working with your class or writing group, look carefully at Allen's essay and his interview notes. What notes did he not use when he wrote the essay? Why do you suppose he left those things out? Is there anything in the notes that he could have—or should have—included in the essay?

Peer Review

Once you have your complete discovery draft, you're ready to start peer reviews. Here's a recap of what you need to do.

- Exchange papers with a classmate.
- Be alert to what the writer both succeeds at doing and is having trouble doing.
- Write your peer review, using one of the forms on pages 77–78 and 79–80.
- Talk over your review with the writer for a few minutes.
- Go through the whole process with another classmate.
- After reading the peer reviews of your own draft, complete the Writer's Response to Peer Review forms that follow the Peer Review forms. These will

help you decide how to follow any good suggestions from reviewers when you revise your discovery draft and will help your reviewers understand how they can provide the most effective information for you.

Revising Your Discovery Draft

By now you should have a small stack of paper: your notes, your completed discovery draft, and peer reviews written by two of your classmates. With these, you can start revising the discovery draft into the final version of your paper—the one you're actually going to turn in. Here's the process for revising.

- Reread your draft.
- Reread your peer reviews, noting what the reviewers found effective and what they suggested to improve the draft.
- Decide which of the comments you agree with and which you disagree with. (Remember, you don't have to agree with or make the changes they suggest; you have the final responsibility for your essay.)
- If the reviewers suggested that you revise your introduction, look again at the sample introductions in this chapter for some approaches that you might try.
- Note the places where the reviewers suggested that you add focusing sentences to your paragraphs. Do these additions make your paragraphs and your essay more focused?
- Add information in the places noted by your reviewers (but be sure that the information is related to the focus of the essay). Do these additions make the essay seem fuller and more interesting?
- Once you have written a second draft, reread your revised version. Do you find it more focused, more interesting, and more detailed? If you are still not completely satisfied, you might wish to have another class member read it and do another peer review for you.

Once you are satisfied with the organization and detail of your essay, you're ready to do the final editing. Let's look at some of the things you should pay careful attention to as you edit your last draft.

Editing Your Draft

After you've revised your discovery draft, making whatever changes you think are necessary, you're pretty close to finished with your essay. What's left is the final editing to make sure your sentences state your ideas exactly as you want them to and that they're grammatically correct. To help you with your final editing, we'll look first at some details about sentences, then at one of the most common grammatical problems.

SOME USEFUL TERMS

Subject   *The subject of a sentence tells who or what the sentence is about. The subject consists of a noun or pronoun plus any words that modify that noun or pronoun.*

Noun   *A noun is a word used to indicate (or "name") a person, place, thing, or concept* (Connie, Toledo, orange, freedom). *A* singular noun *refers to a single person, place, thing, or concept* (idea), *whereas a* plural noun *refers to more than one person, place, thing, or concept* (ideas). *Most plural nouns in English end in* s (dogs, oranges), *but there are plenty of exceptions* (men, women, children, deer, mice).

Pronoun   *A pronoun is a substitute for a noun. The pronouns we most commonly use are the* personal pronouns. *The particular pronoun you use depends not only on the noun it refers to but also* on its function in the sentence. *If you're using a pronoun as a subject, use* I, you, he, she, it, we, *or* they; *if you're using a pronoun as an object, use* me, you, him, her, it, us, *or* them. *See pages 159–62 for a complete discussion of pronouns.*

Verb   *A verb indicates either an action (the dog* drinks *water) or a state of being (the dog* is *brown). It can be either a single word* (drinks, eats) *or a main verb plus a "helping verb" (the dog* can drink *water). Verbs indicate not just that something happened or existed but when it happened or existed (or will happen or exist). This is their* tense: *the dog* drinks *(present tense), the dog* drank *(past tense), the dog* will drink *(future tense).*

Predicate   *The predicate of a sentence consists of the main verb and any words modifying that verb.*

Sentences

All complete sentences have both a subject and a predicate. Here's a short example:

Subject	Predicate
Ralph	moved.

And here's a longer one:

Subject	Predicate
The tall blond student with the nose ring	*moved from Minnesota to Kansas.*

The subject portion of the sentence contains at least one noun or pronoun and any words that modify it, and the predicate portion contains at least one verb and all of its modifiers.

Subject-Verb Agreement

The subject and the verb of a sentence have to agree: If the subject is singular, the verb has to be singular, and if the subject is plural, the verb has to be plural. That seems logical enough, but it gives a lot of people trouble.

Regular Third-Person Singular Verbs

Most English verbs are regular in form. In the present tense, regular verbs take the base form for every subject except those in the third-person singular. The third-person singular is the verb form you use with the pronouns *he, she,* and *it* and with singular nouns like *dog, bus,* and *Martha.* Regular third-person singular verbs add an *s* to the base form.

Base form
Today I *talk,* you *talk,* we *talk,* they *talk,* girls *talk.*

Third-person singular form
Today he *talks,* she *talks,* it *talks,* the girl *talks,* Martha *talks.*

Note that the simple past tense of regular verbs generally won't cause any agreement problems because it's always formed by adding *ed:*

Yesterday I *talked;* she *talked.*

Similarly, the simple future tense is always formed by using *will* before the base form of the verb:

Tomorrow I *will talk;* she *will talk.*

Omitting the final *s* from third-person singular present-tense verbs is one of the most common subject-verb agreement errors. If the subject is *he, she, it,* or a singular noun, a regular verb should always end in *s.*

Irregular Verbs

Not all English verbs are regular. We won't give you all of the irregular verbs here (you can check a handbook for a full list), but we will look at those that cause the most trouble in terms of subject-verb agreement: *be, have,* and *do.* These verbs are used so often because much of what we talk about concerns what we are, what we have, and what we do.

As you can see, *be* has three different forms in the present tense (*am, are, is*) and two in the past tense (*was, were*):

Be

Present		Past	
I *am*	we *are*	I *was*	we *were*
you *are*	you *are*	you *were*	you *were*
he, she, it *is*	they *are*	he, she, it *was*	they *were*

Be is so irregular that its base form (*be*) isn't even used in the present or past tense. Here's a good rule of thumb:

Never use the base form *be* to indicate present or past actions.

Like regular verbs, *have* and *do* change form in the present tense only for third-person singular subjects; the past tense, though formed irregularly (*had, did*), is the same for all subjects.

Have

Present		Past	
I *have*	we *have*	I *had*	we *had*
you *have*	you *have*	you *had*	you *had*
he, she, it *has*	they *have*	he, she, it *had*	they *had*

Do

Present		Past	
I *do*	we *do*	I *did*	we *did*
you *do*	you *do*	you *did*	you *did*
he, she, it *does*	they *do*	he, she, it *did*	they *did*

Here's another rule of thumb:

> If the subject is *he, she, it,* or a singular noun, use *has* or *does* for the present tense; otherwise, use *have* or *do*.

Compound Subjects

It's easy to get confused when a verb has more than one subject, like this: "Royce and Joyce agree that they don't like cold weather." Royce *agrees* and Joyce *agrees,* but when these subjects are joined with *and (Royce and Joyce),* they make a compound subject, which requires a plural verb form (*agree*). A compound subject is plural, so the verb has to be in the plural form.

Intervening Words

Errors in subject-verb agreement also commonly occur when several words separate the subject and the verb—especially when one of those intervening words could be mistaken for the subject:

Subject	Verb
Many houses on Lin's block were for sale.	

In the sentence "Many houses on Lin's block are for sale," *block* is the object of a preposition and can't be the subject of the sentence. For more information on prepositions and their objects, see pages 279–81.

Because *block* (a singular noun) comes close to the verb, it would be easy to assume that the verb should go with it; but the real subject of this sentence is *houses.*

Subjects Following the Verb

In most sentences the subject comes before the verb, but in some sentences the verb comes before the subject. When you write such a sentence, be sure to identify the subject, and make sure that it agrees with the verb. Look at these examples of the verb-subject construction:

> Verb   Subject
> There *were* several peach *trees* in his yard.

> Verb   Subject
> Behind the house *were* two broken-down *cars.*

You can check for subject-verb agreement in such sentences as these by recasting the sentence so that the subject is first:

> Several peach trees were in his yard.
> Two broken-down cars were behind the house.

No matter what their relative positions in a sentence, the subject and the verb still have to agree.

Subject-Verb Checklist

*H*ere's a checklist to help you avoid the most common subject-verb agreement errors:

- Be sure that regular verbs end in *s* when the subject is a singular noun or a third-person singular pronoun (*he, she,* or *it*).
- Be sure that regular verbs end in *ed* when the verb refers to an action or event in the past.
- Be aware of irregular verb forms, especially the forms of *be, have,* and *do.*
- Never use the word *be* to refer to an action or event in the present or the past.

Continued

Continued

- Use a plural verb with two or more subjects joined by *and*.
- Be sure that the subject and verb agree even when words come between them.

- Be sure that the subject and verb agree when the verb comes before the subject.

Metaessays

One of the best ways to help improve your writing is to write about it. Beginning with this chapter, for each major out-of-class paper, we'll ask you to write an essay about your essay—a "metaessay"—in which you'll address some of the writing problems you've faced and discuss how you overcame them. The more aware you are of your own writing processes, the better your writing will become.

METAESSAY

The writing process for the character sketch involved several parts:

- interviewing and gathering information
- focusing your ideas
- organizing your ideas
- writing the discovery draft
- making suggestions in peer reviews
- revising the discovery draft

Which of these parts of the writing process were easy or difficult for you? In a brief essay, discuss each of these parts, and tell how you tried to overcome those that gave you difficulty.

PEER REVIEW FORM 1: A CHARACTER SKETCH

Writer's Name: _____

Reviewer's Name: _____

First number the paragraphs of the work you are reviewing. Then write out your answer to each of the following questions. Use the paragraph numbers for reference, and use the back of this page if you need more space. When you have completed this review, tear out this page and give it to the writer.

1. Does the introduction make you want to read on? If not, can you suggest any approaches that might make it more interesting?

_____

_____

_____

_____

_____

2. What about the person is the writer trying to focus on? (If there is no clear focus, suggest a focus that might prove interesting, judging from the information in the discovery draft.)

_____

_____

_____

_____

_____

3. Does each paragraph have a clear focus that relates to the main idea of the essay? Do any paragraphs need a focusing sentence? If so, which paragraphs?

_____

_____

_____

_____

_____

4. What additional information would help you understand more clearly the person being written about? (Remember, this information should be related to the focus of the character sketch.)

_____

_____

_____

_____

_____

5. Note any information that seems not to fit the focus of the essay.

_____

_____

_____

_____

_____

PEER REVIEW FORM 2: A CHARACTER SKETCH

Writer's Name: _____

Reviewer's Name: _____

First number the paragraphs of the work you are reviewing. Then write out your answer to each of the following questions. Use the paragraph numbers for reference, and use the back of this page if you need more space. When you have completed this review, tear out this page and give it to the writer.

1. Does the introduction make you want to read on? If not, can you suggest any approaches that might make it more interesting?

_____

_____

_____

_____

_____

2. What about the person is the writer trying to focus on? (If there is no clear focus, suggest a focus that might prove interesting, judging from the information in the discovery draft.)

_____

_____

_____

_____

_____

3. Does each paragraph have a clear focus that relates to the main idea of the essay? Do any paragraphs need a focusing sentence? If so, which paragraphs?

_____

_____

_____

_____

_____

4. What additional information would help you understand more clearly the person being written about? (Remember, this information should be related to the focus of the character sketch.)

_____

_____

_____

_____

_____

5. Note any information that seems not to fit the focus of the essay.

_____

_____

_____

_____

_____

WRITER'S RESPONSE TO PEER REVIEW 1

Read the peer reviews you received from the members of your group; then fill out one of these forms for each one. (This exercise will help you decide how you want to follow your reviewers' suggestions when you revise your discovery draft. It will also help your reviewers understand how they can provide the most effective information for you.)

Writer's Name: _____

Reviewer's Name: _____

1. Did this reviewer's comments help you see the strengths and weaknesses of your discovery draft? If they were not helpful, what kind of information and suggestions were you hoping to get?

_____

_____

_____

_____

_____

2. Based on this review, in what ways do you plan to revise your discovery draft?

_____

_____

_____

_____

_____

3. Which of the reviewer's comments and suggestions did you find most helpful? Why?

_____

_____

_____

_____

_____

4. Which of the reviewer's comments and suggestions do you disagree with? Why?

_____

_____

_____

_____

_____

WRITER'S RESPONSE TO PEER REVIEW 2

> *Read the peer reviews you received from the members of your group; then fill out one of these forms for each one. (This exercise will help you decide how you want to follow your reviewers' suggestions when you revise your discovery draft. It will also help your reviewers understand how they can provide the most effective information for you.)*

Writer's Name: _____

Reviewer's Name: _____

1. Did this reviewer's comments help you see the strengths and weaknesses of your discovery draft? If they were not helpful, what kind of information and suggestions were you hoping to get?

_____

_____

_____

_____

_____

2. Based on this review, in what ways do you plan to revise your discovery draft?

_____

_____

_____

_____

_____

3. Which of the reviewer's comments and suggestions did you find most helpful? Why?

_____

_____

_____

_____

_____

4. Which of the reviewer's comments and suggestions do you disagree with? Why?

_____

_____

_____

_____

_____

SELF-EVALUATION FORM: A CHARACTER SKETCH

Name: _____

Essay Title: _____

Date: _____

Complete this evaluation and turn it in with your essay.

1. How much time did you spend on this paper? What did you spend most of your time on (getting started, drafting, revising, something else)? Do you think you needed to spend more time or less time on some of these parts of the writing process?

_____

_____

_____

_____

_____

2. What do you like best about your paper?

_____

_____

_____

_____

3. What changes have you made in your paper since the peer review?

_____

_____

_____

_____

4. If you had an additional day to work on your paper, what other changes would you make?

_____

_____

_____

_____

_____

5. What things would you like your instructor to give you special help with when reading and commenting on this paper?

_____

_____

_____

_____

_____

CHAPTER THREE

RECOGNIZING FACTS AND OPINIONS

Expressing Your Views

GOALS

To help you write about a controversial topic of importance to you, we'll concentrate on the following goals in this chapter:

- Recognizing the major differences between talking and writing

- Distinguishing between facts and opinions

- Organizing a paragraph with the focusing sentence at the end

- Recognizing and correcting sentence fragments

- Varying sentences by using coordinating and subordinating conjunctions

Writing Preview

Using what you learn in this chapter, you'll write about a local issue that's important to you, explaining your views about that issue as clearly as you can, while at the same time carefully distinguishing between your opinions and the facts.

Think about callers you've heard on radio or television talk shows or letters to the editor you've read in the newspaper. People call talk shows or write letters to the editor about issues that are very important to them, and they often seem to think that expressing their opinions will make others agree with them. One of the things that is most noticeable about these callers and writers is the great conviction they express, whether they've analyzed the subject very thoroughly or not.

What sorts of issues do you feel strongly enough about to call a talk show or write a letter to the editor to express your views? Take a few minutes to write down a list of such topics.

> If you're having a hard time thinking of what to say, try some of the prewriting strategies you read about in Chapter 1 to help you get started.

Then discuss your list with your group or class. Have many of you listed the same general topics? Try to explain to the others why you would consider publicly expressing your views about your topics. Why are they so important to you?

TALKING AND WRITING

Even though some people may believe that they can just write the way they talk, there are some major differences between talking and writing. To make this point; let's look at an example of some real talk. The following paragraph is a statement by a woman named Joyce who appeared on the *Oprah Winfrey Show* to tell about her experiences with her adult son, who constantly borrows money and takes advantage of her:

> I don't like it. It's just that I don't want to cause any problems with the kids or anything and—you know, no arguments. It's easier just to say, "Here. Take it. I love you," you know, "but don't keep coming back time after time." I mean, I did get to the point on my phone bill—I mean, it's $600 a month. You've got to cut it off sometime. So, I fixed my phone to where he can't call me collect. . . .

That doesn't look very much like formal writing, does it? There are occasional interjections ("you know," "I mean"), and one sentence even shifts topics halfway through when Joyce interrupts herself to tell how high her telephone bill was. Although Joyce was able to communicate her ideas quite well by talking, when we look at the written transcript of what she said, it's clear that her ideas go off in all directions without the connections or development we would expect if she were expressing herself in writing.

Talking and writing are different ways of expressing ourselves. One is not necessarily better than the other. Sometimes you may feel that you can capture what you truly think and believe when you speak but not when you write. That's only natural, since like most people, you probably talk much more than you write. And when you speak, you have other things to help you express yourself:

- the tone and volume of your voice
- the way you pronounce your words
- your facial expressions—the movement of your eyebrows, eyes, and jaw
- your hand gestures and the movement of your shoulders, arms, legs, and feet

When you talk, you can shrug your shoulders, raise your eyebrows, smirk, cover your face with your hands, wink, and make hundreds of other gestures to aid you in conveying precisely what you mean. Moreover, by watching your listener's responses, you can tell how well you're communicating.

But when you write, none of these resources are available to you. As a result, writing may often seem to you a less effective way of communicating. But of course it's not. It's just that you need to draw on other resources to convey in writing what your gestures, tone of voice, facial expressions, and other physical activities help you convey when you're talking—the words you choose, the way you vary your sentences, the kinds of evidence you include, and so forth.

GROUP ACTIVITY

Spend ten minutes discussing the differences between talking and writing with the members of your group. What are some examples of the differences we've already covered? Can you think of other differences? Have one member of your group serve as recorder, listing the differences you find.

Which of these statements are facts, and which are opinions? Discuss them with your class or group.

FACT AND OPINION

You've probably known several people who have a hard time distinguishing their opinions from facts. These people tend to use their views as clubs: If they believe something, they think, it must be a fact. As an educated speaker and writer, though, if you're really going to convince people that your view is correct—as you would in most college and work-related writing—you need to use both facts and opinions. Sometimes it's very easy to distinguish a fact from an opinion.

Ninety-eight percent of American homes have television sets.

Most people watch too much television.

The first sentence is a fact. A fact is something we can verify, in this case by going house to house (if we have to). When we collect this sort of information to help support a point, we're gathering *evidence.*

The second sentence, on the other hand, is an opinion. After all, people's ideas about what is "too much" may vary quite a bit. Does watching "too much television" mean eight hours a day, which some studies estimate as the average amount that Americans watch? Or is "too much television" two hours a day? Twelve?

Sometimes it's hard to tell an opinion from a fact because so many people share the same opinion that it seems to be unquestionable.

Bill Cosby is a nice man.

This statement may well be true, but only people who know Bill Cosby personally can make such a judgment; the rest of us just know the characters he portrays on television. The

> A fact is a statement that can be verified by looking at evidence. An opinion is a statement that expresses the speaker's point of view.

common view of him as a "nice man" is an opinion, not a fact. And different people may use the word *nice* to mean different things: that he's generous and gives his wife and children new sports cars every year or donates millions of dollars to charities, that he signs lots of autographs without complaining and is always willing to speak to his fans, or maybe something entirely different. Although many people may agree on a particular matter, their agreement doesn't make it a fact.

INDIVIDUAL ACTIVITY

Indicate whether each of the following statements expresses a fact or an opinion by writing "F" or "O" on the line preceding each one:

_____ 1. There are 16 ounces in a pound.

_____ 2. Jesse Jackson is a Democrat.

_____	3.	Cherry pie is delicious.	_____	8.	California is larger than New York.
_____	4.	Going to college is good.	_____	9.	Running is the best form of exercise.
_____	5.	Fords are better than Chevrolets.	_____	10.	Basketball is more fun than baseball.
_____	6.	Fried foods increase your level of cholesterol.			
_____	7.	Teachers have easy jobs.			

R E A D I N G S

The following readings all deal in some way with the media. The first is part of a transcript from the *Oprah Winfrey Show;* the second concerns a controversy over MTV, and the third deals with the issue of violence on television. More important, though, each of these selections also illustrates ways in which people express their views about things that are important to them by using both facts and opinions: in speech, in letters to the editor, and in essays. As you read them, look at the ways the speakers and writers use or fail to use facts and opinions. Also begin to consider what issue you'll want to write about for your next essay. What's really important to you? If you were asked to express your view on a talk show, in a letter to an editor, or in an essay for a newspaper, what sorts of things would you say? What opinions would you express? What facts would you use?

PREREADING EXERCISE

In Chapter 2 you saw that you can get an idea of what an essay is about by reading just the introduction. Here we'd like you to try a different prereading strategy: skimming the entire essay. Before you read each of the following selections, look through them very quickly, just letting your eyes skim over the pages; then write a few sentences telling what you expect the essay to be about.

WHEN SHOULD TEENAGERS BE ALLOWED TO DATE?
The Oprah Winfrey Show

This selection is a transcript of part of the Oprah Winfrey Show *of September 16, 1994. Oprah's guests include a mother who says she will not let her daughter date until she is eighteen and an editor at* YM *magazine who offers an "expert's" view on the subject of dating and curfews.*

1   *Oprah Winfrey:* I remember around junior high school there were a lot of girls started talking about when they were going to be allowed to date. Some kids were allowed to start at something like 12. I couldn't understand that. And others had to wait until they were 16. I was one of those people forced to wait until I was 16, although at 14 I was 36-24-36. Hadn't seen those days anymore. But any way, I don't remember anybody who couldn't date until they were 18. But Pam says her daughter, Ambur, who is now 16, will not date until then — until she is 18.

2   *Pam:* Right.

3   *Winfrey:* And you intend to stand by that?

4   *Pam:* Yes.

5   *Winfrey:* And the reason is why?

6   *Pam:* I just—I want her to go to school. I got married when I was 15, and I know what it's like. And, no, I want her to go to school, get an education. She can worry about dating and boys later.

7   *Winfrey:* OK. And do you think that's reasonable? Do you think it's reasonable? Let me just ask . . .

8   *Pam:* Oh, yes, I think it's reasonable.

9   *Winfrey:* You think that's reasonable?

10   *Pam:* Yeah.

11   *Winfrey:* OK. Do you think that's reasonable, Ambur?

12   *Ambur:* No.

13   *Winfrey:* So you haven't dated ever?

14   *Ambur:* Never. Well, once—I went on a date once.

15   *Winfrey:* Uh-huh.

16   *Ambur:* I went to homecoming.

17   *Winfrey:* Went to a homecoming. You were allowed to go.

18   *Ambur:* I was allowed to go. But when she told me I could go, it took months and months and months to get her to say yes.

19   *Winfrey:* How does that make you feel?

20   *Ambur:* Like I did something wrong, which I didn't.

21   *Winfrey:* Mm-hmm. And does it make you feel, obviously, that she doesn't trust you or something?

22   *Ambur:* Yes.

23   *Winfrey:* Uh-huh. You know, I used to feel this. Let me tell you if—if you felt this, too. It was such a hassle in my house, because we'd have to ask, as you say, so many months in advance and then you'd have to get a check list

of who was going to be there, and did their mother know, and what time it was going to end and what time it was going to start. Then there were a lot of times I wouldn't even ask because it wasn't even worth the trouble. It was better to dry my hair.

24   *Ambur:* Yeah.

25   *Winfrey:* Do you—do you feel that?

26   *Ambur:* Yeah.

27   *Winfrey:* Yeah. That it's not worth the trouble. Because I thought it was bad, I had a—we're not trying to beat up on you, yet. But I had a—because I really don't have an opinion about this. I had a curfew at 11:00 and I was an anchor woman at 19 doing the 10:00 news and had to be home by 11:00. How embarrassing is that? You have to finish the news, wrap it up, get home by 11:00. But you have, I understand, a 9:30 curfew.

28   *Ambur:* 9:30.

29   *The audience groans.*

30   *Winfrey:* Can you believe it? Pam, we don't know what to say about it. Although we don't have no opinion. But we don't know what to say. Do you think that's reasonable?

31   *Pam:* Yes. I think it—I don't think she needs to stay out later.

32   *Winfrey:* What did you say? Can—what did you say?

33   *Audience member:* Are you allowed to go to the prom? Or any other school dances?

34   *Ambur:* She lets me go, but I have to be home earlier than everyone else.

35   *Winfrey:* OK. Well, how do you get asked to a prom if you are not allowed to socialize any time in between? Because don't people ask people who are allowed to . . .

36   *Pam:* Well, she's never been to the prom. She went to a homecoming last—last year.

37   *Winfrey:* Uh-huh.

38   *Pam:* She went to the homecoming. I think I let her stay out until it was, like, 12:00 or 1:00, something like that. And . . .

39   *The audience laughs.*

40   *Winfrey:* I know, we're so happy for you.

41   *Pam:* She had to—she had to be the first one home.

42   *Winfrey:* I know, my dad let me go to a New Year's Eve party once, but told me, "But be home by midnight." What's the point?

43   *Pam:* See, I mean, what—she doesn't need to be out that late.

44   *Winfrey:* I understand.

45   *Pam:* She had to be the first one home that night. She wasn't allowed to be the last one dropped off.

46   *Winfrey:* OK.

47   *Pam:* She has to be first. Her grades dropped after that and that's it.

48   *Winfrey:* Her grades dropped after one night out?

49   *Pam:* Well, we went—my husband and I went to the school for the parents-teachers conference and they said once we allowed her—said she could go to the homecoming—Ambur, like she daydreamed homecoming. They'd have to wake her in class. "Ambur, you know, we're back in school now." And that's all she thought about. So—no.

50   *Winfrey:* That's because it's the one thing she . . .

51   *Ambur:* Yes. Yes.

52   *Winfrey:* Ambur, what do you want to say here?

53   *Ambur:* I don't think it's fair. It was my first time out. And yeah, I did that. That's all I thought about because it was the first time. And it was so exciting. I finally got to go out with all my friends. Because I hang around with someone who's 14, because people my age, I can't hang out with because they get to get in the cars, they go places, they go downtown, they go here, they go there. And I can't go because I have to be home at 9:30 and they have no curfew . . .

54   *Pam:* I—that's just how I feel. I mean, I . . .

55   *Winfrey:* I understand. And you have a right to raise your daughter the way you choose to raise your daughter. . . . But I'm just thinking that—I mean, the whole socialization process, the reason why people start dating around this age—and we'll have somebody come out and address this—is because, you know, you—hormones and you're changing and you're developing and you need to socialize and have friends. And you—you think that you can restrict that?

56   *Pam:* Yes.

57   *Winfrey:* You do. OK. . . .

58   *Audience member:* Ambur, do you have a boyfriend?

59   *Ambur:* No.

60   *Winfrey:* She . . .

61   *Pam:* No.

62   *Winfrey:* Of course not. That's what she's talking about. She doesn't have a boyfriend.

63   *Audience member:* And when you go out with your friends . . .

64   *Ambur:* Pardon me?

65 *Audience member:* . . . and have to come home real early, doesn't that make you feel kind of bad—awful?

66 *Ambur:* My friends, they usually don't call me up to ask me to go out. They . . .

67 *Audience member:* They know you can't go.

68 *Ambur:* They—yeah, and because they know it bothers me. I mean, they call up, and it's like, "Well, I can't go." It makes me feel bad because—and they know, usually I don't—I don't go out. I'm always home because . . .

69 *Pam:* But Ambur can go. She's just not going to stay out—she's not staying out until curfew. I'm not going to let her stay out . . .

70 *Winfrey:* Because the curfew is at 9:30?

71 *Pam:* OK.

72 *Winfrey:* Right?

73 *Pam:* Yeah.

74 *Winfrey:* OK. . . . We invited Sally Lee to join us because Sally reads thousands of questions from teens about their dating concerns. She does that because she is editor-in-chief of *YM* magazine. And the biggest question is always: What age can you date? I bet? Isn't it?

75 *Sally Lee:* Well, whatever age your parents will let you. But at what age are teens generally dating, it's usually about, you know, 14. I'm afraid so, in these days. But you know, the whole issue is . . .

76 *Winfrey:* Yeah. We need to define dating . . .

77 *Lee:* Yes, let's define dating. Chris's parents [previous guests] had an idea about—about what a date was. And they considered that a very old-fashioned date. That is when a guy goes out with a girl one-on-one and maybe takes her to dinner or to the movies. And it's a very intimate situation. That isn't—for the—the most part, dates don't happen like that among 13- or 14-year-olds. Thirteen and 14-year-olds like to go out in a group.

78 *Winfrey:* They pack.

79 *Lee:* They pack.

80 *Winfrey:* Yeah.

81 *Lee:* And it's a lot of fun because it's kind of scary being out with a guy one-on-one. I mean, you got to talk to him. You got to figure him out. You don't know what to say. It's a scary experience. Most teens, at 13 and 14, go out in groups. And that's healthy.

82 *Winfrey:* Yes. Are you allowed to do that, Ambur?

83 *Ambur:* No. She gets mad. No.

84 *Winfrey:* You're not allowed to do that. OK. Do you think it's healthy—I mean . . . you say parents should not be too strict. Isn't what—what is too strict?

85   *Lee:* Well, I think that parents need to set limits. I think teens appreciate limits a great deal. They do appreciate curfews. You know, it's not a matter of don't set a curfew. They do appreciate curfews. But you have to set limits within what the teen's peers are doing. Everybody in the audience groaned here when Pam talked about the curfew for Ambur. And every mother groaned and then, you know, that if every mother groans, then maybe you're being unreasonable, because you're making Ambur an outcast because all her peers have a later curfew. All her peers get to. . . .

86   *Winfrey:* But what about this . . .

87   *Lee:* . . . go with the gang.

88   *Winfrey:* . . . as long as I—I heard this, I think, you know, Pam and my father need to get together and they can do the—that—the speech about, "As long as you're living in my house, under my roof, you will do as I say."

89   *Lee:* Right. Right.

90   *Winfrey:* You hear that speech ever, Ambur?

91   *Ambur:* Oh, I hear it all the time.

92   *Winfrey:* Hear it all the time. And it is, I'm respectful of the fact that it is your house. However, if—I know a lot of parents often say, "You can't do what everybody else is doing just because they're doing it." But you're saying, if the entire peer groups comes home at 11:00, the 9:30 might be unreasonable?

93   *Lee:* 9:30 is unreasonable. I'd say 10:30, if you want to—if you want to set a different standard for your kid, try and set it in parameters that are reasonable. And it's not only a matter of—you know, you can say, "These are my rules under my house." And that's fine. But Ambur doesn't live in your house all the time. Sometimes she has to be in school; she has to walk down the street; she has to deal with guys on a day-to-day basis and she has to learn how to deal with guys. And, you know, if you have—if you keep her in the house, locked up until she's 18 and then finally she leaves your house and she goes out into the world, she's going to have to deal with a lot of scary things coming from guys that she's not learned to deal with in the years from when she was 14 to 18. She's not going to be equipped to deal with them. She's got to know what to do. . . .

94   *Winfrey:* Will Pam agree to loosen up just, I mean, a little bit? Just . . .

95   *Pam:* No.

96   *Winfrey:* Could we get—could we just get Ambur a 10:30 curfew?

97   *Pam:* No. No. No.

98   *Winfrey:* We will try, when we come back. Back in a moment.

POSTREADING EXERCISE

1. Looking back through the transcript, identify five facts used by any of the speakers; write an F in the margin beside each fact. Then identify five opinions and write an O in the margin beside each one. Discuss your selections with members of your group or class. Do you all agree about which statements are facts and which are opinions, or is it difficult to tell whether some statements are facts or opinions?

2. What are some of the facts Pam uses to justify her daughter's curfew? List three of them, and discuss them with your group or class. How could you verify that they are facts?

3. How would some of the statements made in this transcript differ if they were written rather than spoken? Look at paragraph 93, for example. Turn it into a "proper" written statement by correcting errors, making the sentences complete and grammatically correct, and so forth.

STUDENT PROTESTERS WANT THEIR MTV

Mark Smith

In the summer of 1991, a Texas cable TV system canceled MTV in response to complaints about the music network's content. The following article, which appeared in the Houston Chronicle, *tells about the reaction of students at Texas A&M University to the cancellation. Following the article are several letters to the editor written by high school students, expressing their views about whether MTV should be taken off the air.*

1   Two Texas A&M University students stared at the silent blue screen as it continuously scrolled a three-paragraph message saying MTV had been dropped because of "community concern."

2   "Taking MTV away from us is like taking away beer or even our books," said Kevin Early, 21, a psychology student and waiter.

3   "We're college students and have to work until 1 A.M. or 2 A.M. to support ourselves. You get back home and there is nothing to watch."

4   Michelle Slafter, 21, a bartender and A&M psychology student, quickly added: "Now, instead, we have to watch the screaming televangelists. They'll scream for money. MTV never did."

5   "I just can't understand the decision to remove MTV. There is nothing any more obscene on MTV than the daytime soaps or on prime time television."

6   But TCA Cable officials who distribute cable television service to 430,000 subscribers in six states—including 30,000 subscribers in sister cities Bryan and College Station—said they felt differently.

7   After receiving what it claims were "hundreds" of complaints, TCA

Cable of Tyler became the first U.S. cable company to drop MTV because of program content.

8   The music network, which celebrates its 10th anniversary next month, is shown in 40 countries, reaching an estimated 193 million viewers on six continents.

9   But TCA officials said the lewd content of some of MTV's music videos had caused outrage in "Bible Belt" cities such as Bryan and College Station. . . .

10   TCA's decision to eliminate MTV has caused a fierce debate.

11   Those who oppose the decision to drop MTV have held rallies and protested in front of TCA's Bryan/College Station office. Some are discussing attempts to sue TCA, while others have begun a petition to get a second cable company.

12   Those who support MTV's removal have praised TCA for its "courage" and "bold decision" in a college town with 42,000 students.

13   "I haven't found anybody who doesn't have a strong opinion one way or another on this," said Randy Rogers, 31, head of TCA Cable's operations in the Bryan/College Station office.

14   During the past week, Rogers said, his office has received 1,400 phone calls and several hundred letters split "about 50/50" over the decision.

15   "We've gained customers this week from people who say: 'Since you've taken MTV off the cable we're going to subscribe,'" Rogers said. "We've also lost customers."

16   Rogers said he was unsure how many subscribers originally complained about MTV. But he said TCA had received complaints for "several years."

17   Most complaints were about Madonna and her music video "Like a Prayer," Rogers said. Cable viewers complained that the video showed Madonna standing in front of burning crosses and later simulating masturbation.

18   "When your service is offensive to enough people we felt it was necessary to take the stance we did," said Rogers, who added that TCA's service areas include towns in Texas, Arkansas, Idaho, Louisiana, New Mexico and Mississippi.

19   "Most of our communities have average populations of 25,000 to 30,000," Rogers said. "I think you have a different set of morality in smaller communities than larger communities."

20   Rogers said TCA wanted to drop MTV from the basic cable service available to all customers and make it available, instead, to only those who want it.

21   But MTV's owners wanted TCA to continue to offer MTV as a basic cable service. They said TCA customers not wanting the programming could ask TCA to block its broadcast to their homes. . . .

22   "We encourage them to turn or lock MTV out of people's homes who don't want it," said Carrie Robinson, a Viacom spokeswoman . . . , who claims MTV's program standards are "virtually the same" as the broadcast networks. . . .

23   Rogers, however, said he received 350 letters, along with six "Prayergrams," praising him for TCA's decision to drop MTV.

24   "It is a breath of fresh air to have someone finally stand up and say we've had enough of filth and garbage," a "Prayergram" delivered to Rogers said.

25   A local church event sent a 100-name petition saying: "Thank you for caring for your own children's minds. God bless you!"

26   In her letter, Bev Tydlacka, 42, a Bryan mother with two sons, said the content of "so many of the videos aired on MTV depict unacceptable behavior. Daily viewing of this type of behavior eventually leads a child to question what they are taught by their parents and teachers."

27   When reached for further comment, Tydlacka said MTV's videos have steadily become "raunchier" in an attempt by some musical artists to gain greater publicity through selling sex and violence.

28   "This area is not New York or California," Tydlacka said. "This is the Bible Belt—a conservative, Christian community."

29   "Some of the lyrics in the MTV songs are a put-down on women and are racist. If your children hear the songs long enough, even if they are not conscious of it, they may pick up the undercurrent thoughts." . . .

30   Others said they do not believe the dropping of MTV is censorship.

31   "Your decision does not indicate censorship; rather it is a marketing decision," wrote Clark and Susan Gandy, a Bryan couple.

32   "Please do not be swayed by the furor of the vocal minority; stand by your decision—it was the right one."

33   The decision, however, has caused anger and disappointment at Texas A&M University, where some of the students and nearby businesses have charged TCA with censorship.

34   "People watch MTV around the world," said Gwynne Ash, 22, an English literature student who heads Citizens against Censorship.

35   "It's seen in the Soviet Union," Ash said. "The Soviet Union is usually seen as a bastion of censorship, but it's seen 24 hours a day in Leningrad. But we can't get it in College Station."

36   "Once you start censoring things you never know what is next to go. Beer commercials show more flesh than MTV. Many of the same videos shown on MTV are seen on network television. Are they going to try to censor them too?"

37   Ash said she found TCA hypocritical.

38   "TCA talks about consumer concern, but they totally disregard this consumer's concern," Ash said, pointing to herself. "Is ESPN off the air if I

call in and complain? How many people need to complain? Or does it just have to fit within TCA's moral agenda?" . . .

39   Don Anz, owner of three Bryan-College Station restaurants, is one of several businessmen who have donated money and gift certificates for a Citizens Against Censorship rally.

40   "It's embarrassing we don't have the diversity," said Anz, 43. "There are a lot of people who want more diversity with A&M here."

41   "We have two country-western channels, but no MTV. If you watch those country-western channels, they're pretty tasteless too."

42   Anz praised MTV for social programming wedged among music videos, including anti-drug, AIDS education and environmental messages.

43   Jamie Mitchell, 24, of Bryan, said she fears MTV's removal is "veiled racism."

44   "I think many of the people feel threatened by the music," said Mitchell, a black woman who works in a day-care center. "It's not up to TCA Cable to censor."

45   "All parents have to do is flip the channel. I think there are a lot of lazy parents who aren't willing to watch their children and use television as a baby-sitter."

46   Mitchell's 75-year-old grandmother, Alice Patterson, said she has begun praying for MTV's return.

47   "Every time I got a chance I listened to MTV," Patterson said. "It took a part of me when they took it off the air."

48   "MTV had a lot of messages in their music. When I was in the kitchen preparing dinner or working in the house I'd turn on MTV."

49   Others, such as A&M philosophy professor Manuel Davenport, said they are studying a possible lawsuit against TCA Cable for not having replaced MTV with "something of comparable value" as required in TCA's franchise agreement with College Station.

50   "I don't believe TCA Cable's moral argument," said Davenport, 62. "What they have done is reduce their cost and not replaced MTV with anything."

51   "If MTV is so bad why should TCA try to sell it at a higher price?" he asked. "It's like saying a drug is bad for you so we'll not make it available. But if we can sell it at a higher price we'll do it." . . .

POSTREADING EXERCISE

1. Go through this article and label five facts and five opinions, just as you did with the *Oprah Winfrey Show* transcript. Put an F in the margin beside each fact and an O beside each opinion. Can you always clearly identify the facts and the opinions?

2. The reporter gives us a lot of differ-

ent views in this article, using both direct and indirect quotations. Do you have a sense of which side "wins," the pro-MTV side or the anti-MTV side? Do you think the writer is on one side or the other? What about the article makes you think that?

3. In the transcript of the *Oprah Winfrey Show,* you read statements written out exactly as they were spoken; in this article, though, the reporter selected portions of spoken statements and perhaps even cleaned them up somewhat. Which did you find easier to read, the transcript or the article? Why?

4. Have one member of your group or class read part of the MTV article aloud to the others. Next have two or three members of your group or class play the roles of the people on the *Oprah Winfrey Show* and read their statements. Is it easier to follow the article or the transcript when you're listening to them both? Is the transcript easier to follow and understand when you read it or when you hear it?

5. Before you read the letters to the editor that follow, consider how you feel about this issue. Was TCA Cable justified in canceling MTV? Write a one-paragraph letter to the editor of your school or local newspaper expressing your view.

LETTERS TO THE EDITOR ABOUT THE MTV CONTROVERSY

As part of its follow-up on the MTV story, the Houston Chronicle *invited young readers to write in expressing their views about whether MTV should be canceled. Obviously, many readers felt very strongly about the issue; here are some of their responses.*

1   Wake up out there. Hello are you awake? Good, now that I've got your attention, are you crazy? What's this stuff I hear about banning MTV from the Houston airways? Come on, man, get with the program. You're talking about banning the core of rock and roll videos here. So MTV is a little bit suggestive, what's wrong in showing a little bit of bumping and grinding on rock videos? That's what they're here for. And if your parents don't like it, then don't watch it. But if your excuse is, "They watch MTV all day, and I never get to watch the news." Well, that's why you were made parents—buy them their own TV set, then everybody is happy. Also, the banning of MTV would [conflict] with MTV's rights to show what they want when they want. You know, the First Amendment, the thing that this great country is pretty much based on. So don't talk about this neurological deranged stuff about banning MTV and just go with the flow of rock and roll.

*   *   *

2   The banning of MTV is not only unjust and immoral but also anti-American.

3   This is America, where we have freedom of choice; viewers should be able to choose whether or not to watch MTV. Censorship is not the answer to the problem.

4   I don't think it's right for one company to play baby-sitter to hundreds of households. No concern for the viewer has been shown, only the cowardice of a company trying to avoid controversy.

5   The subject of MTV being suggestive and controversial is opinion. The opinion of one company should not interfere with the rights of the viewers to watch what they choose. Instead of concerning themselves with the opinions of those who disapprove of MTV, they should ask those who like it.

*   *   *

6   Personally, I do not want MTV banned anywhere. Don't we have freedom of choice in America? Don't I deserve the right to choose whether or not to watch these "suggestive" images? Why is MTV accepted [and not censored] in Leningrad, while the opposite is true in Texas? Could the Soviet Union be more progressively democratic than we are?

*   *   *

7   MTV should not be taken off cable because they update us on our favorite groups and singers. And they're the only ones who play rap, pop, and heavy metal. Who's going to tell us about the new groups coming out and who's going to interview them? I'm deaf in one ear caused by nerve damage. MTV is the only source that I can understand unless it is real loud because I can read their lips, and I'm good at it. MTV does a lot. A person can't walk into a record store and say, well, I've never heard of the group, so I'm not going to buy the tape. How are pop and rock and roll groups supposed to make a living? The paper said that there are 830,000 people who watch MTV a day just in the Houston area. There are comedy hours for parents, prime times for teens and television for children. MTV should be kept!

POSTREADING EXERCISE

1. Go back through these letters and distinguish between facts and opinions. Write an F in the margin beside five facts and an O beside five opinions. Do the writers always carefully distinguish between facts and opinions?

2. Do any of these letters seem to you more like speech than writing? Do some seem more like speech (or writing) than others? Why?

TV CAUSES VIOLENCE? SAYS WHO?
Patrick Cooke

In this essay, from the Op-Ed page of the New York Times, *the writer expresses a view of television violence that many might find surprising. As you read Cooke's essay, pay attention to the way he expresses his views. How does it differ from the speaking on the* Oprah Winfrey Show *and the letters to the editor? How is it similar?*

1   As the Beverly Hills conference on violence on television showed this month, academia's dire warnings about the dangers of watching the tube have always been an easy sell. But with Senator Paul Simon hinting darkly at Government censorship unless the industry does a better job of policing itself, the ante has been raised. The question is: Do TV researchers know what they're talking about?

2   Since the late 1940's, there have been more than 3,000 reports on the effect of watching television, and TV research itself has become a cottage industry. Most of the conclusions have been grim; many have been baffling. Here are some of the findings of the past few decades: TV leads to hyperactivity in children; TV makes children passive. TV isolates viewers; TV comforts the lonely. TV drives families apart; TV brings families together.

3   Not even the Public Broadcasting Service has been spared. In 1975, when researchers noticed 2-year-old children obsessively reciting numbers and letters, one study cautioned parents about a new disorder called the "Sesame Street Hazard."

4   Four years ago, the Department of Education financed the most extensive survey to date of the research on childhood development and TV. It concluded that a disturbing amount of scholarship had been slipshod or influenced by a prevailing attitude that TV is harmful.

5   Despite the difficulty of obtaining reliable information on how television influences people, some beliefs, particularly about violence, are as persistent as *Cheers* reruns. The National Coalition on Television Violence, for example, has for years asserted that murders and rapes are more likely to occur because of TV violence. According to the organization, "It increases the chances that you will be mugged in the street or have your belongings stolen."

6   Many Americans agree with this conclusion; the link between mayhem on TV and a real-life violent society, after all, seems to make sense. But consider this possible area for research: Why doesn't anyone ever talk about the many occasions when people are nice to one another on TV? What effect has that had?

7   Much of the hand-wringing at the Beverly Hills conference centered on the sheer volume of brutality young people witness on TV and how, at the very least, such incidents desensitize them to real violence. But if teenagers have seen 18,000 TV murders by the age of 16, as one study estimated, isn't it possible, given the popularity of shows like *Fresh Prince of Bel Air, Brooklyn Bridge* and *Beverly Hills 90210,* that they have seen many more incidents of kindness?

8   From *Little House on the Prairie* to *The Golden Girls,* there is no end of people discovering their love for one another. Singles, marrieds, siblings, punks and homeboys share so much peace, tolerance and understanding that you might even call it gratuitous harmony.

9   It is tempting to conclude that a young person bombarded with hours of dramas in which characters are good-hearted becomes more sensitized to niceness. The conclusion might be wrong, but it's just as plausible as arguing that TV encourages evil.

10   These issues have been around longer than television has, of course. In the 1930's and 40's, studies warned of the harmful effects radio was having on children's school performance and their ability to distinguish fantasy from reality. "This new invader of the privacy of the home has brought many a disturbing influence in its wake," a psychologist wrote in 1936. "Parents have become aware of a puzzling change in the behavior of their children." . . .

11   Comic books were once blamed for young people's poor reading ability, and the early days of film prompted books like *Movies, Delinquency, and Crime.* . . .

12   Comic books? Films? Those comics and films are classics now. And it's a shame many of us weren't around to hear those wonderful shoot-'em-up *Gangbusters* in the golden days of radio.

13   It is possible that today's kids will survive the effects of new technology as well as earlier generations did—provided they aren't forced to watch panel discussions by the TV experts.

POSTREADING EXERCISE

1. Cooke suggests that some TV shows might expose people to good behavior and thus help them learn how to behave toward others. List three TV shows that you've seen recently that Cooke could use to support this view, and explain in a couple of sentences for each why they would be good examples. In your explanation, be sure to give your opinion clearly, but also use at least one fact for each show. Then do the same thing for three TV shows that you think Cooke or others could use as an example of shows that might lead people to bad behavior.

2. If Cooke were recounting this information to someone in speech rather than

in writing, he would no doubt say many things differently. Select one paragraph from Cooke's article, and rewrite it as you would imagine it to sound if it were informal speech rather than formal writing. What sorts of things should you add? What other kinds of changes should you make so that it will sound more like "real" talk?

GROUP ACTIVITY

Now that you've read all three selections, spend fifteen minutes writing a paragraph on the differences you've observed between speaking and writing, using some examples from the three selections you've just read.

After you've written your paragraph, spend fifteen minutes discussing the differences with your class or group. Given the differences you've observed, what sorts of changes would you make in the essays you wrote for earlier chapters? What kinds of things will you keep in mind for future essays?

INDIVIDUAL ACTIVITY

Select a controversial topic important enough to you to write an essay about. Write a single sentence in which you tell what that topic is; then write five sentences in which you express your opinions about it. Next write out five facts about it.

PARAGRAPHING AGAIN

In some of the paragraphs you wrote for your character sketch, we asked you to write your focusing sentence first and then follow it with supporting statements.

Another way of paragraphing is to place your focusing sentence near the end, building up to it with supporting statements. In this type of paragraphing, your focusing sentence serves as a *conclusion* that is based on the sentences that come before it.

The following paragraph from an editorial about rap music operates this way.

Queen Latifah introduces her video, "Ladies First," performed with the English rapper Monie Love, with photographs of black political heroines like Winnie Mandela, Sojourner Truth, Harriet Tubman and Angela Davis. With a sound that resembles scat as much as rap, Queen Latifah chants "Stereotypes they got to go" against a backdrop of newsreel footage of the apartheid struggle in South Africa. The politically sophisticated Queen Latifah seems worlds apart from the adolescent, buffoonish sex orientation of most rap. In general, women rappers seem so much more grown up.

Michelle Wallace, "When Black Feminism Faces the Music
and the Music Is Rap"

The focusing sentence of this paragraph is at the end: "In general, women rappers seem so much more grown up." All the earlier sentences build up to that statement by presenting details of the Queen Latifah video. The focusing sentence doesn't have to be at the end; it could have been near the beginning, like this:

> In general, women rappers seem so much more grown up. Queen Latifah introduces her video, "Ladies First," performed with the English rapper Monie Love, with photographs of black political heroines like Winnie Mandela, Sojourner Truth, Harriet Tubman and Angela Davis. With a sound that resembles scat as much as rap, Queen Latifah chants "Stereotypes they got to go" against a backdrop of newsreel footage of the apartheid struggle in South Africa. The politically sophisticated Queen Latifah seems worlds apart from the adolescent, buffoonish sex orientation of most rap.

Wallace made a choice to build up to her general statement about women rappers based on the specific example of Queen Latifah. When you want your focusing statement to have particular force and make a strong point, putting it at the end of the paragraph can be effective because you can build up to it with specific examples and details.

INDIVIDUAL ACTIVITY

To practice writing a paragraph with the focusing sentence at the end, write a paragraph in which you use two or three of the facts you listed for the individual activity on page 105 and lead up to a general conclusion based on them. That conclusion should be the focusing sentence of your paragraph and should come at the end.

WRITING ASSIGNMENT: EXPRESSING YOUR VIEWS

Think about an issue in your community or on your campus that's very important to you. It may be as simple as the number of students who cut across lawns rather than use sidewalks or as complex as safety in certain parts of town at night. Write a paper that could run as an editorial in your campus or local newspaper, expressing your views on this issue and suggesting what can be done about it.

Summary of Steps

Here's a summary of steps to take in completing this assignment. Check off each step after you've completed it.

_____ Determine what issue you're going to deal with. It should be at least controversial enough that not everyone would agree with your view.

_____ Write down your opinion of the issue.

_____ Make a list of the main points you want to cover.

_____ List as many relevant facts as you can.

_____ Determine which facts fit with the main points you want to cover. Be sure that you distinguish carefully between facts and opinions both before you write and as you are writing.

_____ Arrange the main points in the order you want to present them in your essay. Consider alternate orders for the main points, too.

_____ Write an introduction in which you state your topic clearly and indicate what your view is.

_____ Make sure that each paragraph in your essay actually deals with your main topic; don't drift off the topic into other issues you care about, no matter how important they may be to you.

GROUP ACTIVITY

Talk about your topic with your group or class. Explain why it's important to you, what your opinions are, and some facts you plan to use to support your views. As you listen to other members of your group or class, offer suggestions about the kinds of facts or opinions they might consider including.

Student Sample

In the following essay, the writer, Chi Nguyen, expresses her concern about suicide among teenagers. Note that Chi makes her views on this issue clear in her very first paragraph and that she uses some facts and personal examples to support her opinions.

TEEN SUICIDE
Chi Nguyen

1   In 1989, one of my closest friends thought that her life was useless, that it had no meaning, so she killed herself. While her parents were away for the weekend, she locked herself in the garage and started the engine of her father's station wagon. She sat in the car and inhaled the carbon monoxide fumes. She fell asleep shortly afterward. The police found her there, after the neighbors heard the loud noises the car was making and went to investigate. Her parents did not know until they came back on Monday that their daughter had taken her own life. It was a great shock, not just to them, but to all her friends and classmates, because she seemed like the kind of person that people think have it all; we never thought she was the kind who would do anything like that.

2   While alcohol, drugs, and accidents are also high on the list, suicide is one of the leading causes of death among young people in the United States. According the 1994 *World Almanac and Book of Facts,* in 1992, almost 9,000 people between the ages of 15 and 24 committed suicide. Many teenagers in America turn to suicide to solve their problems with life. They see no way of getting better. They see no light at the end of the tunnel, no rainbows and blue skies. They are so depressed that they totally disregard their personal and social lives.

3   How can we solve this problem? How can we keep these kids from killing themselves? Mostly what we need to do as a community, society, family members, and friends is encourage our teenagers to have a better sense of self-esteem. Parents especially shouldn't put them down every time they make a mistake; they should tell them that it is all right and that they can try to do better.

4   Don't lecture your teenagers or tell them how it was different in your days. That's the point. Those were *your* days, not theirs. Things were different then, so you can't expect them to do everything the

way you did or the way you want them to. Let them live their own lives, just as you wanted your parents to let you live your life.

5   Parents often set their standards too high, so that teenagers get depressed because they think they have failed. The standards are so high that the goal can't be reached. All we need to do is let the children grow up and make their own mistakes, live their own lives, and be happy that they are doing the best they can.

6   Just give them a little space and be patient with them. When you think they are doing something wrong, give them some advice, not a lecture. Have more trust in your children because they are your children; be confident that you have raised your children to the best of your ability and they'll try to do their best.

7   I wish that I had known what to do when my friend was in danger. I wish other people had known, too. We couldn't see the signs that she gave us then, and now it's too late. But maybe we can save someone else if we'll just pay attention.

INDIVIDUAL ACTIVITY

1. What issue is Chi Nguyen dealing with in this essay? What is her opinion?

2. Put an F beside three of the facts in this essay; put an O beside three of the opinions.

3. Do you think the facts Nguyen uses are all relevant to her main points?

4. What other kinds of facts could Nguyen have used in this essay?

Peer Review

Once you have your complete discovery draft, you're ready to start peer reviews. Here's a recap of what you need to do.

- Exchange papers with a classmate.
- Be alert to what the writer succeeds at doing and is having trouble doing.
- Write your peer review, using one of the forms on pages 111–12 and 113–14.
- Talk over your review with the writer for a few minutes.

- Go through the whole process with another classmate.
- After reading the peer reviews of your own draft, complete the Writer's Response to Peer Review forms that follow the Peer Review forms.

Revising Your Discovery Draft

By now you should have a small stack of paper: your notes, your completed discovery draft, and peer reviews written by two of your classmates. With these you can start revising the discovery draft into the final version of your paper—the one you're actually going to turn in. Here's the process for revising.

- Reread your draft.
- Reread your peer reviews, noting what the reviewers found effective and what they suggested to improve the draft.
- Decide which of the comments you agree with and which you disagree with. (Remember, you don't have to agree with or make the changes they suggest; you have the final responsibility for your essay.)
- If the reviewers weren't sure what single issue you are focusing on or what your opinion is, revise your opening and closing paragraphs so that the issue and your views are more clearly stated.
- Note any places where the reviewers suggested that you add facts or other details to make the importance of your topic clearer. Are there additional facts or details you could add?
- Did the reviewers find any paragraphs that need a clearer focus? If so, what sort of focusing sentence could you use? Would it be more effective at the beginning of the paragraph or at the end? What other changes will you have to make in the paragraph to make it more sharply focused?
- Once you have written a second draft, reread your revised version. Do you find it more focused, more interesting, and more detailed? Have you distinguished carefully between your opinions and the facts? If you are still not completely satisfied, you might wish to have another class member read it and do another peer review for you.
- Once you are satisfied with the organization and detail of your essay, read it carefully to be sure that you've expressed your opinion clearly and that the facts you've used are appropriate.

You're now ready to do the final editing of your essay. First, go over your draft carefully to make sure that all the subjects and verbs agree (see the checklist on pages 75–76). Then read the next section for some advice on how to revise your sentences to make them more effective.

Editing Your Draft

Once you've gone over your peer reviews and revised your discovery draft, you're ready to do some editing to make sure that none of your sentences are fragments and to combine sentences so that the relationship between ideas is clear.

Sentence Fragments

In Chapter 2, we showed that every sentence has a subject and a predicate. A *phrase* is a group of related words that may contain either a subject or a predicate, but not both: *the music videos on MTV* is a phrase; so is *cause children to be violent*.

A phrase should never stand by itself as a sentence; if it does, it is considered a fragment, which is not grammatically acceptable in most academic writing.

Another kind of fragment that does contain a subject and a verb is a dependent clause. Unlike a phrase, a *clause* contains both a subject and a predicate. It may be a complete sen-

> **A** sentence can have almost any number of phrases or clauses, but it always has to have at least one *independent clause.*

tence, in which case it's called an *independent clause*. A clause that begins with a subordinator can't stand by itself as a sentence; it's called a *dependent* or *subordinate clause* and must be attached to a main (independent) clause to make a complete sentence.

Because the videos on MTV are often vulgar is a dependent clause. It has a subject *(videos)* and a predicate *(are often vulgar),* but it starts with a subordinator *(because)* and is thus a subordinate clause. Such a clause is also called a *dependent clause* because it depends on another clause—always an independent clause—to make the sentence complete: *Because the videos on MTV are often vulgar, parents should not let young children watch.* Dependent clauses are always attached to independent clauses.

*H*ere are some common subordina-   of these, you'll make it a subordinate
tors; if you start a clause with any   clause:

after	before	so	what	while
although	(even) though	that	when	
as	if	unless	where	
because	since	until	which	

Which of the following clauses are phrases, which are dependent clauses, and which are independent clauses? Write a P beside each phrase, an I beside each independent clause, and a D beside each dependent clause. Then revise the dependent clauses to make them independent clauses.

_____ 1. the link between mayhem on TV and a real-life violent society

_____ 2. if MTV is so bad

_____ 3. who oppose the decision to drop MTV

_____ 4. TCA's decision to drop MTV has caused a fierce debate

_____ 5. wanted TCA to offer MTV as a basic cable service

_____ 6. many of the videos on MTV depict unacceptable behavior

_____ 7. when they took it off the air

_____ 8. beer commercials show more flesh than MTV

_____ 9. which celebrates its 10th anniversary next month

_____10. including antidrug, AIDS education and environmental messages

Sentence Combining

Sometimes an idea can be most effectively expressed in a simple sentence:

Henry didn't check his facts.

At other times, though, simple sentences don't express relationships as clearly as you'd like them to:

Henry didn't check his facts. The editor fired Henry.

There's pretty clearly an implied cause-and-effect relationship between those two ideas—Henry's failure to check the facts and his getting fired—but that relationship isn't expressed in those two sentences. But look what happens when we put them together. We can make the first sentence a subordinate clause and link it to the second sentence:

> Because Henry didn't check his facts, the editor fired him.

When we combine the two sentences, the cause-and-effect relationship is clear: We've shown not just that Henry wasn't a careful reporter but also that his bad reporting resulted in the editor's firing him.

The easiest kind of sentence combining takes two or more sentences and links them with a conjunction, just as we did. There are two main types of conjunctions:

- coordinating conjunctions
- subordinating conjunctions

Using Coordinating Conjunctions

Coordinating conjunctions join words, phrases, or clauses of equal importance. Think of them as a kind of plus sign. You use them to link two or more words or phrases or clauses and give equal stress to each. Here's a list of coordinating conjunctions:

> and, but, or, so, yet, nor, for

Obviously, not all of these words will work in all situations. You can say "The reporter wrote the story, and the editor read it" or "The reporter wrote the story, so the editor read it." But it doesn't make much sense to say, "The reporter wrote the story, nor the editor read it." You should use the coordinating conjunction that indicates the *relationship* you see between the two linked elements.

Here's how the coordinating conjunctions are used:

And indicates an *equal linking*. When elements are linked with *and*, one isn't more important than the other or the cause of the other. If you say, "The tuition has doubled, and fees have tripled," you're indicating something about costs, but that's the only relationship between these two clauses.

But indicates a *contrast*. Something exists or happens, while at the same time something contrary exists or happens: "He paid his fees, but he didn't have enough money for books."

Or indicates *exclusion*. If one thing happens or exists, then another does not. "He'll pay his fees, or he'll buy a car." *Either* and *or* are often used together: "Either he'll pay his fees, or he'll buy a car."

So indicates *result*. It suggests a causal relationship between the two elements.

In the sentence "The scholarship money decreased, so I didn't get an award," it's understood that there was no award *because* the scholarship money decreased.

Yet indicates a *contrast*. *Yet* is similar to *but,* but the contrast it indicates is greater. *Yet* usually indicates that something was expected but failed to happen or exist: "Funding increased, yet fees went up."

Nor indicates an *equal linking* between two elements that are negative. "He did not have a job, nor did he go to school." As with *and,* there's no cause-and-effect link between these elements. (*Nor* is often used with *neither:* "He neither had a job, nor did he go to school.")

In the examples we've used here, note that there's a comma before the conjunctions that link the two independent clauses. This is one of the proper (and required) uses of the comma. If you need more information on commas, see pages 203–4 and the appendix, "A Survivor's Guide to English," pages 347–49.

For indicates *cause or effect*. It indicates that the first item caused the other. If you say, "College enrollment is down, for there is less funding available to students," you imply that the decrease in college enrollment is *caused by* reduced funding. We generally use *for* as a preposition ("He saved money *for* tuition"). But when it's used as a conjunction to connect two clauses, think of it as indicating about the same thing as *because*.

Knowing how coordinating conjunctions work will help you use them to better effect when you combine your sentences.

INDIVIDUAL ACTIVITY

Combine each pair of sentences with a coordinating conjunction, following the directions. Feel free to revise the wording if you think changes will make the combined sentences sound better.

1. Some students stay on the sidewalks.

   Some students cut across the grass.

   Indicate equal linking: _____

   _____

   _____

2. Students have to park far from their classrooms.

   They are often late for class.

   Indicate that the second sentence is a result: _____

   _____

   _____

3. Trash cans have been placed all over campus.

   Students still throw garbage on the ground.

   Indicate a contrast: _____

   _____

   _____

4. The administration promised to improve dining hall service.

   The quality of the food is actually worse this year.

   Indicate a strong contrast: _____

   _____

   _____

5. These students do not respect the feelings of others.

   They do seem to respect themselves.

   Indicate a negative linking: _____

   _____

   _____

6. We must stand up for our rights today.

   We may find ourselves with no rights at all.

   Indicate exclusion: _____

   _____

   _____

INDIVIDUAL ACTIVITY

Select two sentences from your draft that will make sense when they are combined. Link them with a coordinating conjunction to show equality, contrast, or cause and effect. (Remember, you will probably have to revise your sentences as you combine them. You don't have to keep exactly the same wording.)

How many other sentences in your draft can you combine in this way?

Using Subordinating Conjunctions

When you use a coordinating conjunction to link two independent clauses, the two clauses are still independent; each one could stand on its own as a sentence. You can even still punctuate the two clauses as separate sentences: "The boy walked. And the dog ran" is as grammatically correct as "The boy walked, and the dog ran," although there are several reasons to prefer the latter version.

When you use a subordinating conjunction, though, you make one of the clauses dependent on the other, so it can no longer stand by itself.

There are only seven coordinating conjunctions in English, so they're pretty easy to remember. There are a lot more subordinating conjunctions, though. Here's a partial list of them, arranged according to the relationships they indicate:

Time To indicate a time relationship, you can use *after, before, since, while, until, once, whenever,* or *when:*

Before he could buy his text, the bookstore ran out of used books.

Contrast To indicate a contrast, use *although, though,* or *even though:*

Although the used books are badly marked up, they're all he can afford.

Cause or effect To indicate a cause or effect, use *as* or *because:*

Because the books are so badly marked, they're hard to use.

Location To indicate a physical location, use *where* or *wherever:*

Wherever he went, he saw his classmates.

Condition To indicate that a choice or an action depends on a particular condition, use *if, even if, provided,* or *unless:*

If students can't get their books, they can't pass their courses.

Obviously, not all of these subordinating conjunctions will work with every sentence. You can't logically say, "If he could buy his text, the bookstore ran out of books." You have to choose an appropriate subordinating conjunction according to the relationship you're trying to show.

INDIVIDUAL ACTIVITY

Use subordinating conjunctions to combine each pair of sentences, following the directions. You may need to revise the wording so that the combined sentences are clear.

1. Some students stay on the sidewalks.

    Some students cut across the grass.

    Indicate a time relationship: _____

    _____

    _____

2. Students have to park far from their classrooms.

    They are often late for class.

    Indicate a cause-and-effect relationship: _____

    _____

    _____

3. Trash cans have been placed all over campus.

    Students still throw garbage on the ground.

    Indicate a contrast: _____

    _____

    _____

4. The administration promised to improve dining hall service.

    The quality of the food is actually worse this year.

    Indicate a contrast: _____

    _____

    _____

5. These students do not respect the feelings of others.

    They do seem to respect themselves.

    Indicate a strong contrast: _____

    _____

    _____

6. We must stand up for our rights today.

    We may find ourselves with no rights at all.

    Indicate that the second point depends on the first: _____

    _____

    _____

INDIVIDUAL ACTIVITY

Select two sentences from the draft of your opinion essay that suggest a relationship of time, contrast, or cause and effect. Using appropriate subordinating conjunctions, combine them.

Now read through your whole draft very carefully. Are there other sentences in it that would benefit from sentence combining? If so, be sure to make the appropriate changes as you revise the draft into the final version of your opinion essay.

METAESSAY

The process for this essay assignment required you to do the following:

- Select a local issue of importance to you.
- Determine what opinions you would express about the issue.
- Determine what facts you would cite about the issue.
- Write a discovery draft expressing your opinions and using the facts.
- Review your classmates' papers and offer suggestions for improvement.

- Revise your discovery draft following suggestions made by your classmates.

How did you go about selecting the facts and opinions you used for this essay? Did any part of the selection process seem especially difficult for you? If so, how did you overcome the difficulty; if not, why do you suppose selecting facts and opinions was easy?

Write a brief essay exploring these questions. If you need more description of metaessays, see page 76.

PEER REVIEW FORM 1: EXPRESSING YOUR VIEWS

Writer's Name: _____

Reviewer's Name: _____

First number the paragraphs of the work you are reviewing. Then write out your answer to each of the following questions. Use the paragraph numbers for reference, and use the back of this page if you need more space. When you have completed this review, tear out this page and give it to the writer.

1. What single problem or issue does the writer focus on in this essay? What is the writer's opinion of this issue?

_____

_____

_____

_____

_____

2. Are there any places where the writer uses opinions as if they're facts? If so, can you suggest some facts that the writer might use?

_____

_____

_____

_____

_____

3. What additional facts or other details would help you understand more clearly the importance of the issue the writer is writing about?

_____

_____

_____

_____

4. Do all of the paragraphs have a clear focus? Do any of them need a focusing sentence, either at the beginning or at the end? If so, make a note in the margin of the essay.

_____

_____

_____

_____

_____

5. Do all of the subjects and verbs agree? (See pages 72–76 for information on subject-verb agreement.) Underline any subjects and verbs that you think may not agree. Also point out any fragments and any sentences that you think might be combined.

_____

_____

_____

_____

_____

PEER REVIEW FORM 2: EXPRESSING YOUR VIEWS

Writer's Name: _____

Reviewer's Name: _____

First number the paragraphs of the work you are reviewing. Then write out your answer to each of the following questions. Use the paragraph numbers for reference, and use the back of this page if you need more space. When you have completed this review, tear out this page and give it to the writer.

1. What single problem or issue does the writer focus on in this essay? What is the writer's opinion of this issue?

_____

_____

_____

_____

_____

2. Are there any places where the writer uses opinions as if they're facts? If so, can you suggest some facts that the writer might use?

_____

_____

_____

_____

_____

3. What additional facts or other details would help you understand more clearly the importance of the issue the writer is writing about?

_____

_____

_____

_____

_____

4. Do all of the paragraphs have a clear focus? Do any of them need a focusing sentence, either at the beginning or at the end? If so, make a note in the margin of the essay.

_____

_____

_____

_____

_____

5. Do all of the subjects and verbs agree? (See pages 72–76 for information on subject-verb agreement.) Underline any subjects and verbs that you think may not agree. Also point out any fragments and any sentences that you think might be combined.

_____

_____

_____

_____

_____

WRITER'S RESPONSE TO PEER REVIEW 1

> *Read the peer reviews you received from the members of your group; then fill out one of these forms for each one. (This exercise will help you decide how you want to follow your reviewers' suggestions when you revise your discovery draft. It will also help your reviewers understand how they can provide the most effective information for you.)*

Writer's Name: _____

Reviewer's Name: _____

1. Did this reviewer's comments help you see the strengths and weaknesses of your discovery draft? If they were not helpful, what kind of information and suggestions were you hoping to get?

_____

_____

_____

_____

_____

2. Based on this review, in what ways do you plan to revise your discovery draft?

_____

_____

_____

_____

_____

3. Which of the reviewer's comments and suggestions did you find most helpful? Why?

_____

_____

_____

_____

4. Which of the reviewer's comments and suggestions do you disagree with? Why?

_____

_____

_____

_____

_____

WRITER'S RESPONSE TO PEER REVIEW 2

Read the peer reviews you received from the members of your group; then fill out one of these forms for each one. (This exercise will help you decide how you want to follow your reviewers' suggestions when you revise your discovery draft. It will also help your reviewers understand how they can provide the most effective information for you.)

Writer's Name: _____

Reviewer's Name: _____

1. Did this reviewer's comments help you see the strengths and weaknesses of your discovery draft? If they were not helpful, what kind of information and suggestions were you hoping to get?

_____

_____

_____

_____

_____

2. Based on this review, in what ways do you plan to revise your discovery draft?

_____

_____

_____

_____

_____

3. Which of the reviewer's comments and suggestions did you find most helpful? Why?

_____

_____

_____

_____

4. Which of the reviewer's comments and suggestions do you disagree with? Why?

_____

_____

_____

_____

_____

SELF-EVALUATION FORM: EXPRESSING YOUR VIEWS

Name: _____

Essay Title: _____

Date: _____

Complete this evaluation and turn it in with your essay.

1. How much time did you spend on this paper? What did you spend most of your time on (getting started, drafting, revising, something else)? Do you think you needed to spend more time or less time on some of these parts of the writing process?

_____

_____

_____

_____

_____

2. What do you like best about your paper?

_____

_____

_____

_____

_____

3. What changes have you made in your paper since the peer review?

_____

_____

_____

_____

_____

4. If you had an additional day to work on your paper, what other changes would you make?

_____

_____

_____

_____

_____

5. What things would you like your instructor to give you special help with when reading and commenting on this paper?

_____

_____

_____

_____

_____

CHAPTER FOUR

SUPPORTING YOUR OPINIONS

An Essay on the Media

GOALS

To help you write an essay supporting your opinions about some issue dealing with the media, we'll concentrate on the following goals in this chapter:

- Using facts to support your opinions so that your readers will understand and be more likely to accept your point of view

- Responding critically to the articles you read

- Producing different kinds of paragraphs and using paragraph blocs

- Combining sentences with modifiers

- Using pronouns to make your writing smoother, clearer, and more cohesive

Writing Preview

Using what you learn in this chapter, you'll write an essay in which you express your opinion about daytime talk shows or another issue related to the media (TV, radio, newspapers). In this essay you'll support your views with facts you get from your own experiences with the media, from the readings in this chapter, and perhaps even from interviews with family members, friends, or experts.

ike nearly everyone else, you've probably watched an occasional daytime TV
talk show; perhaps you even watch one or
more of them regularly. Even if you've
never watched a whole talk show, though,
you almost surely have some opinions
about them and about particular TV talk
show hosts.

Before you read the essays in this chapter, consider your views about talk shows
and talk show hosts. Do you like or dislike
such TV shows? What do you think about
particular daytime talk show hosts (for
example, Oprah Winfrey, Sally Jessy
Raphael, Phil Donahue, or Geraldo Rivera)?

Take about ten minutes to write a
paragraph expressing your views about
daytime talk shows, being as specific as
possible. Then compare your ideas with
those of your classmates or group members. Do you share many of the same
ideas? How are your ideas similar? How
do they differ?

USING FACTS

Facts by themselves aren't of much use. Not many people like to see a whole
paragraph full of facts; we need to know the point of all the information. You must
use facts, but you can't just write them down one after another without indicating
why they're important. Facts are useful as support for your ideas; you can use them to
help persuade your readers that your point of view is correct.

Using Facts to Make a Point

Few of us like to read paragraphs like the following because it overwhelms the
reader with facts without really making any point:

> There are thirty students in this class. Fourteen of them are men, and sixteen
> of them are women. The oldest is 31 and the youngest is 17. Their average age
> is 21.7 years. This is a writing class. The students write seven papers each; that
> is, the thirty of them will write 210 papers. Each paper takes the instructor
> approximately twenty-five minutes to grade. Thus the instructor will spend
> 750 minutes grading each set of papers, or 5,750 minutes for the full set, or
> 87.5 hours of grading time.

Here's another way of using the same facts; this time, though, they're used to
make a point about the importance of class size:

> Class size is a very important issue, particularly for writing classes. In this class,
> for example, there are thirty students, each of whom has to write seven papers.
> If the instructor spends just twenty-five minutes on each paper, she'll have to

devote a total of nearly ninety hours each term to grading them. However, if we reduce the class to twenty students, grading time falls to just under sixty hours—leaving the instructor with additional time to spend in conferences and in individual work to help students.

The second paragraph uses a focusing sentence at the beginning to provide a clear stance. Then it presents some of the facts in the first paragraph (the number of papers and grading time) to help make the central point that class size is important because smaller classes allow teachers more time to spend with students individually. In other words, the facts actually are used for a reason rather than just listed for their own sake.

INDIVIDUAL ACTIVITY

What facts aren't used in the second of the two preceding paragraphs? Why do you think the writer omitted them? List two facts that the writer left out of the sec- ond paragraph, and write a couple of sentences about each, telling why you think they were left out.

Some Facts about Television

- Ninety-eight percent of all U.S. households have at least one television set. That's over 93 million households. Of these, more than 91 million have color television.

- In 1975, there were 9,196,690 cable subscribers in the United States. In 1992, there were 57,211,600.

- In 1983, the three major broadcast networks had a 69 percent share of all TV viewing. In 1992, that share had dropped to 54 percent. During the same period, public television had 3 percent of the viewers.

- With 61,600,000 subscribers, ESPN is the most popular cable network. The Family Channel has 57,400,000 subscribers, MTV has 57,300,000, and Nickelodeon has 59,000,000.

- The most popular television broadcast of all time was the final episode of *M*A*S*H* in 1983, with 50,150,000 households tuned in, followed by a 1980 episode of *Dallas* (41 million) and the final part of the miniseries *Roots* in 1977.

- Super Bowl games account for six of the top ten most watched broadcasts of all time (in 1976, 1978, 1979, 1982, 1983, and 1986).

- *60 Minutes, Home Improvement,* and *Roseanne* were among the most popular television shows in 1994.

Continued

Continued

- Automobile advertisers spend almost $33 billion each year on TV advertising. Beer and wine advertisers spend close to $660 million each year.

- In 1991, the leading U.S. advertiser was Procter and Gamble, which spent over $2 billion on all types of advertising. General Motors was third with $1.4 billion; and Ford was ninth with $676 million.

INDIVIDUAL ACTIVITY

Write a paragraph in which you make a point about television in the United States, using some of the facts in the box to help support your view. Read your paragraph to the members of your group or class, and explain why you selected the particular facts you used.

Some Problems with Using Facts

Facts are easy to use, and they can certainly help you convince your readers that you know what you're talking about and that your opinions are worth listening to. Facts can also be misused or overused, though, and sometimes they are even irrelevant to the topic you're discussing.

Misleading Facts

Although it's important to learn to use facts to convince your reader, you must be careful not to misuse them to mislead. We've all seen TV commercials in which the announcer says, "Ninety-nine out of one hundred doctors who expressed a preference chose our brand over all others." That may be true. But suppose that the manufacturer asked 10,000 doctors which brand they prefer, and 9,900 of them said that there's no significant difference among brands, ninety-nine preferred Brand X, and one preferred Brand Y. In that case, the advertiser's statement is indeed a fact: ninety-nine out of one hundred doctors who expressed a preference chose Brand X. But it's also misleading, for 9,900 out of 10,000 doctors didn't prefer Brand X—or any other brand.

Sometimes you can get away with misleading your readers; after all, most won't bother to check your facts. But those who do will know that you're being dishonest in your use of facts, and they're not likely to believe anything you say after that.

Overused Facts

It's also possible to overuse facts, as we mentioned when discussing the paragraph that listed seemingly unrelated details about a writing class. If you use so many facts, especially unrelated facts, that you overwhelm your reader, there's not much chance that you'll also convince the reader to agree with you.

Irrelevant Facts

Finally, when you use facts in your essays, you must be certain that they are relevant. Even if the facts you use are accurate and don't overwhelm the reader, if they aren't actually relevant to your point, they won't help your case.

You're not likely to include facts about a new car's performance in an essay in which you discuss your feelings about talk shows; you would realize that such facts were clearly irrelevant to your point. It is more likely that you would get sidetracked and include facts that *seem* to be relevant but really aren't.

Suppose, for example, that you find out that the average male teenager spends 22.5 hours each week watching television and that the most popular programs among teenagers are situation comedies. Would those facts be relevant to an essay about whether teenagers should be permitted to watch Geraldo Rivera's show? Probably not. And including them simply because you've got them won't serve any purpose at all. So be sure that the facts you use support the point you're trying to make.

READING CRITICALLY

Reading critically—closely analyzing what writers are saying and how they make their points—is an important skill that we'll encourage you to practice as you read the selections in this text. To help your understanding of what you read, first underline or highlight any words you don't understand. See if you can figure out the meaning of any unfamiliar word from the context of the sentence or paragraph in which it appears. Then look up the word in your dictionary and check the meaning. Write the meaning, in your own words, in the margin. This strategy will improve your reading and enlarge your own vocabulary as well.

Another way to be a thoughtful reader is to carry on a discussion with the writers of the essays you read by writing your own comments and questions in the margins. Carrying on a sort of dialogue with a writer will help you come to a far better understanding of what an article or book is all about.

As you read, think about what the writer says and test it against your own observations and knowledge. Many times, as you read and reflect on what you're reading, you'll want to note in the margin whether you agree or disagree with the writer, ask questions when you're unsure of the writer's point, and express your own views.

This is not exactly the same thing as talking to the writer, but it's almost like having a conversation with him or her. Here are some marginal notes on an excerpt from "Gawk Shows," an essay that appears later in this chapter:

These are noble thoughts, and not entirely hypocritical. Compassion and understanding are always in short supply. There is an outside chance that some of each might be spread around in this exercise. We may also be witnessing exploitation. "These children are risking their lives to be here," says Sally, introducing children who will die if exposed to light. What may she be risking if they don't appear? As Donahue says, "If I don't draw a crowd, I could be parking cars for a living." . . .

> He's just justifying the exploitation. I'm sure he'd get a better job than this!

Do you find yourself addicted to sex with prostitutes? Tell Oprah Winfrey and her audience all about it. Did you engage in an affair with a priest? Have your breast implants started slipping?

> This is an important medical issue. It should be discussed.

Geraldo Rivera wants to know. Do you wish you could reverse your sex-change operation? Are you a celebrity subject to diarrhea at odd moments? Does your mother keep stealing your boyfriends?

> But these are just private. That's different.

We care, we are interested. Whatever your problem, there's a television talk show that will accommodate you.

As you read the following selections, keep a pencil in hand and make similar notes of your own.

READINGS

Just about everyone has seen a television talk show on which people talk about their problems and interact with the host and the audience. These shows have become so popular that they're on at all hours of the day and night. Some people say that such shows are popular because they inform viewers about topics that are important or because they help us solve our own problems by seeing how others have solved them. Other people, though, feel that talk shows are the lowest form of entertainment, appealing mainly to our desire to view sleaziness and exploitation. To such critics, talk shows are just television versions of the supermarket tabloids with headlines about alien babies and living Elvises.

The articles that follow all concentrate on these kinds of talk shows, but their authors have very different views. As you read, consider whether they state their views clearly. What facts, if any, do they use to help support their views?

GROUP ACTIVITY

Before you read the three essays in this chapter, consider what you already know about daytime talk shows on television. If you're a regular viewer, you're probably aware of the differences among the various hosts and their shows. But even if you don't watch these shows regularly, chances are that you still know quite a bit about them from advertising and from talking with your friends.

1. With the members of your discussion group or class, list as many daytime talk show topics as possible that you've actually seen or heard advertised.

2. Given what you already know about talk shows, what sorts of topics would you expect to see?

3. What topics would you like to see on a talk show?

4. What sorts of topics would you intentionally avoid seeing if they were being shown?

PREREADING EXERCISE

In earlier chapters, you tried two prereading strategies—reading just the introduction to see what an article is about and skimming the entire selection to get some ideas about it before reading it through. In this chapter, we'd like you to combine these prereading strategies: read the introductory paragraph or paragraphs to get a forecast of the main ideas, skim the article, and then look at the conclusion as well.

GAWK SHOWS
Nicols Fox

gawk: to stare at something that is really none of your concern

In this essay, which originally appeared in Lear's *magazine, the writer attempts to explain our fascination with TV talk shows. What facts does he use? What conclusions does he reach? Are his conclusions supported by the facts? Do you agree with him? Note that Fox begins his essay by comparing talk shows to old-fashioned carnival sideshows where visitors paid to gawk at freaks.*

1   I remember the dusty heat of late summer, the yellow and white tent, and the barker strutting on the platform. His voice rose above the sounds of the carnival, hinting of the wonders within the tent, wonders

painted in cheap colors on the cracked backdrop: the two-headed baby, the world's fattest man, the bearded woman. I remember the sideshows. I thought they were long behind us.

2   I turn on the television and see an astonishing sight: a woman. Her soul is beautiful. It penetrates the atmosphere, even across the airwaves. Her body is not. It is covered with the lumps and bumps of Elephant Man disease. Sally Jessy Raphael, wearing her trademark red spectacles, cocks her blond head and asks what the woman's life is like. A window is opened into pain. There are more victims of the disease sitting in the audience. We are treated to its various *manifestations*. We are horrified and amazed: We gawk.

manifestations: the ways in which something shows itself

3   Phil Donahue interviews tiny, *wizened* children. They have progeria, "the aging disease." With their outsize, hairless heads and huge eyes imparting solemnity and even wisdom, they offer us themselves as a sacrifice to our curiosity. We are compelled into silence, fascinated. We are back in the tent. . . .

wizened: dry and wrinkled; old looking

4   The carnival plays on, and we have returned to the sideshows—minus the honesty that made no pretense about what lay behind the curtain, the honesty that divided the world into those who were able to resist their curiosity at the expense of others and those who were not. Gawking is painted in shades of *solicitude* now. We justify much in the name of compassion, but we are in fact being entertained in the same ancient tradition. Gawk shows sell.

solicitude: care, concern

5   "I offer no apology," says Donahue. "These children have been *unmercifully* pressured by their very distinctive appearance." The purpose of the show? "To humanize people who have suffered. It becomes a vehicle for examining our prejudices. Just because it may be true that this kind of show draws a crowd does not condemn it," he says.

unmercifully: without care for their feelings

6   For Sally Jessy Raphael the rationale is the same: "Teaching the lessons of compassion. Man's triumph over adversity."

7   These are noble thoughts, and not entirely *hypocritical*. Compassion and understanding are always in short supply. There is an outside chance that some of each might be spread around in this exercise. We may also be witnessing exploitation. "These children are risking their lives to be here," says Sally, introducing children who will die if exposed to light. What may

hypocritical: falsified

she be risking if they don't appear? As Donahue says, "If I don't draw a crowd, I could be parking cars for a living.". . .

8   Do you find yourself addicted to sex with prostitutes? Tell Oprah Winfrey and her audience all about it. Did you engage in an affair with a priest? Have your breast implants started slipping? Geraldo Rivera wants to know. Do you wish you could reverse your sex-change operation? Are you a celebrity subject to diarrhea at odd moments? Does your mother keep stealing your boyfriends? We care, we are interested. Whatever your problem, there's a television talk show that will accommodate you.

9   Donahue, Oprah, Sally, Geraldo: They are the *virtuosos* of *voyeurism,* lifting the skirts of our culture, peering into the closets, airing the national soiled linen. . . .

virtuosos: people with mastery or skill in a certain field

10   Nothing is sacred. There are no memories, no mysteries too precious to reveal. A woman discusses her husband's sexual addiction. Geraldo asks the husband for details—and gets them. There is nothing we won't share, or watch someone else share, with a million strangers.

voyeurism: enjoying secretly watching others, especially in sexual situations

11   We have invented a new social contract on the talk shows: Lay bare your body, your bed, your soul, your emotions, your worst fears, your innermost secrets, and we will give you a moment or two of fame. Every sacrifice can and should be made to the video god.

12   Are there topics too hot to talk about?

13   "How to blow up your local post office," says Donahue. He'd draw the line there.

14   There is no topic Sally wouldn't consider if it "concerns the human condition." She draws the line only at being boring. We have to want to watch it. So we set the *agenda.*

15   Donahue, a man obviously in conflict between his natural honesty and better instincts and his ambition, admits that his audience calls the shots. Devoting a recent show to strippers—both male and female—he says, "It must be ratings week. I don't want to do these shows. . . . they make me." Sure they do. But who is making us watch?

agenda: list of things to be discussed or done

16   Freedom of expression is not the issue here. Nobody's suggesting censorship or even *paternalistic* decisions based on what someone else thinks is good for us. The issue is honesty—honesty about why we watch. The talk shows are merely giving us what we want. The question is, Why do we want it? . . .

paternalistic: fatherly, controlling

17   The potential is there on the TV talk shows for real entertainment—
and for service. Oprah scored with a terrific show on female comics. Programs on health matters or economic questions are valuable. During the
first days of the war in the Persian Gulf, Donahue aired shows that were
serious and important contributions to our understanding of the conflict.
"I do have a conscience," he says.

18   Geraldo, however, ever subject to the temptations of the flesh,
spoiled what could have been a serious discussion of breast implants by
having Jessica Hahn as the honored guest and by fondling examples of
implants *interminably*. Does he have a right? Are   *interminably:* end-
we a people who need to watch breast implants   lessly
being fondled?

19   What happens when we set aside our last   *taboo:* something
taboo? What happens when we've finally been *titil-*   forbidden
lated to a terminal numbness, incapable of shock,
on the prowl for a new high? What manner of stim-   *titillated:* stimulated
ulation will we need next? Are we addicted? Talk   or excited
show codependent?

20   Which topic affects us more: the discussion   *S&L:* savings and
of the *S&L* crisis Donahue did last summer or the   loan associations;
interviews with the strippers? Which do you think   the crisis occurred
got the better ratings?   when a number of
                                                        S&Ls went bankrupt

21   In a free society we get what we want. We
shouldn't be surprised when we end up with what we deserve. But we can't
transfer blame. It's not the hosts' fault—it's the viewers'.

POSTREADING EXERCISE

Here you will analyze how factual information is sometimes used with opinions in the same sentence. For example, in
paragraph 17, Fox states, "Oprah scored
with a terrific show on female comics."
That Oprah did a show on female comics is
a fact; that it was "terrific" is an opinion.

Sometimes facts and opinions may be
woven together in several sentences. In
paragraph 2, Fox states, "Sally Jessy
Raphael, wearing her trademark red spectacles, cocks her blond head and asks what
the woman's life is like. A window is
opened into pain." The first sentence contains factual information about Sally Jessy
Raphael's glasses, her hair, the way she
moves, and the question she asks. The next
sentence is an opinion; it is Fox's interpre-
tation of what happened next.

Look through "Gawk Shows" and find at
least three places where Fox weaves facts
and opinions together either in single sentences or in consecutive sentences. Underline the factual information, and circle the
opinions. Once you have identified some
facts and opinions, discuss them with your
group or class. Do you all agree on which
are facts and which are opinions?

INDIVIDUAL ACTIVITY

Write out your answers to these questions; then compare answers with the other members of your group or class.

1. Do the things we see on talk shows teach us "the lessons of compassion," as Sally Jessy Raphael says (paragraph 6)? Or do they serve some other less lofty purpose?

2. Fox says that "there is nothing we won't share, or watch someone else share, with a million strangers" (paragraph 10). Would you be willing to discuss the most intimate details of your life on a talk show—especially if it meant you might be seen by thousands of viewers? Are there some things you would rather not hear about other people? What are they?

3. Phil Donahue says that there are some things he just wouldn't use on his show. " 'How to blow up your local post office,' says Donahue. He'd draw the line there" (paragraph 13). Where would you draw the line?

4. "The talk shows," Fox says, "are merely giving us what we want. The question is, Why do we want it?" (paragraph 16). Why do you suppose we want such things? What answers does Fox provide to his question? Are they facts, opinions, or both? Do you agree with them?

TELEVISION'S SHOW-AND-TELL
Stephen Lowery

In this article, the writer looks at both positive and negative aspects of talk shows. Which way do you think he leans by the end of his article? What facts does he use? What evidence that he provides do you find most persuasive? As you read this essay, don't forget to look up words you don't know.

1   Stephie Berezowskyj was 15 years old when she was raped.

2   Nothing, not her Ukrainian-born parents or her small Connecticut hometown, gave her any hope that talking about what happened in 1974, or about her subsequent abortion, would do any good.

3   She told no one. She married but refused to have children, convinced that God would give her deformed babies as punishment for the abortion and the rape. Her days she crammed full of work, while at night she woke screaming.

4   "I was going wacky," she said, adding that thoughts of suicide became common. It was at that point, at age 25, that Stephie Berezowskyj believes God gave her a miracle and delivered it in the person of talk-show host Sally Jessy Raphael.

5   "If it wasn't for Sally," she said, "I probably wouldn't be alive today."

6   The parade is endless, relentless, amazing, disturbing. Celebrities, wannabes, disgustoids and homemakers barge into homes *via* Phil, Oprah, Geraldo and Sally, revealing

via: by way of

to a live audience of hundreds and a TV audience of millions the most intimate, painful and private details of their lives.

7   They talk about marrying a porn star or the man who raped them. They talk about big breasts or having multiple wives or molesting children. They talk about things that would mean removal from a respectable restaurant. They talk about things they were too ashamed and scared to share with their own family and friends.

8   And as shocking as what they have to say is the fact that they've agreed to go before an entire nation and say it.

9   "Sometimes I would be absolutely amazed at what people were willing to reveal about themselves," said Darlene Hayes, supervising producer of *The Montel Williams Show,* taped in Los Angeles. "Even if it's your job, you can't help but sometimes be shocked by it." . . .

10   Doug Fizel, press liaison at the American Psychological Association, has frequent dealings with talk-show producers who attempt to line up psychologists to discuss the issue *du jour.* But even he is *taken aback* at times, never more so than when a producer called him for a show about women who marry the men who rape them.

du jour: of the day

taken aback: shocked

11   "I said, 'Geez! Where do you find these people?' " said Fizel, his voice shrill in the retelling. "He said, 'Find them? Three different people wrote me asking to be on the show.' "

12   It was a letter that got Berezowskyj, unable to talk about her rape even to her therapist, on Raphael's show. She had heard Raphael on her syndicated radio call-in show and trusted her. In 1984, she called the show three times, hanging up the first two, finally blurting out something about the rape and quickly hanging up on the third try. She wrote a letter to the TV show, asking it to do a report on rape victims.

13   "They called me and asked me if I wanted to be on the show," she said. "I said, 'Are you kidding? I can't talk to a therapist and you want me to go on television?'

14   "We kept talking, I don't know how it happened, but I agreed to be on the show. I really think it was God that made it all happen."

15   She flew to St. Louis, where Raphael was then taping, without telling anyone why she was going. She went on the show, blocked out the audience and concentrated only on Sally.

16   "It was like having a private conversation," she said. "It was like just me and Sally. I really believed if I talked to Sally she could solve this." . . .

17   Producers say that doing talk shows provides a *cathartic release* for many people, that being able to talk about a problem before many people represents beating it or, at least, being in control of it.

cathartic release: getting rid of intensely negative emotions

18   But others see far less high-minded motives at work.

19   "What you have in many cases is mutual exploitation," said Stuart Fischoff, a psychologist who has been on all the major talk shows.

20   He said he has little respect for those who put on talk shows.

21   "With the way they so cruelly use people, I can't imagine what they think when they see themselves in the mirror."

22   But he does have empathy for those who go on the shows, many of whom have low self-esteem because of the circumstances that land them on television. Talking about their problems many times means taking control of something that controlled them. There also is a bit of exhibitionism involved and the fact that, for many, it's easier to talk to a crowd of strangers than to a friend or relative one-on-one.

23   "They serve several masters," said Fischoff, who said he did talk shows merely for the experience and now refuses to do any more. "It's an incredible release to tell millions something you've carried around for years. It's also about your 15 minutes of fame."

24   Though he may have sympathy, Fischoff said people are kidding themselves if they believe that talk-show hosts care about them any further than the ratings they provide. His experience has been that hosts do not talk to guests before or after the show or during breaks.

25   "Many of these people are basically hallucinating their relationships," Fischoff said.

26   To illustrate the point, he told about a limousine ride to the airport after taping a Sally Jessy Raphael show about women who marry the men who rape them. He shared the ride with one such woman who, he said, was *ravaged* verbally by him, Raphael and the studio audience during the show.

ravaged: attacked and almost destroyed

27   "I was feeling uncomfortable with having to share a limo with someone I had helped totally humiliate in front of millions," he said. "And yet, all she could talk about was how wonderful the show was, how much she liked Sally, and how everyone in the audience loved her.

28   "We're talking many times about people who are out of touch with reality. On that same show, a woman who dated a rapist said she hoped no one ever found out about it. The woman was on TV saying this. Some of these people have simply lost the ability to reason."

29   But producers say they will continue to put these people on because in airing their problems, they help others in similar straits.

30   "We don't have people on our show to solve their problems," said Burt Dubrow, executive producer of the *Sally Jessy Raphael* show. "They come on our show to help someone else."

31   For every criticism leveled at them, producers can point to shows that benefit the public. [*Geraldo* producer Dan] Weaver has spent nights

in Grand Central Station researching the homeless and in AIDS wards putting together shows. [Montel Williams's producer Darlene] Hayes is particularly proud of a show she produced that introduced many new prosthetic devices largely unknown to amputees.

32   Cindy Spaid, who volunteers time at an alcoholism crisis center in Pennsylvania, said the phones always light up after a talk show dealing with drinking. Spaid, a recovering alcoholic, told her story on Geraldo after she was asked to do the show by Weaver, her brother.

33   She talked about her abusive husband and about being so desperate for a drink that she once drank two bottles of cold medicine for the alcohol.

34   "People tell me how courageous I was," she said. "It's not about courage, it's about doing your part to make the world a better place."

35   After her appearance on Raphael's show, Berezowskyj went back to her hometown of Guilford, Conn., where she said the response was rather cool. But, she said, the important thing is that she can now move on with her life. She volunteers time at a rape-crisis center when she isn't taking care of her 5-year-old son, Artie.

36   Artie, the child Berezowskyj vowed she would never have, is perfectly healthy and has a particularly attentive godmother. Her name is Sally Jessy Raphael.

POSTREADING EXERCISE

Here we will examine how facts can be used to establish the authority of the writer or of someone the writer quotes. For example, in paragraph 9, Lowery writes " 'Sometimes I would be absolutely amazed at what people were willing to reveal about themselves,' said Darlene Hayes, supervising producer of *The Montel Williams Show,* taped in Los Angeles." The quotation reveals Hayes's opinion of the talk show guests; the factual information—that she is supervising producer of the show—establishes her authority as someone knowledgeable about talk shows and their guests.

Look for three other places in "Television's Show-and-Tell" where factual information is used to establish the authority of a speaker. Compare what you find with others in your group or class, and discuss how the passages you identify establish this authority.

TALK SHOWS
The New Yorker

In this article, from The New Yorker *magazine's "Talk of the Town" column, the unnamed writer doesn't start off by taking a stand on the issue of talk shows. Rather, the writer seems only to provide a series of facts. As you read, consider whether the writer's choice of facts suggests a particular point of view. Remember to look up any words you don't know the meaning of.*

1   We understand talk shows, about how having one has displaced the house with the two-car garage as the thing to aspire to these days. We understand those polls reporting that to young Americans fame is more important than money, and we understand how being a talk-show host represents some sort of apogee in the achievement of fame for its own sake. We understand the feeling of I can do that which everyone experiences while watching Oprah, Sally Jessy Raphael, Donahue, and Montel Williams do their jobs. We understand that talk shows are cheap to produce, and that, what with syndication services, regular network television, and cable access, there is an almost infinite supply of airtime that can be filled with chatter. We understand that the gabfest must go on. . . .

2   In recent months, we've seen on *Montel Williams* women who will date only rich men, and on *Jane* we've seen couples who've dumped each other, and on a show called *Cristina* we've seen a woman who will date only Cuban men (its very blond hostess happens to be Cuban), and on *Sally Jessy Raphael* we've seen Siamese twins joined at the head, and on *Home* we've seen teen-agers with silicone breast implants. On several shows we've seen a former Miss America talk about being a victim of incest, and we've seen Roseanne Arnold and LaToya Jackson do the same. On a *Donahue* rerun we've seen Jamie Lee Curtis and her mom, Janet Leigh, and on a show called *One on One with John Tesh* we've seen Laura Dern and her mom, Diane Ladd. On *Montel Williams* we've seen white supremacists who want to kill blacks. We've seen debates on the welfare state, the beauty myth, the men's movement, the women's movement, Japan bashing, health insurance, Magic Johnson, Ross Perot, Sister Souljah, M.I.A. conspiracy theories, and J.F.K. conspiracy theories so many times that we're not quite sure where we stand on any of these issues any longer.

3   It's not that we were fascinated by any of the stories or psychodramas that the guests on these shows were relating; it's more that we couldn't quite believe that people would actually go on television to discuss this stuff. We said to ourself over and over again "Who cares?" and yet we kept watching. We told ourself that this allowed us a direct view into the American psyche—that by tuning in to *Sally Jessy Raphael* and *Donahue* and *Jane* and *Geraldo* we were able to learn certain basic truths about this nation we live in. But when we tried to decide exactly what those little pearls of insight were, we couldn't. Mostly, we just became more and more aware of our own voyeurism.

4   One day, on *Sally Jessy Raphael,* a man appeared with a representative of something called the Lingerie of the Month Club, and models came out displaying two different underwear outfits: the first, in demure and

lacy white, was for the man's wife; the second, a bright-red merry widow with a tangle of garters and ribbons, was for his mistress. For the rest of the show, the studio audience tried to figure out how the man intended to keep his adultery a secret from his wife after he'd appeared on national television and talked about it. He kept saying that he would take her out on the day the show was going to be broadcast, to insure that she didn't see it—as if that would prevent her family, her friends, and everyone she knew from seeing it. But then we realized that if this man could attend a television taping without his wife's being any the wiser, perhaps the show's broadcast wouldn't affect her, either. After all, with so many talk shows to choose from, a person's appearance on any one of them has diminished in significance to the point where his closest friends might not even notice it. We decided that if things were as trivial as all this we didn't want to watch anymore. . . .

POSTREADING EXERCISE

In this essay, the writer offers many facts and includes only a few directly stated opinions, compared to Nichols Fox, for example, who includes in "Gawk Shows" a greater number of opinions than facts. Does that mean that this writer is more objective than Fox? Not necessarily. Look at the way facts are used in "Talk Shows." The author selects facts and links them together to lead the readers to a conclusion.

Underline all the facts the writer uses in paragraphs 2 and 3.

Then write a paragraph in which you discuss what conclusion you draw from those facts. Discuss what you have written with other members of your group or class. Did you all reach the same conclusion? How did the facts in these paragraphs lead you to your conclusions?

MORE PARAGRAPH TYPES

When we talked about paragraphing in Chapters 2 and 3, we showed you two major types of paragraphs: those with the focusing sentence at or near the beginning and those with the focusing sentence at or near the end. We also told you that these aren't the only kinds of paragraphs. Some paragraphs, in fact, don't even have a focusing sentence.

Short Paragraphs

Newspaper articles, for example, are almost always made up mostly of very short paragraphs, many only one sentence long. (Look back at Stephen Lowery's "Television's Show-and-Tell," which originally appeared in a newspaper.) To understand why, you have to think about how people often read them—while eating breakfast, riding

Not Every Paragraph Has a Focusing Sentence.

on a bus, or standing in line at a checkout counter. By keeping the paragraphs very short, news writers give the readers a great number of places to stop without losing their place.

In more formal essays, a one-sentence paragraph can be used for special emphasis. Look at the way Nicols Fox uses a one-sentence paragraph in his essay to put special emphasis on "hot" topics:

> We have invented a new social contract on the talk shows: Lay bare your body, your bed, your soul, your emotions, your worst fears, your innermost secrets, and we will give you a moment or two of fame. Every sacrifice can and should be made to the video god.
>
> *Are there topics too hot to talk about?*
>
> "How to blow up your local post office," says Donahue. He'd draw the line there.

As you read articles with fairly well-developed paragraphs, look for such one-sentence paragraphs. You won't find them often, but when you do, try to figure out what special effect the writer is aiming for. Used sparingly, one-sentence paragraphs can be very effective in formal essays, but if they're overused, they give the impression that the essay isn't very well developed.

Paragraphs without Explicit Focusing Sentences

Sometimes a paragraph doesn't really have a focusing sentence—or at least doesn't have a sentence that provides all of the focusing information. Look at another paragraph from Nicols Fox's essay:

> These are noble thoughts, and not entirely hypocritical. Compassion and understanding are always in short supply. There is an outside chance that some of each might be spread around in this exercise. We may also be witnessing exploitation. "These children are risking their lives to be here," says Sally, introducing children who will die if exposed to light. What may she be risking if they don't appear? As Donahue says, "If I don't draw a crowd, I could be parking cars for a living."

In this paragraph Fox is suggesting a contradiction: while talk show hosts claim that their goal is to encourage "compassion and understanding," what really seems to be going on is "exploitation." No single sentence summarizes this point. Nevertheless, every sentence in the paragraph contributes to making the point. The first three sentences examine the "noble" goal of encouraging compassion and understanding, "always in short supply." The fourth sentence introduces the idea of exploitation, and the sentences that follow offer examples to support the idea that the shows result mainly in exploitation, not compassion.

Experienced writers often write paragraphs without explicit focusing sentences; you'll encounter them in much of the reading you do in and out of class. In your own writing, you may sometimes find that a focusing sentence is so general that it isn't really necessary to make your point or that your examples and details make your point clearly without an explicit focusing sentence.

Be very careful in composing such paragraphs, though. Readers can find them hard to follow, particularly when an essay has more than one or two of them. In addition, by not using a focusing sentence, you run the risk of writing an unfocused paragraph, one that includes unnecessary or contradictory details. Make sure that you can summarize the focus of the paragraph for yourself, even if you don't include that full summary as a sentence in the paragraph.

Paragraph Blocs

Sometimes a focusing sentence provides the focus for more than one paragraph. A group of paragraphs that are all under a single focusing sentence is called a "paragraph bloc." Look at this paragraph bloc from Nicols Fox's essay:

> Are there topics too hot to talk about?
> "How to blow up your local post office," says Donahue. He'd draw the line there.
> There is no topic Sally wouldn't consider if it "concerns the human condition."
> She draws the line only at being boring. We have to want to watch it. So we set the agenda.

The first paragraph has just one sentence, and it provides the focus for the next two paragraphs. Fox uses his one-sentence paragraph to get our attention, then follows it with two paragraphs that provide two different answers to the question.

INDIVIDUAL ACTIVITY

Stephen Lowrey's "Television's Show-and-Tell" (pages 141–44) was written as a newspaper article, so it has lots of one-sentence paragraphs. It also has several longer paragraphs, though, and some paragraph blocs. Go back through that article and find one example of each of the following:

- *A paragraph bloc.* Underline the sentence that provides the focus for that bloc.

- *A paragraph with the focusing sentence at the beginning.* Underline the focusing sentence.

- *A paragraph with the focusing sentence at the end.* Underline the focusing sentence.

- *A paragraph with no focusing sentence.* Write a focusing sentence for the paragraph.

WRITING ASSIGNMENT: AN ESSAY
ON THE MEDIA

In this chapter we've focused on some of the reasons that television talk shows are so popular and whether they are good or bad for viewers. Just about everyone has an opinion on these subjects or others related to the media, such as whether news programs put too much emphasis on sensational events, whether violence on television should be censored, and whether children's programming and advertising need to be more strictly regulated.

For this essay, you should express your own opinion about the media. You may want to write on TV or radio talk shows, news programming, advertising, children's TV, violence on television, newspaper coverage of local or national events, or some other issue related to the media. Whatever topic you decide to write on, be sure to use facts—from your own experiences, from material you've read, perhaps even from interviews with family members, friends, or experts—to help support your views.

Summary of Steps

Here's a summary of steps to take in completing this assignment. Check off each step after you've completed it.

_____ Clarify your ideas about your topic.

- Use the prewriting techniques on pages 10–15 to help develop your ideas.
- Watch the kind of shows or read the kinds of articles you plan to write about to get some further ideas; keep notes on your ideas as you're watching the shows or reading the articles.

_____ Gather some facts about your topic. For example, for talk shows you could do any of the following.

- Check the local TV listings to see how many different talk shows are broadcast in your area.
- Check the local TV listings to see how many hours are devoted to talk shows each week.
- Observe the TV viewing habits of students to see which talk shows they seem to be watching in public television viewing areas on your campus.
- Interview other students, friends, and relatives to see what talk shows they prefer and why.

_____ Decide which of the facts you can use to help support your point of view.

_____ Write down the major points you want to make and the facts and opinions you'll use to support each one.

_____ Organize your points so that your readers can follow your ideas clearly.

_____ Be sure that your point of view is clearly indicated, probably in your introduction, and that each paragraph supports that view.

_____ Try to make sure that your paragraphs are unified, each focusing on a particular topic or idea.

Student Sample

After years of watching television, student Krista Muller concludes that TV commercials, as she says in her second sentence, "are really unrealistic." As you read, look closely at how Krista uses facts to support her opinions. Does her argument convince you that she is correct?

NOT MY WORLD
Krista Muller

1   People complain a lot because there are so many TV commercials that interrupt shows. But my complaint about commercials is that they are really unrealistic. The products and the lifestyle they show are very different from the way things really are. The media try to make you think that their products are going to change your life. But all they want to do is to make you buy what they're selling. When I look at most commercials, all I can think is, "That's not how things are in my world."

2   Food commercials are some of the most unrealistic ones around. When you see a Taco Supreme or a Whopper on TV, they look really great. They're piled high with meat and cheese, and the lettuce and tomatoes look bright and fresh. But when you buy them at Taco Bell or Burger King, they're half as tall, the lettuce is wilted and greasy, and the sauce is oozing out of the hamburger, usually onto your clothes.

3   Even the commercials for food you prepare at home are unrealistic. Mothers stand around in sparkling clean kitchens thinking about what to prepare for their families. Meanwhile, little boys are outside plotting about how they can get their mothers to make more Stove-Top stuffing. Don't they know that most mothers work? None of the moms I know come

home to shiny clean kitchens, and none of the kids I know sit around talking about Stove-Top stuffing. Usually most mothers come home to find dirty dishes in the sink and on the counters. And most often they're so tired that the last thing they want to do is plan a big dinner. The kids just want to get dinner over with as soon as possible so they can be with their friends. But the commercials for beef show a big happy family gathered around a roast or steaks as though this is typical.

4   Food commercials aren't the only ones that show a false view of life. Car commercials are very often seen on TV in settings that most of us don't drive in. People are always driving on open roads in beautiful mountains or along the ocean. There is usually never any traffic to stop them from driving as fast as they want. And there certainly aren't any police to give them tickets for speeding. When most of us drive, we're on our way to work, school, or the store. Usually instead of having a beautiful drive through the country, we get stuck in traffic. Other drivers cut us off and yell at us when we do something they don't like, and police give us tickets when we speed.

5   Another way that car commercials are unrealistic is that a car can't change who you really are. But advertisers want us to think that if you buy their car, it'll change your personality. Ford has a commercial that shows how people will change if they buy Ford cars. They show a nerdy guy with glasses and a bad haircut, and then they give him a Ford Probe and the next thing you know, he's at the beach with a surfboard, surrounded by a bunch of gorgeous girls. They also show a girl who looks really shy and proper. And just by getting a Ford she turns into someone who looks ready to party. These kinds of things just don't happen. A car takes you where you need to go. It doesn't totally change your personality.

6   Everybody eats, and most people drive. We all know that the commercials about food and cars are very unrealistic, but we continue to buy these prod-

ucts anyway. Why do we do it? Maybe it's because we
wish that instead of living in our world, we lived
in the happy, carefree world shown in TV commercials.

INDIVIDUAL ACTIVITY

1. Look closely at each paragraph of Muller's essay. For each paragraph, what is the proportion of facts to opinions? Which paragraphs include mostly facts? Which include mostly opinions? Why do you think the writer includes facts and opinions as she does?

2. How well do you think Muller has focused each paragraph in her essay? Does every paragraph have a focusing sentence?

Does every sentence in each paragraph clearly deal with the main topic of that paragraph?

3. How has Muller organized her essay? Does her organization make sense to you, or would you suggest any changes?

4. Evaluate Muller's introduction. Does her introduction make you want to keep reading? Why or why not?

Peer Review

Once you have your complete discovery draft, you're ready to start peer reviews. Here's a recap of what you need to do.

- Exchange papers with a classmate.
- Be alert to what the writer succeeds at doing and is having trouble doing.
- Write your peer review, using one of the forms on pages 165–66 and 167–68.
- Talk over your review with the writer for a few minutes.
- Go through the whole process with another classmate.
- After reading the peer reviews of your own draft, complete the Writer's Response to Peer Review forms that follow the Peer Review forms.

Revising Your Discovery Draft

By now you should have a small stack of paper: your notes, your completed discovery draft, and peer reviews written by two of your classmates. With these you can start revising the discovery draft into the final version of your paper—the one you're actually going to turn in. Here's the process for revising.

- Reread your draft.
- Reread your peer reviews, noting what the reviewers found effective and what they suggested to improve the draft.

- Decide which of the comments you agree with and which you disagree with. (Remember, you don't have to agree with or make all the changes they suggest; you have the final responsibility for your essay.)
- If the reviewers weren't sure of your subject or could not tell your view about your subject, revise your introduction to state your view more clearly.
- Note any places where the reviewers suggested that you add facts to support your opinions more effectively, and consider what facts you could add.
- Also note any places where the reviewers said your facts are misused, overused, or irrelevant, and consider ways to use them accurately and relevantly.
- Did the reviewers find any paragraphs that need a clearer focus? If so, what sort of focusing sentence could you use? Would it be more effective at the beginning of the paragraph or at the end? Would paragraph blocs be effective?
- If the reviewers recommended that you combine some of your sentences, try using conjunctions to combine them.
- Once you have written a second draft, reread your revised version. Do you find it more focused, more interesting, and more detailed? Have you carefully distinguished between opinions and facts? If you are still not completely satisfied, you might wish to have another class member read your paper and do another peer review for you.
- Once you are satisfied with the organization and detail of your essay, read it carefully to be sure that you've expressed your opinion clearly and that the facts you've used are appropriate.
- At this point you're ready to do the final editing of your essay. Go over your draft carefully to make sure that all the subjects and verbs agree (see the checklist on pages 75–76. Then read the following section for more advice on ways to make your sentences as effective as possible.

Editing Your Draft

Combining Sentences with Modifiers

In Chapter 3, we looked at some ways to combine sentences using coordinating and subordinating conjunctions. Using these conjunctions can help show relationships between ideas. Sometimes, however, you may want to combine sentences by reducing them to just a word or two. For example, look at the following sentences:

The room was old. It was badly decorated. The paint was gray. It was peeling. It was flaking.

These can be combined into a single sentence:

The old room was badly decorated, its gray paint peeling and flaking.

That combined sentence took four of the short sentences and reduced each one to a modifier—a word or phrase that somehow qualifies or describes another word or phrase. *Old, gray, peeling,* and *flaking* are all modifiers describing things about the room. Modifiers like these, describing nouns or pronouns, are known as adjectives.

Adjectives and Adverbs

*A*djectives modify nouns, describing or qualifying them: *the* short *man, the* fast *car.*

Adverbs modify verbs or adjectives: *the man ran* quickly; *the* blindingly *fast car.*

Adding adverbs can be a bit tricky. It's generally easy to spot the adjectives you want to use in sentence combining, but spotting the adverbs often takes a bit more effort because you have to change the form of the word and sometimes even have to come up with a new word meaning about the same thing. Here are some examples where the form of the modifier must be changed slightly:

The guest spoke. Her speech was quick. Her speech was loud.

These three sentences can become one:

The guest spoke *quickly* and *loudly.*

The modifiers *quick* and *loud* are adjectives. But when we add *-ly* to them, they become adverbs that modify the verb *spoke* in the combined sentence.

In the following example, we need to find a completely different word.

The host talked. He was silly.

Long Sentences versus Short Sentences

Are longer sentences better? Although a lot of people believe that professional writers use longer sentences than beginning writers, that isn't always the case. Sometimes a short sentence is better. Look at these from Richard Rodriguez's "Aria: Memoir of a Bilingual Childhood":

In the early years of my boyhood, my parents coped very well in America. My father had steady work. My mother managed at home. They were nobody's victims. When we moved to a house many blocks from the Mexican-American section of town, they were not intimidated by those two or three neighbors who initially tried to make us unwelcome.

There are five sentences here; the first and last are relatively long, but the three in the middle are quite short. In fact, Rodriguez could have combined them into a single sentence: "They were nobody's victims because my father had steady work and my mother managed at home." But he elected to keep them as individual sentences—and their shortness adds emphasis. You may find that reading your work aloud will help you decide what sentences can be combined. Use sentence length as a tool to help you emphasize ideas, add variety, and keep your reader's attention.

You can't change the adjective *silly* into an adverb by adding *-ly* because there's no such word as *sillily*. But you can use *idiotically* or *foolishly,* words that convey about the same meaning. The following new sentence expresses the same meaning but uses an adverb as a modifier:

The host talked foolishly.

Combining sentences using adjectives and adverbs will help add liveliness, clarity, and variety to your writing.

GROUP ACTIVITY

Working with your group or class, follow the directions to combine these sets of sentences. Keep in mind that adjectives in a series are separated by commas: "Her big, red glasses are her trademark."

1. Combine the following sets of sentences by making sentences (b) and (c) adjectives.
   a. The talk show host asked questions.
   b. The host was young.
   c. The host was arrogant.

   _____

   _____

   a. The talk show host asked questions.
   b. The questions were probing.
   c. The questions were embarrassing.

   _____

   _____

   a. I read the transcript.
   b. The transcript is long.
   c. The transcript is marked up.

   _____

   _____

   a. The book is mine.
   b. The book is unopened.
   c. The book is unmarked.

   _____

   _____

2. Combine the following sets of sentences by making sentences (b) and (c) adverbs.
   a. The producer works.
   b. Her work is efficient.
   c. Her work is careful.

   _____

   _____

   a. The VCR works.
   b. It is noisy.
   c. It is bad.

   _____

   _____

   a. The audience reacted.
   b. It was loud.

c. It was wild.

_____

_____

a. The guest reacted.
b. He was indignant.
c. He was furious.

_____

_____

3. Combine each of the following sets of sentences by using modifiers. Use adjectives or adverbs to combine the sentences in any way you think works.
    a. The guest shouted.
    b. He was angry.
    c. He was violent.
    d. He was loud.

_____

_____

a. The audience asks questions.
b. The questions are personal.
c. The questions are long.
d. The questions are silly.

_____

_____

a. The band played.
b. The band was all-female.
c. The band was loud.

_____

_____

INDIVIDUAL ACTIVITY

Try using modifiers to combine some sentences of your own. Select three sentences from your draft that contain adjectives or adverbs and could be combined into a single sentence using modifiers. Circle the modifiers in your three sentences. Write ADJ above the adjectives and ADV above the adverbs. Next combine these three sentences into a single sentence that uses adjectives or adverbs to modify the subject or the verb.

Sentence Parts

*H*ere's a review of the sentence parts we've covered so far.

- A *phrase* is a group of related words that may contain either a subject or a predicate but not both. See page 111.

- A *clause* is a group of related words that contains *both* a subject and predicate. See page 111.

- An *independent clause* has a subject and a predicate and can stand by itself as a complete sentence. See pages 111–15.

- A *dependent clause* must be attached to an independent clause; it cannot stand alone as a complete sentence. See pages 111–15.

- A *coordinating conjunction* is a word (like *and* or *but*) used to join words, phrases, or clauses of equal importance. See pages 114–16.

- A *subordinating conjunction* is a word (like *if* or *when*) used to introduce a dependent, or subordinate, clause, linking it to an independent, or main, clause. See pages 116–19.

- An *adjective* is used to describe or qualify a noun or a pronoun. See pages 154–56.

- An *adverb* describes or qualifies a verb, an adjective, or an adverb. See pages 155–56.

Pronouns

Pronouns help writers avoid the awkward repetition of nouns. Look at the way Nicols Fox uses pronouns in this paragraph (the pronouns are all in italics):

> *I* turn on the television and see an astonishing sight: a woman. *Her* soul is beautiful. *It* penetrates the atmosphere, even across the airwaves. *Her* body is not. *It* is covered with the lumps and bumps of Elephant Man disease. Sally Jessy Raphael, wearing *her* trademark red spectacles, cocks *her* blond head and asks what the woman's life is like. A window is opened into pain. There are more victims of the disease sitting in the audience. *We* are treated to *its* various manifestations. *We* are horrified and amazed: *We* gawk.

There's no absolute rule that says that Fox had to use pronouns, but look what happens when we use nouns in their place:

> The present writer turns on the television and sees an astonishing sight: a woman. The woman's soul is beautiful. The woman's soul penetrates the atmos-

phere, even across the airwaves. The woman's body is not. The woman's body is covered with the lumps and bumps of Elephant Man disease. Sally Jessy Raphael, wearing Sally Jessy Raphael's trademark red spectacles, cocks Sally Jessy Raphael's blond head and asks what the woman's life is like. A window is opened into pain. There are more victims of the disease sitting in the audience. All of the people watching the television show are treated to the disease's various manifestations. All of the people watching the television show are horrified and amazed: All of the people watching the television show gawk.

As you can see, pronouns help avoid unnecessary repetition and make prose easier to read. There are just three things you need to keep in mind to use pronouns effectively:

- A pronoun must have a clear antecedent.
- A pronoun must agree with its antecedent in gender and number.
- A pronoun must be in the appropriate case.

Let's look at these three rules one at a time.

1. *A pronoun must have a clear antecedent.*

The *antecedent* of a pronoun is the noun to which the pronoun refers. If your readers can't tell what noun a pronoun refers to, they're likely to be confused. Look at this paragraph, for example:

For more information about pronouns, see pages 343–44 in *A Survivor's Guide to English*.

They watched their favorite talk show host with her and her friend. She really seemed to enjoy her guests, and they seemed to have a good time, too. So after the show, they said they should all get together and watch the show again.

That's pretty confusing, isn't it? Every sentence is grammatically correct—each has a subject and a verb, and the words all work together—but you can't really tell which person we're talking about. With names substituting for pronouns, you can tell what's going on:

Norman and Sarah watched their favorite talk show host, Oprah Winfrey, with Carole and her friend Bob. Sarah really seemed to enjoy her guests, and they seemed to have a good time, too. So after the show, Norman and Sarah said that they should all get together and watch the show again.

There are still some pronouns in this version—*their* is used once, and *her* and *they* are used twice—but this time the pronouns have clear antecedents.

You'll notice that the noun generally comes before the pronoun—that's why it's called the pronoun's *antecedent* (*ante* means "before"). A pronoun may occasionally come before the noun it refers to, when the pronoun is in an introductory clause or phrase and the noun is part of the main clause: "Knowing that she would miss her favorite soap opera if she didn't hurry, Martha left the library early."

2. *A pronoun must agree with its antecedent.*

First, the pronoun must agree with its antecedent in gender. In "Gawk Shows," for example, Nicols Fox uses *she* and *her* to refer to *a woman* and uses *it* to refer to the woman's body. When the antecedent is female, the pronoun should be feminine *(she, her, hers);* when the antecedent is male, the pronoun should be masculine *(he, him, his);* when the antecedent isn't normally thought of as female or male (*car, movie,* and so forth), the pronoun should be neutral *(it, its).*

A pronoun must also agree with its antecedent in number. If the antecedent is singular *(man, woman, car),* the pronoun should be singular *(he, she, it).* If the antecedent is plural *(men, women, cars),* the pronoun should be plural also *(they, their, them).* In the following sentence from Stephen Lowery's "Television's Show-and-Tell," the plural pronoun *their* refers to the plural noun *people:*

> "We don't have people on our show to solve their problems," said Burt Dubrow, executive producer of the *Sally Jessy Raphael* show.

One of the most common pronoun errors involves using a plural pronoun when the antecedent is singular. For example, words like *everyone, everybody, no one, nobody, anyone,* and *anybody* are singular. Often, in informal speech, people will use plural pronouns to refer to these words: "Every student should bring their books to class." But to be grammatically correct, the pronoun should be singular (in this case, *his* or *her*): "Every student should bring his or her book to class." Such constructions tend to sound awkward, especially if they get long and complex: "Every student should bring his or her book to class so that he or she will be ready to work." The solution is often to rewrite the sentence using a plural noun: "All students should bring their books to class so that they will be ready to work."

3. *A pronoun must be in the appropriate case.*

Finally, you have to be sure that any pronoun you use is in the appropriate case. That is, if the pronoun serves as the subject of a verb, it should be in the subjective case *(I, you, he, she, it; we, you, they);* if the pronoun is the object (of a preposition, for example), it should be in the objective case *(me, you, him, her, it; us, you, them).*

Incorrect case is one of the most common pronoun errors. If you listen carefully, you'll hear people do it all the time: "He gave the ball to George and I" (should be "to George and me") or "George and me went to the store" (should be "George and

Pronoun Checklist

*H*ere's a brief checklist to help you avoid the most common noun-pronoun agreement errors:

- Be sure that the antecedent of the pronoun is clear. If you haven't recently used the noun the pronoun refers to, use the noun instead of the pronoun.
- Be sure that the pronoun agrees with its antecedent in number and gender.

    If the antecedent is plural, the pronoun must be plural; if the antecedent is singular, the pronoun must be singular.

    If the antecedent is feminine *(woman, Maria),* the pronoun must be feminine *(she, her);* if the antecedent is masculine *(George, man),* the pronoun must be masculine *(he, his);* if the antecedent is neither masculine nor feminine, the pronoun must be neutral *(it, its).*

- Be sure that the pronoun is in the appropriate case, either subjective or objective.

I"). This kind of mistake happens most often with compound subjects or objects—when you're using both a noun and a pronoun together. An easy way to help avoid the problem is to try the sentence without the accompanying noun: "He gave the ball to I," or "He gave the ball to me"? "I went to the store," or "Me went to the store"? The correct case is generally clear.

Subjective Case		Objective Case	
I	we	me	us
you	you	you	you
he	they	him	them
she		her	
it		it	

METAESSAY

*T*he process for writing an essay on the media required that you do the following:

- Consider your views about a subject pertaining to the media

- Find some facts about your subject
- Decide which of the facts support your opinions best
- Plan and write a discovery draft in which you express your opinions and use facts to support them
- Complete peer reviews and offer suggestions for improvement
- Revise your essay based on the peer reviews you received

Which one of these parts of the writing process was the most difficult for you? Discuss the one most difficult part of the process, and explain how you overcame that difficulty.

How did you go about choosing your subject, clarifying your views, and finding facts to support your opinions? What problems, if any, did you face while drafting? While revising? What were the hardest or easiest parts of the process for you?

Write a brief essay exploring these questions. If you need a fuller description of metaessays, see page 76.

PEER REVIEW FORM 1: AN ESSAY ON THE MEDIA

Writer's Name: _____

Reviewer's Name: _____

First number the paragraphs of the work you are reviewing. Then write out your answer to each of the following questions. Use the paragraph numbers for reference, and use the back of this page if you need more space. When you have completed this review, tear out this page and give it to the writer.

1. What is the writer's subject, and what is his or her opinion about the subject?

_____

_____

_____

_____

_____

2. Are there any places where the writer should use more supporting facts?

_____

_____

_____

_____

_____

3. What kinds of additional facts would help support the writer's opinions?

_____

_____

_____

_____

_____

4. Are there any places where facts are misused, overused, or irrelevant to the writer's point? If so, underline them and make a note in the margin.

_____

_____

_____

_____

_____

5. Do all of the paragraphs have a clear focus? Do any of them need a focusing sentence? If so, make a note in the margin of the paper beside those paragraphs.

_____

_____

_____

_____

_____

6. Do any of the sentences need to be combined? If so, draw brackets around them, and explain why you think so.

_____

_____

_____

_____

_____

7. Do all of the subjects and verbs agree? Circle any verbs that you think don't agree with their subjects, and explain why you've done so. See the subject-verb checklist on pages 75–76.

_____

_____

_____

_____

_____

PEER REVIEW FORM 2: AN ESSAY ON THE MEDIA

Writer's Name: _____

Reviewer's Name: _____

First number the paragraphs of the work you are reviewing. Then write out your answer to each of the following questions. Use the paragraph numbers for reference, and use the back of this page if you need more space. When you have completed this review, tear out this page and give it to the writer.

1. What is the writer's subject, and what is his or her opinion about the subject?

_____

_____

_____

_____

_____

2. Are there any places where the writer should use more supporting facts?

_____

_____

_____

_____

_____

3. What kinds of additional facts would help support the writer's opinions?

_____

_____

_____

_____

_____

4. Are there any places where facts are misused, overused, or irrelevant to the writer's point? If so, underline them and make a note in the margin.

_____

_____

_____

_____

_____

5. Do all of the paragraphs have a clear focus? Do any of them need a focusing sentence? If so, make a note in the margin of the paper beside those paragraphs.

_____

_____

_____

_____

_____

6. Do any of the sentences need to be combined? If so, draw brackets around them, and explain why you think so.

_____

_____

_____

_____

_____

7. Do all of the subjects and verbs agree? Circle any verbs that you think don't agree with their subjects, and explain why you've done so. See the subject-verb checklist on pages 75–76.

_____

_____

_____

_____

_____

WRITER'S RESPONSE TO PEER REVIEW 1

> *Read the peer reviews you received from the members of your group; then fill out one of these forms for each one. (This exercise will help you decide how you want to follow your reviewers' suggestions when you revise your discovery draft. It will also help your reviewers understand how they can provide the most effective information for you.)*

Writer's Name: _____

Reviewer's Name: _____

1. Did this reviewer's comments help you see the strengths and weaknesses of your discovery draft? If they were not helpful, what kinds of information and suggestions were you hoping to get?

_____

_____

_____

_____

_____

2. Based on this review, in what ways do you plan to revise your discovery draft?

_____

_____

_____

_____

_____

3. Which of the reviewer's comments and suggestions did you find most helpful? Why?

_____

_____

_____

_____

_____

4. Which of the the reviewer's comments and suggestions do you disagree with? Why?

_____

_____

_____

_____

_____

WRITER'S RESPONSE TO PEER REVIEW 2

> *Read the peer reviews you received from the members of your group; then fill out one of these forms for each one. (This exercise will help you decide how you want to follow your reviewers' suggestions when you revise your discovery draft. It will also help your reviewers understand how they can provide the most effective information for you.)*

Writer's Name: _____

Reviewer's Name: _____

After you have turned in the final version of your paper, tear out this form and give it to your reviewer.

1. Did this reviewer's comments help you see the strengths and weaknesses of your discovery draft? If they were not helpful, what kinds of information and suggestions were you hoping to get?

_____

_____

_____

_____

_____

2. Based on this review, in what ways do you plan to revise your discovery draft?

_____

_____

_____

_____

_____

3. Which of the reviewer's comments and suggestions did you find most helpful? Why?

_____

_____

_____

_____

_____

4. Which of the reviewer's comments and suggestions do you disagree with? Why?

_____

_____

_____

_____

_____

SELF-EVALUATION FORM: AN ESSAY ON THE MEDIA

Name: _____

Essay Title: _____

Date: _____

Complete this evaluation and turn it in with your essay.

1. How much time did you spend on this paper? What did you spend most of your time on (getting started, drafting, revising, something else)? Do you think you needed to spend more time or less time on some of these parts of the writing process?

_____

_____

_____

_____

_____

2. What do you like best about your paper?

_____

_____

_____

_____

_____

3. What changes have you made in your paper since the peer review?

_____

_____

_____

_____

_____

4. If you had an additional day to work on your paper, what other changes would you make?

_____

_____

_____

_____

_____

5. What things would you like your instructor to give you special help with when reading and commenting on this paper?

_____

_____

_____

_____

_____

USING EVIDENCE EFFECTIVELY

An Essay on Language

GOALS

To help you write an essay on the effects of language, we'll concentrate on the following goals in this chapter:

- Using evidence to support generalizations

- Drawing inferences from evidence and making sure that these inferences are well founded and relevant

- Summarizing essays written by others

- Making sure that paragraphs are unified

- Varying sentences by using verbals

- Using commas appropriately

Writing Preview

Using the information covered in this and earlier chapters, you'll write an essay about how language can make people feel excluded, first drawing a generalization about language and then supporting that generalization using the readings in this chapter and your own and other people's experiences.

Most of us have experienced situations when we felt excluded from a group or unable to communicate ideas or feelings to a group when it was important to do so. Many such situations arise when we're not comfortable speaking the language of a particular group, even if everyone is speaking English (or Spanish or whatever). Think about your own experiences. You may have been surrounded by people speaking a foreign language, or you may have noticed that a group of students, your teachers, or your bosses and co-workers speak English in a way that you're not comfortable with, that isn't natural to you.

What incident comes to mind first when you think about being left out? In what ways was this feeling related to language?

> **I**f you can't think of what to say, use the prewriting strategies from Chapter 1.

Spend ten minutes writing about that incident, trying to recall as many of the details as you can. Exactly what happened, and how did you feel?

Then discuss your experience with your group or class. Do the members of your group or class recall similar incidents, or is each person's incident unlike the others?

USING EVIDENCE

Even though we haven't yet focused on it directly, you've already had a lot of practice using evidence. When you included what you learned from an interview as you wrote your character sketch, you were using evidence. When you used facts to support your opinions about the media, you used evidence. In fact, you use evidence all the time, even in casual conversations with friends. Look at this statement, for example:

> School really exhausts me. I have to get up at 5:30 every morning to go to work, and by the time I get home at night, I'm beat—but I have to stay up until after midnight doing my homework. By this point in the semester, I'm just about worn out.

The second sentence ("I have to get up at 5:30 . . .") provides the specific evidence that supports the general statements made in the first and third sentences. You wouldn't have to provide such evidence for a friend, of course; most people are willing to take your word for it if you tell them you're tired. But by providing evidence, you can make your case stronger and more persuasive.

You may think of evidence as things that we can handle or point to, like the items that television lawyers label "Defense Exhibit One." But evidence can take on any form. For written work, evidence is what we present to support our ideas and statements.

Evidence can be

- facts
- statements by authorities
- results of experiments
- statistics

But it can also be

- others' opinions
- inferences
- experiences
- memories

Evidence is what we use to reach our own conclusions, and it's what we present to others to help them understand or agree with those conclusions.

Evidence can be formal or informal. If you include quotations from a published article or book to support a point you're making, you're using formal evidence. (We'll look at using quotations as evidence in Chapter 6.) Formal evidence also includes statistics, surveys, and other published information.

But informal evidence can be effective too. Things that your friends or family members have said, your own thoughts on a subject, your experiences and memories—all these can help support your point of view and convince your readers that what you're saying is valid.

Look back in earlier chapters at the kinds of evidence speakers and writers use. For example, when Pam on the *Oprah Winfrey Show* uses statements from teachers to help support her contention that her daughter Ambur should not be allowed to date (page 94), she's using evidence. When Dorothy Regner recalls the contents of the steamer trunk (page 20), she's using evidence to help us understand an important experience in her life. Dick Wingerson (pages 47–49) presents all sorts of memories to help show how special his father was: those memories are Wingerson's evidence.

For any writing assignment you may have, whether in school or on the job, you should be sure that you include enough evidence to support the ideas you present. It's usually not enough just to state that something is true, that it happened, or that it should happen. Generally, you have to show that it's true or explain why it happened or should happen by offering evidence.

INDIVIDUAL ACTIVITY

Look back at the essay Chi Nguyen wrote on teenage suicide (pages 108–9). How many different kinds of evidence can you find in that essay? List two instances each of facts, experiences, and opinions that Nguyen uses as evidence.

Drawing Inferences Based on Evidence

When you write the final version of any essay, of course, you should already have reached your conclusions, and you should know how the evidence you use supports your points. As you think about your topic, though, and as you write early versions of an essay, you may not know just what conclusions you'll reach or even what sorts of evidence will be appropriate.

Often, in fact, the very process of gathering evidence will help you form your views on a topic. And if you try to keep an open mind as you're working, you may even reach conclusions opposite the ones that you originally expected to reach.

Suppose, for example, that you were planning an essay about the level of physical fitness in America. Perhaps you and many of the people you know run several miles a day and eat a healthy diet, and you initially expected to say that the level of fitness is quite high. But as you begin to talk to others, read articles, and gather information, you will probably find that although most of the people you know are quite fit, this is not true of Americans as a whole. You would then need to revise your conclusions. Simply put, you've got to keep an open mind and be willing to change your conclusions based on the evidence.

Avoiding Misuses of Evidence

In Chapter 4 we looked at some ways in which facts can be misused. Obviously, if you're misusing facts, you're also misusing evidence. But there are some different ways in which evidence can be misused that people aren't always aware of. If you pay attention to a few commonsense principles, though, you can avoid misusing evidence.

1. *Be careful in defining cause-and-effect relationships.*

Just because one thing happened after another, don't assume that the first caused the second. For example, if you hear a loud boom just before your window shatters, there could be a cause-and-effect relationship: an exploding gas pipe or the sonic boom of a low-flying jet might have knocked out the window. But the fact that the boom preceded the breakage doesn't mean that there must be a cause-and-effect relationship. It could be that as the gas line exploded or the jet flew overheard, a vandal on the street threw a rock through your window, breaking the glass. You have to think carefully about cause-and-effect relationships, examining them thoroughly to be sure you aren't misassigning causes or effects.

2. *Be sure that your conclusions are warranted by the evidence.*

Anne Sullivan taught her blind and deaf pupil, Helen Keller, about language by holding the child's hand under running water and then spelling out the word *water* into her hand using sign language. You wouldn't want to use that fact as evidence that holding a hand under water is a good way to teach children to spell. Sometimes events are related in one instance but in no other. You've got to take all the circumstances into account.

3. *Be sure that your evidence is relevant.*

Sometimes what might seem on the surface to be evidence for a particular conclusion really isn't. For example, here a writer uses statistics that are related to the main point but don't really support it:

> It's no wonder that I sometimes feel out of place when I hear people speaking other languages. After all, almost 32 million people in the United States speak languages other than English at home. With that many people speaking other languages, those of us who speak only English are bound to feel out of place.

It may be true that nearly 32 million people speak other languages at home (a figure that comes from the 1994 *World Almanac and Book of Facts*), but that fact can't logically support the writer's point that he or she feels out of place at times: the languages that people speak at home would hardly affect the writer. The statistic is not relevant.

4. *Be sure that any authority you cite is accepted as an authority.*

We often see pseudo-authorities acting as if they were real authorities: professional athletes, for example, endorse a variety of products, and their endorsement is supposed to make us believe that the product is superior. A football player endorsing a brand of shoulder pads might be an appropriate use of authority because we assume that he is an expert when it comes to athletic equipment. But if a star halfback endorses a particular brand of computer, we would want to know what makes him an authority in this area.

GROUP ACTIVITY

The following statements involve some misuse of evidence. What's wrong with them, and how can they be corrected? Discuss the statements with your group or class, and correct any problems you see in them.

1. Reg should know a lot of languages because he's lived in three different countries.

2. Those people talking in a different language are looking at me; they must be talking about me.

3. As soon as I started studying German, my English grades improved. Knowing a foreign language helped me a lot in my other classes.

4. The only reason those people talk in their own language is so that

we won't be able to understand them.

5. Marta must be really smart; she speaks three different languages.

6. The whole idea of language isolating people is silly; it's never happened to me.

7. I'll never be accepted by most people because my parents don't speak English very well.

8. The only reason for studying a for-

eign language is so that you can order from the menu in a fancy restaurant.

9. English must be the most efficient language because most air traffic controllers speak it on the job.

10. All the signs in Canada are printed in both English and French; that's probably because many French Canadians are too lazy to learn English.

READINGS

Most people don't spend much time thinking about language until they have a problem with it. For example, most of us don't think about how we use words to express our ideas and feelings until we're faced with a situation in which we're having trouble getting someone else to understand us. But even when we're not thinking about it actively, language is central to our lives. It is our link to the world around us, our primary method of communicating with others.

In the readings that follow, three writers—Maxine Hong Kingston, Helen Keller, and Richard Rodriguez—each look back at their childhood and remember how language changed them and changed for them. As you read these essays, be sure to carry on a dialogue with the writers as we've described in earlier chapters, writing your questions and other ideas in the margins. And pay particular attention to the kinds of evidence they use and how they present it.

PREREADING EXERCISE

In earlier chapters, we've asked you to preview the first paragraph of each essay before reading it or to skim the entire essay. This time we'd like you to try a third prereading strategy: go through each essay, and read just the first sentence of each paragraph. This is another technique that will help you get an initial overview of what a writer is saying and thus comprehend the essay more fully.

KINDERGARTEN

Maxine Hong Kingston

Maxine Hong Kingston, an essayist and novelist, is the child of immigrant parents who moved to California from China before she was

*born. She grew up speaking Chinese and learned English only when she
started school. In this selection from her book* The Woman Warrior,
Hong Kingston describes her earliest experiences with English.

1   When I went to kindergarten and had to speak English for the first
time, I became silent. A dumbness—a shame—still cracks my voice in
two, even when I want to say "hello" casually, or ask an easy question in
front of the check-out counter, or ask directions of a bus driver. . . .

2   My silence was thickest—total—during the three years that I covered my school paintings with black paint. I painted layers of black over
houses and flowers and suns, and when I drew on the blackboard, I put a
layer of chalk on top. I was making a stage curtain, and it was the moment
before the curtain parted or rose. The teachers called my parents to
school, and I saw they had been saving my pictures, curling and cracking,
all alike and black. The teachers pointed to the pictures and looked serious, talked seriously too, but my parents did not understand English.
("The parents and teachers of criminals were executed," said my father.)
My parents took the pictures home. I spread them out (so black and full of
possibilities) and pretended the curtains were swinging open, flying up,
one after another, sunlight underneath, mighty operas.

3   During the first silent year I spoke to no one at school, did not ask
before going to the lavatory, and
flunked kindergarten. My sister
also said nothing for three years,
silent in the playground and
silent at lunch. There were other
quiet Chinese girls not of our family, but most of them got over it sooner
than we did. I enjoyed the silence. At first it did not occur to me I was
supposed to talk or to pass kindergarten. I talked at home and to one or
two of the Chinese kids in class. I made motions and even made some
jokes. I drank out of a toy saucer when the water spilled out of the cup,
and everybody laughed, pointing at me, so I did it some more. I didn't
know that Americans don't drink out of saucers. . . .

> Remember to carry on your dialogue with the writer; take notes and write your comments as you read.

4   It was when I found out I had to talk that school became a misery,
that the silence became a misery. I did not speak and felt bad each time
that I did not speak. I read aloud in first grade, though, and heard the
barest whisper with little squeaks come out of my throat. "Louder," said
the teacher, who scared the voice away again. The other Chinese girls did
not talk either, so I know the silence had to do with being a Chinese girl.

5   Reading out loud was easier than speaking because we did not have
to make up what to say, but I stopped often, and the teacher would think
I'd gone quiet again. I could not understand "I." The Chinese "I" has
seven strokes, intricacies. How could the American "I," assuredly wearing
a hat like the Chinese, have only three strokes, the middle so straight?

Was it out of politeness that the writer left off strokes the way a Chinese has to write her own name small and crooked? No, it was not politeness; "I" is a capital and "you" is lower-case. I stared at that middle line and waited so long for its black center to resolve into tight strokes and dots that I forgot to pronounce it. The other troublesome word was "here," no strong consonant

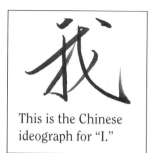

This is the Chinese ideograph for "I."

to hang on to, and so flat, when "here" is two mountainous ideographs. The teacher, who had already told me every day how to read "I" and "here," put me in the low corner under the stairs again, where the noisy boys usually sat.

6   When my second grade class did a play, the whole class went to the auditorium except the Chinese girls. The teacher, lovely and Hawaiian, should have understood about us, but instead left us behind in the classroom. Our voices were too soft or nonexistent, and our parents never signed the permission slips anyway. They never signed anything unnecessary. We opened the door a crack and peeked out,

This is the Chinese ideograph for "here."

but closed it again quickly. One of us (not me) won every spelling bee, though. . . .

7   After American school, we picked up our cigar boxes, in which we had arranged books, brushes, and an inkbox neatly, and went to Chinese school, from 5:00 to 7:30 P.M. There we chanted together, voices rising and falling, loud and soft, some boys shouting, everybody reading together, reciting together and not alone with one voice. When we had a memorization test, the teacher let each of us come to his desk and say the lesson to him privately, while the rest of the class practiced copying or tracing. Most of the teachers were men. The boys who were so well behaved in the American school played tricks on them and talked back to them. The girls were not mute. They screamed and yelled during recess, when there were no rules; they had fistfights. Nobody was afraid of children hurting themselves or of children hurting school property. The glass doors to the red and green balconies with the gold joy symbols were left wide open so that we could run out and climb the fire escapes. We played capture-the-flag in the auditorium, where Sun Yat-sen and Chiang Kai-shek's pictures hung at the back of the stage, the Chinese flag on their left and the American flag on their right. We climbed the teak ceremonial chairs and made fly-

ing leaps off the stage. One flag headquarters was behind the glass door and the other on stage right. Our feet drummed on the hollow stage. During recess the teachers locked themselves up in their office with the shelves of books, copybooks, inks from China. They drank tea and warmed their hands at a stove. There was no play supervision. At recess we had the school to ourselves, and also we could roam as far as we could go—downtown, Chinatown stores, home—as long as we returned before the bell rang.

8   At exactly 7:30 the teacher again picked up the brass bell that sat on his desk and swung it over our heads, while we charged down the stairs, our cheering magnified in the stairwell. Nobody had to line up.

9   Not all of the children who were silent at American school found voice at Chinese school. One new teacher said each of us had to get up and recite in front of the class, who was to listen. My sister and I had memorized the lesson perfectly. We said it to each other at home, one chanting, one listening. The teacher called on my sister to recite first. It was the first time a teacher had called on the second-born to go first. My sister was scared. She glanced at me and looked away; I looked down at my desk. I hoped that she could do it because if she couldn't, then I would have to. She opened her mouth and a voice came out that wasn't a whisper, but it wasn't a proper voice either. I hoped that she would not cry, fear breaking up her voice like twigs underfoot. She sounded as if she were trying to sing though weeping and strangling. She did not pause or stop to end the embarrassment. She kept going until she said the last word, and then she sat down. When it was my turn, the same voice came out, a crippled animal running on broken legs. You could hear splinters in my voice, bones rubbing jagged against one another. I was loud, though. I was glad I didn't whisper.

POSTREADING EXERCISE

Hong Kingston discusses how painful school was for her because of language:

It was when I found out I had to talk that school became a misery, the silence became a misery. I did not speak and felt bad each time that I did not speak. (paragraph 4)

Underline any evidence that Hong Kingston presents in her essay to support this point. Does she persuade you that the experience was very painful for her? Have you had any similar experiences because of language, cultural differences, or other reasons? What evidence could you present to support your own point of view?

THE MOST IMPORTANT DAY
Helen Keller

Maxine Hong Kingston describes the difficulty of coping with a new language. She struggled to learn English, but at the same time she was comforted by the confidence she felt in her native language. Helen Keller's situation was quite different. At about the same age that Hong Kingston began learning a second language, Keller—blind, deaf, and mute—made the startling discovery that language exists at all. Before that time, all she could really experience was a "wordless sensation." In this selection from The Story of My Life, *Keller's autobiography, she describes this momentous event.*

1   The most important day I remember in all my life is the one on which my teacher, Anne Mansfield Sullivan, came to me. I am filled with wonder when I consider the immeasurable contrast between the two lives which it connects. It was the third of March, 1887, three months before I was seven years old.

2   On the afternoon of that eventful day, I stood on the porch, dumb, expectant. I guessed vaguely from my mother's signs and from the hurrying to and fro in the house that something unusual was about to happen, so I went to the door and waited on the steps. The afternoon sun penetrated the mass of honeysuckle that covered the porch and fell on my upturned face. My fingers lingered almost unconsciously on the familiar leaves and blossoms which had just come forth to greet the sweet southern spring. I did not know what the future held of marvel or surprise for me. Anger and bitterness had preyed upon me continually for weeks and a deep languor had succeeded this passionate struggle. . . .

3   I felt approaching footsteps. I stretched out my hand as I supposed to my mother. Someone took it, and I was caught up and held close in the arms of her who had come to reveal all things to me, and, more than all things else, to love me.

> Are you writing any notes in the margins? Underlining words you need to look up? Thinking carefully about what the writer is saying?

4   The morning after my teacher came she led me into her room and gave me a doll. The little blind children at the Perkins Institute had sent it and Laura Bridgman had dressed it; but I did not know this until afterward. When I played with it a little while, Miss Sullivan slowly spelled into my hand the word "d-o-l-l." I was at once interested in this finger play and tried to imitate it. When I finally succeeded in making the letters correctly I was flushed with childish pleasure and pride. Running downstairs to my

mother I held up my hand and made the letters for doll. I did not know that I was spelling a word or even that words existed; I was simply making my fingers go in monkeylike imitation. In the days that followed I learned to spell in this uncomprehending way a great many words, among them pin, hat, cup and a few verbs like sit, stand and walk. But my teacher had been with me several weeks before I understood that everything has a name.

5   One day, while I was playing with my new doll, Miss Sullivan put my big rag doll into my lap also, spelled "d-o-l-l" and tried to make me understand that "d-o-l-l" applied to both. Earlier in the day we had had a tussle over the words "m-u-g" and "w-a-t-e-r." Miss Sullivan had tried to impress it upon me that "m-u-g" is mug and that "w-a-t-e-r" is water, but I persisted in confounding the two. In despair she had dropped the subject for the time, only to renew it at the first opportunity. I became impatient at her repeated attempts and, seizing the new doll, I dashed it upon the floor. I was keenly delighted when I felt the fragments of the broken doll at my feet. Neither sorrow nor regret followed my passionate outburst. I had not loved the doll. In the still, dark world in which I lived there was not strong sentiment or tenderness. I felt my teacher sweep the fragments to one side of the hearth, and I had the sense of satisfaction that the cause of my discomfort was removed. She brought me my hat, and I knew I was going out into the warm sunshine. This thought, if a wordless sensation may be called a thought, made me hop and skip with pleasure.

6   We walked down the path to the well-house, attracted by the fragrance of the honeysuckle with which it was covered. Someone was drawing water and my teacher placed my hand under the spout. As the cool stream gushed over one hand she spelled into the other the word water, first slowly, then rapidly. I stood still, my whole attention fixed upon the motions of her fingers. Suddenly I felt a misty consciousness as of something forgotten—a thrill of returning thought; and somehow the mystery of language was revealed to me. I knew then that "w-a-t-e-r" meant the wonderful cool something that was flowing over my hand. The living word awakened my soul, gave it light, hope, joy, set it free! There were barriers still, it is true, but barriers that could in time be swept away.

7   I left the well-house eager to learn. Everything had a name, and each name gave birth to a new thought. As we returned to the house every object which I touched seemed to quiver with life. That was because I saw everything with the strange, new sight that had come to me. On entering the door I remembered the doll I had broken. I felt my way to the hearth and picked up the pieces. I tried vainly to put them together. Then my eyes filled with tears; for I realized what I had done, and for the first time I felt repentance and sorrow.

8   I learned a great many new words that day. I do not remember what they all were; but I do know that mother, father, sister, teacher were among them—words that were to make the world blossom for me, "like Aaron's rod, with flowers." It would have been difficult to find a happier child than I was as I lay in my crib at the close of that eventful day and lived over the joys it had brought me, and for the first time longed for a new day to come.

POSTREADING EXERCISE

Keller describes her breakthrough as a moment of great importance in her life: "The living word awakened my soul, gave it light, hope, joy, set it free!" (paragraph 6). Underline the evidence that Keller offers to support this statement. Can you recall a time when you struggled to learn something and how you felt when you made a breakthrough? What evidence could you present to support your description of the way you felt?

ARIA: MEMOIR OF A BILINGUAL CHILDHOOD
Richard Rodriguez

Richard Rodriguez was born in 1944 in San Francisco. His parents immigrated from Mexico, and the language spoken in their home was Spanish until Rodriguez's teachers told them their children must practice English at home. In this selection from his autobiography, Hunger of Memory, *published in 1982, Rodriguez talks about how learning English at school eventually made him successful in some ways but also made him more distant from his family.*

1   I remember, to start with, that day in Sacramento, in a California now nearly thirty years past, when I first entered a classroom—able to understand about fifty stray English words. The third of four children, I had been preceded by my older brother and sister to a neighborhood Roman Catholic school. But neither of them had revealed very much about their classroom experiences. They left each morning and returned each afternoon, always together, speaking Spanish as they climbed the five steps to the porch. And their mysterious books, wrapped in brown shopping-bag paper, remained on the table next to the door, closed firmly behind them.

2   An accident of geography sent me to a school where all my classmates were white and many were the children of doctors and lawyers and business executives. On that first day of school, my classmates must certainly have been uneasy to find themselves apart from their families, in

the first institution of their lives. But I was astonished. I was fated to be the "problem student" in class.

3   The nun said, in a friendly but oddly impersonal voice: "Boys and girls, this is Richard Rodriguez." (I heard her sound it out: *Rich-heard Road-ree-guess.*) It was the first time I had heard anyone say my name in English. "Richard," the nun repeated more slowly, writing my name down in her book. Quickly I turned to see my mother's face dissolve in a watery blur behind the pebbled-glass door.

4   Now, many years later, I hear of something called "bilingual education"—a scheme proposed in the late 1960s by Hispanic-American social activists, later endorsed by a congressional vote. It is a program that seeks to permit non-English-speaking children (many from lower-class homes) to use their "family language" as the language of school. Such, at least, is the aim its supporters announce. I hear them, and am forced to say no: It is not possible for a child, any child, ever to use his family's language in school. Not to understand this is to misunderstand the public uses of schooling and to trivialize the nature of intimate life.

5   Memory teaches me what I know of these matters. The boy reminds the adult. I was a bilingual child, but of a certain kind: "socially disadvantaged," the son of working-class parents, both Mexican immigrants.

6   In the early years of my boyhood, my parents coped very well in America. My father had steady work. My mother managed at home. They were nobody's victims. When we moved to a house many blocks from the Mexican-American section of town, they were not intimidated by those two or three neighbors who initially tried to make us unwelcome. ("Keep your brats away from my sidewalk!") But despite all they achieved, or perhaps because they had so much to achieve, they lacked any deep feeling of ease, of belonging in public. They regarded the people at work or in crowds as being very distant from us. Those were the others, *los gringos.* That term was interchangeable in their speech with another, even more telling: *los americanos.*

7   I grew up in a house where the only regular guests were my relations. On a certain day, enormous families of relatives would visit us, and there would be so many people that the noise and the bodies would spill out to the back-yard and onto the front porch.

> Take time to make notes in the margin as you read. Ask questions, express ideas that come to you, and respond to what the writer says.

Then for weeks no one would come. (If the doorbell rang, it was usually a salesman.) Our house stood apart—gaudy yellow in a row of white bungalows. We were the people with the noisy dog, the people who raised chickens. We were the foreigners on the block. A few neighbors would smile and wave at us. We waved back. But until I was seven years old, I did not know the name of the old couple living next door or the names of the kids living across the street.

8   In public, my father and mother spoke a hesitant, accented, and not always grammatical English. And then they would have to strain, their bodies tense, to catch the sense of what was rapidly said by *los gringos*. At home, they returned to Spanish. The language of their Mexican past sounded in counterpoint to the English spoken in public. The words would come quickly, with ease. Conveyed through those sounds was the pleasing, soothing, consoling reminder that one was at home.

9   During those years when I was first learning to speak, my mother and father addressed me only in Spanish; in Spanish I learned to reply. By contrast, English *(ingles)* was the language I came to associate with gringos, rarely heard in the house. I learned my first words of English overhearing my parents speaking to strangers. At six years of age, I knew just enough words for my mother to trust me on errands to stores one block away—but no more. . . .

10   I knew that I spoke English poorly. My words could not extend to form complete thoughts. And the words I did speak I didn't know well enough to make distinct sounds. (Listeners would usually lower their heads to hear better what I was trying to say.) But it was one thing for *me* to speak English with difficulty; it was more troubling to hear my parents speaking in public: their high-whining vowels and guttural consonants; their sentences that got stuck with "eh" and "ah" sounds; the confused syntax; the hesitant rhythm of sounds so different from the way gringos spoke. I'd notice, moreover, that my parents' voices were softer than those of gringos we would meet.

11   I am tempted to say now that none of this mattered. (In adulthood I am embarrassed by childhood fears.) And, in a way, it didn't matter very much that my parents could not speak English with ease. Their linguistic difficulties had no serious consequences. My mother and father made themselves understood at the county hospital clinic and at government offices. And yet, in another way, it mattered very much. It was unsettling to hear my parents struggle with English. Hearing them, I'd grow nervous, and my clutching trust in their protection and power would be weakened.

12   There were many times like the night at a brightly lit gasoline station (a blaring white memory) when I stood uneasily hearing my father talk to a teenage attendant. I do not recall what they were saying, but I cannot forget the sounds my father made as he spoke. At one point his words slipped together to form one long word—sounds as confused as the threads of blue and green oil in the puddle next to my shoes. His voice

rushed through what he had left to say. Toward the end, he reached falsetto notes, appealing to his listener's understanding. I looked away at the lights of passing automobiles. I tried not to hear any more. But I heard only too well the attendant's reply, his calm, easy tones. Shortly afterward, headed for home, I shivered when my father put his hand on my shoulder. The very first chance that I got, I evaded his grasp and ran on ahead into the dark, skipping with feigned boyish exuberance.

13   But then there was Spanish: *español,* the language rarely heard away from the house; *español,* the language which seemed to me therefore a private language, my family's language. To hear its sounds was to feel myself specially recognized as one of the family, apart from *los otros.* A simple remark, an inconsequential comment could convey that assurance. My parents would say something to me and I would feel embraced by the sounds of their words. Those sounds said: *I am speaking with ease in Spanish. I am addressing you in words I never use with* los gringos. *I recognize you as someone special, close, like no one outside. You belong with us. In the family. Ricardo. . . .*

POSTREADING EXERCISE

Early in his essay, Rodriguez says that he has reached a conclusion about bilingual education:

Now, many years later, I hear of something called "bilingual education"—a scheme proposed in the late 1960s by Hispanic-American social activists, later endorsed by a congressional vote. It is a program that seeks to permit non-English-speaking children (many from lower-class homes) to use their "family language" as the language of school. Such, at least, is the aim its supporters announce. I hear them, and am forced to say no: It is not possible for a child, any child, ever to use his family's language in school. (paragraph 4)

What does Rodriguez mean by "family language"? What evidence does he present in his essay to support this conclusion? Do you agree or disagree with the conclusion? What evidence could you present to support your own point of view?

SUMMARIZING

One way to be sure that you're getting everything possible from your reading is to take extensive notes on what you've read. Sometimes it's best to take those notes directly in the margins of the book (provided, of course, it's your own book), as we've suggested earlier. But when you want to make sure that you've understood a piece of writing as completely as possible, it's best to summarize what you've read in your own words.

We summarize all the time. If a friend asks you what you've done over the weekend, you don't give every detail, quoting every word you said or heard and describing everything that happened. Rather, you give brief versions of the highlights of what happened. You do the same thing when a friend interrupts you twenty minutes into a TV program you're watching and says, "What's happened so far?" You don't try to repeat all the dialogue or even to put it into your own words. You just condense what has happened so that your friend gets the general idea of what the movie is about: "This woman killed her husband by bashing him over the head with a frozen leg of lamb; then she served the murder weapon to the detective for dinner."

Sometimes you'll use summaries to help you recall what's in a book or article you've read. This is especially important when you're doing research for a project or paper: if you write a brief summary of each article or chapter as soon as you finish reading it, you can use these summaries later to help you recall what each was about. Summarizing this way is also helpful when you're preparing for exams. You can also use summaries in your own essays to tell your readers what someone else has said on a subject or what happened.

When you summarize, the main point is to select the most important events, details, or experiences, and recount them in your own words. Obviously, when you're talking about something that happened to you, you won't have any trouble using your own words. But when you summarize something you've read, you have to be careful to use your words and not the other writer's.

Sometimes you may find that you can use a summary of something you've read to help support a point you're trying to make. For example, one of our students, writing about how people feel when they are first able to understand a difficult concept, included in her essay the following summary of paragraphs 6 through 8 of Helen Keller's "Most Important Day":

> Sometimes understanding comes suddenly and leaves a person feeling very excited. Helen Keller—deaf, blind, and mute—first connected words with the objects they stand for when her teacher one day ran water from a well pump over her hand and spelled "w-a-t-e-r" over and over again into her other hand. Keller couldn't really explain what happened; she just suddenly realized that "w-a-t-e-r" referred to what she felt flowing over her hand. When that happened, she felt thrilled, as if she had been set free, and began to learn as many words as she could. For the first time in her life, she felt she had something to live for.

If you look back at the original paragraphs from Keller's autobiography, you'll see that the writer here has summarized more than fifteen sentences into only four, enough to serve her purpose of supporting her opening statements. You'll usually find it necessary only to summarize a portion of an article, as this writer did, but an entire article of several pages can most often be reduced to just a paragraph or so.

INDIVIDUAL ACTIVITY

Read the following paragraph in which Richard Rodriguez describes an occasion when he was embarrassed by his father's limited English. Then summarize this passage in one sentence.

There were many times like the night at a brightly lit gasoline station (a blaring white memory) when I stood uneasily hearing my father talk to a teenage attendant. I do not recall what they were saying, but I cannot forget the sounds my father made as he spoke. At one point his words slipped together to form one long word—sounds as confused as the threads of blue and green oil in the puddle next to my shoes. His voice rushed through what he had left to say. Toward the end, he reached falsetto notes, appealing to his listener's understanding. I looked away at the lights of passing automobiles. I tried not to hear any more. But I heard only too well the attendant's reply, his calm, easy tones. Shortly afterward, headed for home, I shivered when my father put his hand on my shoulder. The very first chance that I got, I evaded his grasp and ran on ahead into the dark, skipping with feigned boyish exuberance.

GROUP ACTIVITY

Select one of the three readings in this chapter to summarize in one paragraph.

- First, discuss the reading you choose to be sure that each of you understands it well.
- Next, decide on the major points you want to include in your summary.
- Finally, develop the summary, selecting one member of your group to be the recorder, and write out what you, as a group, agree you want to say.

Keep in mind that you aren't trying to tell everything—just the major points, the highlights, of the reading.

PARAGRAPH UNITY

We've already seen how many different types of paragraphs there are. Some are long; some are short. Some have a focusing sentence at the beginning, others at the end; some have no focusing sentence at all or are part of a bloc of paragraphs. As we've said before, sometimes it seems that there are just about as many different types of paragraphs as there are writers to produce them.

In general, however, special kinds of paragraphs, such as one-sentence paragraphs, should be reserved for special occasions. Most paragraphs in papers written for college courses will have several sentences, and if they're to be effective, the various sentences should all focus on a single topic—they should create a sense of unity, of fitting together, rather than feel like a random collection of statements, ideas, or information. Look at this paragraph, for example, from Richard Rodriguez's "Aria" (we've numbered the sentences to make them easier to refer to):

> (1) I grew up in a house where the only regular guests were my relations. (2) On a certain day, enormous families of relatives would visit us, and there would be so many people that the noise and the bodies would spill out to the backyard and onto the front porch. (3) Then for weeks no one would come. (4) (If the doorbell rang, it was usually a salesman.) (5) Our house stood apart—gaudy yellow in a row of white bungalows. (6) We were the people with the noisy dog, the people who raised chickens. (7) We were the foreigners on the block. (8) A few neighbors would smile and wave at us. (9) We waved back. (10) But until I was seven years old, I did not know the name of the old couple living next door or the names of the kids living across the street.

Everything in this paragraph deals with Rodriguez's sense of his parents' home as isolated from its Anglo neighborhood. The paragraph doesn't have a specific focusing sentence; rather, Rodriguez implies a focus that can be summarized as follows: "With the exception of occasional visits from relatives, we lived an isolated life in our neighborhood."

Every sentence in the paragraph helps reinforce the family's sense of isolation. There are, of course, the relatives who visit (sentences 1 and 2), but no other visitors (sentence 3), except the occasional door-to-door salesman (sentence 4). Usually the family was alone, clearly isolated from and different than their neighbors. Sentences 5, 6, and 7 emphasize that difference: their house is a different color (5); their animals are different (6); they are, in short, "foreigners" (7). (In fact, it would be possible to start a new paragraph here, and many writers might have chosen to do so, but Rodriguez uses these details as support for the main topic of his paragraph.)

Rodriguez finishes the paragraph by showing that there were some attempts at contact between his family and their neighbors (sentences 8 and 9), but that contact was clearly not enough to make them real members of the neighborhood, for they still didn't know their neighbors' names for years (10).

The whole paragraph, then, stresses the family's isolation in an Anglo neighborhood. By sticking to this one topic, Rodriguez creates a unified paragraph.

INDIVIDUAL ACTIVITY

Reread the paragraph you wrote about being left out for the "Before We Start" exercise at the beginning of this chapter. Are there any sentences in it that don't seem to fit with the main idea you tried to express? If so, what can you do to make the paragraph more unified?

Select one sentence from that paragraph

that you think you will be able to use for your next essay, and write a fully developed, unified paragraph with that sentence as your focusing sentence.

WRITING ASSIGNMENT: ESSAY ON LANGUAGE

At the start of this chapter, you wrote a paragraph about a time when you felt left out because of language. You've talked about these incidents with the members of your group or class and read three essays dealing with the same topic.

By this time, you should have some ideas about how language can make us feel isolated. Write a discovery draft in which you draw a generalization about how language can exclude people from activities or groups. To support your generalization, use examples from your own experience, the experiences of others in your class, and the essays by Hong Kingston, Keller, or Rodriguez.

Summary of Steps

Here's a summary of steps to take in completing this assignment. Check off each step after you've completed it.

_____ Clarify your ideas about your topic. In what ways do you think language can exclude people or create barriers between individuals or groups? Use the prewriting techniques described in Chapter 1 to help develop your ideas.

_____ Write out a generalization about how language excludes people from activities or groups. A generalization is a statement that summarizes a basic idea or truth about a topic, such as the first sentence in the student paragraph on page 190 ("Sometimes understanding comes suddenly and leaves a person feeling very excited").

_____ Make a list of all of the experiences you might use to support your generalization.

- List your own experiences first.
- Next, list the experiences of your classmates.
- Then list the experiences you might use from the essays in this chapter.

_____ Select from these lists relevant experiences that you can use to support your generalization.

_____ Organize your points so that your readers can follow your ideas clearly.

_____ Make sure that your generalization is clearly indicated in your introduction or conclusion.

_____ Try to make your paragraphs unified, each focusing on a particular topic or idea.

Student Sample

Sometimes you can feel isolated from others even when they speaking your native language. In this essay, Eleni Soekadis recounts her confusion when she was faced with the kind of language her husband and his friends use when they talk about computers.

IT JUST DOESN'T COMPUTE!
Eleni Soekadis

1   Normally I feel fairly comfortable around my family, friends, and co-workers. But when my husband and his friends come over and start talking about computers, I feel completely lost. Even though they're speaking English, it may as well be another language.

2   The first time I heard them mention "meg" and "K," I thought they were talking about some women at work or maybe some people they were going out with. Instead of answering me when I asked about these names, they just looked at each other and then started to laugh. I didn't know what was going on, and I felt really stupid. Later on after they had all gone home, my husband explained that they really weren't laughing at me. He said they were just surprised that I didn't know what they were talking about. Then he explained to me that "meg" means "megabyte" and that "K" means "kilobyte," units of measurement for computers.

3   Since that time I've tried to listen to their conversations and learn more about computers. But it's really hard. In fact, I think it's harder than learning another language. They talk about "bits" and "bytes" and "RAM." They also discuss "memory," but they don't use it the way most of us do. I think of memory as the part of your brain that helps you remember things, like where you left your keys or when your mother-in-law's birthday is. But when they use it, they mean something about computer storage.

They also get upset when their hard drives crash, but these drives and crashes have nothing to do with cars or wrecks. Lately they talk a lot about the information superhighway, but this too has nothing to do with cars or driving.

4   I've learned a little bit about computers, but not enough to keep up with my husband and his friends. I know enough to type my school papers, save what I've typed, and print it. But anything beyond that has me confused. When I ask for help, all I can really do is say that the "whatchamacal-lit" doesn't work.

5   I may not feel as bad as Maxine Hong Kingston did when she was unable to speak in an American school, but in some way I know what she felt. It's hard when you don't know what people are talking about and you can't communicate with them. It makes me feel like I don't fit in. But it also makes me try to explain things better to people when I think they don't know what I'm talking about.

6   For example, when I talk about the real estate office where I work, I don't assume that everyone understands what a mortgage is or what *amortization* means. And when I talk about my studies with my friends and family who didn't go to college, I'm careful to explain what it means when I say I'm working on a "discovery draft" or doing some "clus-tering." Basically, what it all comes down to is remembering that people know different things and if you want them to feel included and understand what you're saying, you have to speak their language or help them learn yours.

INDIVIDUAL ACTIVITY

1. Reread this essay, and underline the generalization that Soekadis makes about language and isolation. Why do you think she positions it where she does in the essay?

2. What kind of evidence does Soekadis use to support her generalization? Does she include enough evidence to convince you that her generalization is valid?

3. Look closely at each of Soekadis's paragraphs in this essay. Are they all clearly unified? How can you tell?

Peer Review

Once you have completed your discovery draft, you're ready to start peer reviews. Here's a recap of what you need to do.

- Exchange papers with a classmate.
- Be alert to what the writer succeeds at doing and is having trouble doing.
- Write your peer review, using one of the forms on pages 207–8 and 209–10.
- Talk over your review with the writer for a few minutes.
- Go through the whole process with another classmate.
- After reading the peer reviews of your own draft, complete the Writer's Response to Peer Review forms that follow the Peer Review Forms.

Revising Your Discovery Draft

By now you should have a small stack of paper: your notes, your completed discovery draft, and peer reviews written by two of your classmates. With these you can start revising the discovery draft into the final version of your paper—the one you're actually going to turn in. Here's the process for revising.

- Reread your draft.
- Reread your peer reviews, noting what your reviewers found effective and what they suggested to improve the draft.
- Decide which of the comments you agree with and which you disagree with. (Remember, you don't have to agree with or make all the changes they suggest; you have the final responsibility for your essay.)
- If the reviewers recommend that you rearrange the paragraphs, try putting them in a different order, using scissors and tape or the cut-and-paste function on a word processor. Do you see any improvement with this new organization?
- Note the places where the reviewers suggested that you delete information. Take out these words and phrases. Do the points in the draft seem more relevant and well-founded?
- Note the places where your reviewers wanted additional information. Could you include additional evidence that would support your generalizations more convincingly?
- Are the paragraphs all in the most effective form? Could some benefit from having a focusing sentence at the beginning or at the end? Can your reader

easily tell what the main idea of each paragraph is? Are the paragraphs unified?

- Have you used several long or short sentences in a row? Do you need to vary sentence length to eliminate such a problem? Would combining sentences help?

- Once you have written a second draft, reread your revised version. Do you find that your essay is better supported by relevant and well-founded evidence? If you are still not completely satisfied, you might wish to have another class member read it and do another peer review for you.

- Once you are satisfied with the organization, detail, and evidence in your essay, read it carefully to be sure that you've expressed your generalization clearly and that you've used relevant evidence to support and explain it.

- At this point you're ready to do the final editing of your essay. First, go over your draft carefully to make sure that all the subjects and verbs agree (see the checklist on pages 75–76) and that the pronouns are used appropriately (see the checklist on page 162). Then read the following section for more advice on ways to make your sentences as effective as possible.

Editing Your Draft

Combining Sentences with -*ing* Verbals

In Chapter 3 we looked at ways of combining sentences using subordination and coordination; in Chapter 4 we covered combining sentences with modifiers. In this chapter we're going to examine another method of sentence combining, and learn yet another grammatical term—*verbals*.

Sentence Fragments

Using a verbal as a verb is a fairly common mistake, one of the most frequent causes of sentence fragments. "My nose runs" can be a complete sentence because it has both a subject ("My nose") and a predicate ("runs"). "My running nose," by contrast, can't be a complete sentence because it has only a subject. My and running both modify the noun nose; there's no verb. For more information on sentence fragments and how to correct them, see the appendix, "A Survivor's Guide to English" (pages 336–37).

A verbal is a verb form that functions as a noun or a modifier (an adverb or adjective). One such verb form is the *-ing* form, which can function as an adjective. *Run* is a verb; the *-ing* form of this verb is *running.* In the sentences "I run" and "The track stars run," *run* is used as a verb. And *running* can be used as a verb in combination with another verb form: "I am running"; "They were running." But in the sentence "My running nose is driving me crazy," *running* is a verbal because it's acting as an adjective, modifying *nose.* Two sentences can sometimes be combined by converting the verb in one sentence to its *-ing* form as an adjective. For example, the two sentences "My nose runs" and "It really hurts" can be combined into a single sentence: "My running nose really hurts."

Keep in mind, though, that the *-ing* form cannot function by itself as the main verb of a sentence ("my nose running"), so when you convert a verb to a verbal, you have to combine the clause it's in with another sentence, or you'll have a sentence fragment.

Let's look at another example. Following are two sentences that can be combined.

I could not understand a word they said. I was mystified.

One way of combining these two sentences is to use coordination:

I could not understand a word they said, so I was mystified.

Another way is to use subordination:

Because I could not understand a word they said, I was mystified.

A better way in this case might be to combine the two sentences using the *-ing* verbal *understanding* rather than the verb *understand:*

Not understanding a word they said, I was mystified.

INDIVIDUAL ACTIVITY

Following are two sets of sentences to combine according to the directions below. As an example, we've combined the first pair of sentences in each case; your job is to combine pair B in a similar way.

A. Luz was tired of not understanding her classmates. She decided to improve her English.

B. Luz felt strongly about her decision. She begged her parents to hire her a tutor.

1. Combine the sentences in pair B using a coordinating conjunction. (See page 114 for a list of coordinating conjunctions.)

> *Example:* Luz was tired of not understanding her classmates, so she decided to improve her English.

_____

_____

2. Combine the sentences in pair B using a subordinating conjunction. (See page 111 for a list of subordinating conjunctions.)

> *Example:* Because she was tired of not understanding her classmates, Luz decided to improve her English.

_____

_____

3. Combine the sentences in pair B using an *-ing* verb form.

> *Example:* Being tired of not understanding her classmates, Luz decided to improve her English.

_____

_____

GROUP ACTIVITY

Working with your group or class, convert the following verbs to verbals using the *-ing* ending. Then use each *-ing* verbal in a sentence. Remember that a verbal cannot be the main verb of a sentence, so you'll need to be sure that each sentence you come up with has both a main verb and a verbal.

> Verb: sing   Verbal: singing
> Sentence: Singing badly, Ralph was embarrassed.

1. Verb: speak

   Verbal: _____

   Sentence: _____

   _____

   _____

2. Verb: read

   Verbal: _____

   Sentence: _____

   _____

   _____

3. Verb: listen

   Verbal: _____

   Sentence: _____

   _____

   _____

4. Verb: hear

   Verbal: _____

   Sentence: _____

   _____

   _____

5. Verb: think

   Verbal: _____

   Sentence: _____

   _____

   _____

6. Verb: concentrate

   Verbal: _____

Sentence: _____

_____

_____

7. Verb: play

   Verbal: _____

   Sentence: _____

   _____

   _____

8. Verb: feel

   Verbal: _____

   Sentence: _____

   _____

   _____

9. Verb: leave

   Verbal: _____

   Sentence: _____

   _____

   _____

10. Verb: misunderstand

    Verbal: _____

    Sentence: _____

    _____

    _____

INDIVIDUAL ACTIVITY

Select two sets of sentences from your revised draft that you think will benefit from sentence combining. Combine each set into a single sentence using any of the techniques we've looked at so far: coordination, subordination, modifiers, or *-ing* verbals.

Using Commas Appropriately

Nearly every writer has trouble with punctuation at times. We'll begin, in this chapter, with the most frequently used mark of punctuation, the comma, and then cover the others in the next few chapters.

Commas are used for a variety of purposes: to indicate a pause, to show a relationship, to separate modifiers or main ideas, and so forth. Here we discuss the most common uses of the comma.

1. *Use commas to separate three or more items in a series.*

Conveyed through those sounds was the pleasing, soothing, consoling reminder that one was at home.

Richard Rodriguez

After American school, we picked up our cigar boxes, in which we had arranged books, brushes, and an inkbox. . . .

Maxine Hong Kingston

In the first of these sentences, the three items in series are adjectives *(pleasing, soothing, consoling),* all modifying *reminder.* In the second sentence, the three items are nouns (*books, brushes, inkbox*). Often the final item in such a list will be preceded by *and* (as it is in "books, brushes, and an inkbox"). Some writers consider most commas before *and* optional (and they are almost never used in journalistic writing, which differs in style from academic writing in a number of ways). But we suggest that you use a comma before *and* in a series. If you get into this habit, you won't omit such commas when they're needed.

2. *Use a comma to separate independent clauses linked with a coordinating conjunction.*

I do not recall what they were saying, but I cannot forget the sounds my father made as he spoke.

Richard Rodriguez

These two independent clauses could each stand alone as a sentence: "I do not recall what they were saying. I cannot forget the sounds my father made as he spoke." When you link such clauses with a coordinating conjunction *(and, but, nor, or, yet, for, so),* use a comma before the conjunction as a way of making each of the clauses distinct.

3. *Use a comma after an introductory word, phrase, or clause.*

But until I was seven years old, I did not know the name of the old couple living next door or the names of the kids living across the street.

Richard Rodriguez

If the introductory element is just a word or two, some writers will omit the comma:

> Soon [,] the baby's babbling turned into words.

But be sure to set off longer phrases or clauses with commas:

> After studying in Paris for two years, Marlene learned to speak French.

4. *Use commas to set off such interrupting elements as transitional terms and parenthetical phrases.*

I'd notice, moreover, that my parents' voices were softer than those of gringos we would meet.

Richard Rodriguez

This thought, if a wordless sensation may be called a thought, made me hop and skip with pleasure.

Helen Keller

There are, of course, many other uses for commas. But if you follow these guidelines, you'll be able to deal with the most common uses of the comma.

INDIVIDUAL ACTIVITY

Using sentences from your own draft, find an example of each of these uses of the comma. Add needed commas as appropriate. If you don't have an example in your draft, rewrite one of your sentences so that it includes the example.

1. Commas separating three or more items in a series.

2. A comma separating independent clauses linked with a conjunction.

3. A comma used after an introductory word, phrase, or clause.

4. Commas used to set off a transitional term or parenthetical phrase.

METAESSAY

The process for writing an essay about language required you to do the following:

- Talk about being excluded by language
- Read essays by others who were excluded by language
- Plan and write a discovery draft using your own and others' experiences
- Review your classmates' drafts and offer suggestions for improvement
- Revise your draft following suggestions made by your classmates

How did you go about determining your central generalization and coming up with supporting evidence? What problems, if any, did you face while drafting? While revising? What were the hardest and easiest parts of the process for you?

Write a brief essay exploring these questions. If you need a fuller description of metaessays, see page 76.

PEER REVIEW FORM 1: AN ESSAY ON LANGUAGE

Writer's Name: _____

Reviewer's Name: _____

First number the paragraphs of the work you are reviewing. Then write out your answer to each of the following questions. Use the paragraph numbers for reference, and use the back of this page if you need more space. When you have completed this review, tear out this page and give it to the writer.

1. What main idea, or generalization, is the writer trying to convey about language? Quote the sentence or sentences in which this main idea is expressed. If you can't identify the main idea, tell the writer why you're having trouble finding it.

_____

_____

_____

_____

2. What evidence does the writer use from personal experience?

_____

_____

_____

_____

3. What evidence does the writer use from other students or the essays you've read?

_____

_____

_____

_____

4. How does the writer connect his or her own experience with the experiences of other students or those of the writers in this chapter?

_____

_____

_____

5. In referring to their work, does the writer accurately and effectively summarize the experiences of Hong Kingston, Keller, or Rodriguez?

_____

_____

_____

_____

6. Are there sentences that would benefit from being combined? If so, put brackets around the sentences that could go together, and explain why you think so.

_____

_____

_____

_____

7. Do all of the subjects and verbs agree? Circle any verbs that you think don't agree with their subjects, and explain why you've done so. (See the subject-verb checklist on pages 75–76.)

_____

_____

_____

_____

8. Do all of the pronouns have clear antecedents? Are all of the pronouns in the correct gender, number, and case? Circle any pronouns you think might be incorrect, and explain why. (See the pronoun checklist on page 162.)

_____

_____

_____

_____

PEER REVIEW FORM 2: AN ESSAY ON LANGUAGE

Writer's Name: _____

Reviewer's Name: _____

First number the paragraphs of the work you are reviewing. Then write out your answer to each of the following questions. Use the paragraph numbers for reference, and use the back of this page if you need more space. When you have completed this review, tear out this page and give it to the writer.

1. What main idea, or generalization, is the writer trying to convey about language? Quote the sentence or sentences in which this main idea is expressed. If you can't identify the main idea, tell the writer why you're having trouble finding it.

_____

_____

_____

_____

2. What evidence does the writer use from personal experience?

_____

_____

_____

_____

3. What evidence does the writer use from other students or the essays you've read?

_____

_____

_____

_____

4. How does the writer connect his or her own experience with the experiences of other students or those of the writers in this chapter?

_____

_____

_____

_____

5. In referring to their work, does the writer accurately and effectively summarize the experiences of Hong Kingston, Keller, or Rodriguez?

_____

_____

_____

_____

6. Are there sentences that would benefit from being combined? If so, put brackets around the sentences that could go together, and explain why you think so.

_____

_____

_____

_____

7. Do all of the subjects and verbs agree? Circle any verbs that you think don't agree with their subjects, and explain why you've done so. (See the subject-verb checklist on pages 75–76.)

_____

_____

_____

_____

8. Do all of the pronouns have clear antecedents? Are all of the pronouns in the correct gender, number, and case? Circle any pronouns you think might be incorrect, and explain why. (See the pronoun checklist on pages 162.)

_____

_____

_____

_____

WRITER'S RESPONSE TO PEER REVIEW 1

> *Read the peer reviews you received from the members of your group; then fill out one of these forms for each one. (This exercise will help you decide how you want to follow your reviewers' suggestions when you revise your discovery draft. It will also help your reviewers understand how they can provide the most effective information for you.)*

Writer's Name: _____

Reviewer's Name: _____

After you have turned in the final version of your essay, tear out this form and give it to your reviewer.

1. Did this reviewer's comments help you see the strengths and weaknesses of your discovery draft? If they were not helpful, what kinds of information and suggestions were you hoping to get?

_____

_____

_____

_____

_____

2. Based on this review, in what ways do you plan to revise your discovery draft?

_____

_____

_____

_____

_____

3. Which of the reviewer's comments and suggestions did you find most helpful? Why?

_____

_____

_____

_____

_____

4. Which of the reviewer's comments and suggestions do you disagree with? Why?

_____

_____

_____

_____

_____

WRITER'S RESPONSE TO PEER REVIEW 2

> *Read the peer reviews you received from the members of your group; then fill out one of these forms for each one. (This exercise will help you decide how you want to follow your reviewers' suggestions when you revise your discovery draft. It will also help your reviewers understand how they can provide the most effective information for you.)*

Writer's Name: _____

Reviewer's Name: _____

After you have turned in the final version of your essay, tear out this form and give it to your reviewer.

1. Did this reviewer's comments help you see the strengths and weaknesses of your discovery draft? If they were not helpful, what kinds of information and suggestions were you hoping to get?

_____

_____

_____

_____

_____

2. Based on this review, in what ways do you plan to revise your discovery draft?

_____

_____

_____

_____

_____

3. Which of the reviewer's comments and suggestions did you find most helpful? Why?

_____

_____

_____

_____

4. Which of the reviewer's comments and suggestions do you disagree with? Why?

_____

_____

_____

_____

_____

SELF-EVALUATION FORM: AN ESSAY ON LANGUAGE

Name: _____

Essay Title: _____

Date: _____

Complete this evaluation and turn it in with your essay.

1. How much time did you spend on this paper? What did you spend most of your time on (getting started, drafting, revising, something else)? Do you think you needed to spend more time or less time on some of these parts of the writing process?

_____

_____

_____

_____

_____

2. What do you like best about your paper?

_____

_____

_____

_____

_____

3. What changes have you made in your paper since the peer review?

_____

_____

_____

_____

_____

4. If you had an additional day to work on your paper, what other changes would you make?

_____

_____

_____

_____

_____

5. What things would you like your instructor to give you special help with when reading and commenting on this paper?

_____

_____

_____

_____

_____

CHAPTER SIX

THINKING ABOUT YOUR AUDIENCE

An Essay on Your Community

GOALS

To help you write an essay about your community, we'll concentrate on the following goals in this chapter:

- Understanding your audience—who your readers are—and how you can write for them most effectively.

- Writing an opening that will both get your readers' attention and help them understand what your essay is about.

- Writing a strong, effective conclusion.

- Linking paragraphs with transitions so that your readers can easily follow your ideas.

- Using apostrophes and semicolons effectively.

Writing Preview

Using what you've learned in this and earlier chapters, you'll write an essay about your community, trying to help an outsider understand just what the culture you live in is like. "Culture" and "community" can be very broadly defined—your school, your class, your neighborhood, your city, your state, even your nation. You'll pick a few telling details and use those details to characterize your community, just as the writers of the essays in this chapter characterized their communities.

First decide what "community" you think you'd like to write about. If you are initially unsure, do some brainstorming. Then pick out something about your community that's significant and write four or five sentences about it. Imagine that you are writing to someone preparing to visit your community for the first time—a relative, a friend, an exchange student. What should that person know about your community before coming to visit?

Think about things to avoid in the community, things not to be missed, and activities in the community that you especially enjoy.

Once you have written some notes, compare them with those of the other members of your group or your class. Did you all select the same "community" or different ones? Do you all agree about what's significant—things to be avoided, to be seen, or to be done?

DEFINING YOUR READERS

In Chapter 3, we compared talking and writing, and we noted that there are some significant differences in how we say things in speech and in writing. But not even all speaking is the same. We change the way we talk when we're speaking to different types of listeners. You might angrily declare, "I got suckered on that midterm!" to a friend or classmate, but if you were talking to your history professor, your remark would more likely be something along the lines of "Professor Smith, I found your midterm exam a bit too difficult," spoken in a calm, respectful voice.

It's obvious that we adjust our speech—both the words we use and our tone of voice—according to the person or group we're speaking to. We all do this; it's perfectly natural. And such shifts apply to writing as well.

Different Readers, Different Choices

Imagine writing two letters complaining about something happening on your campus: one to your best friend and one to a college administrator. Those letters would be quite different, wouldn't they? You'd probably describe things to your best friend very differently than you would to someone in charge of correcting the problem. And even if the content of the two letters were the same, wouldn't the style—the choice of words, the sentence structure—be very different? An opening sentence like "I'm so mad, I could choke someone" is obviously not appropriate for a letter to an administrator, but it may be perfectly fine for a letter to a friend.

Obviously, you have to think about your readers when you write. That seems pretty simple; after all, you think about your listeners when you speak. But it's often more difficult to identify your readers than to tell who your listeners are. You can almost always see the people you're speaking to, and even if you're not sure how best to get your ideas across, you can watch their reactions and listen to their questions and comments, adjusting what you say accordingly.

But you can't watch and listen to your readers to judge how well they're understanding and accepting what you've written. And, of course, you can't change what you've said after you've mailed your letter or submitted your paper. So for many writing tasks—particularly important or formal ones—you need to do some analysis of your readers before you even start putting words on paper. If you write a paper without taking your reader into account, you're not very likely to achieve the best results because the evidence you provide, the vocabulary you use, and even the tone you exhibit may not really communicate your ideas to that audience.

Obviously, if you're writing a letter to your best friend, you don't have to do much conscious analysis; you already know your reader pretty well, and you can anticipate the likely reaction to what you have to say. When you write papers for your composition courses, you also know something about your readers—you've talked with your instructor, the other members of your group, and perhaps even the class as a whole—so you should be able to figure out some of the things these readers already know and what they expect from you. In other situations, however—particularly in the world beyond your college courses—you often won't even know who your specific readers are, so the job of analyzing your reader can be a lot tougher. But for now let's concentrate on writing for an audience you can identify fairly easily.

Thinking about What Readers Know

For most types of writing, it helps to categorize potential readers according to how much they know about a subject. We may learn about things in a variety of ways: through direct personal experience, from reading and observing, and by talking with others. Regardless of the source of their knowledge, readers can be categorized in three ways: well-informed, partially informed, and uninformed readers.

Well-Informed Readers

Well-informed readers already know a great deal about the subject. In fact, a well-informed reader may know more about the subject than you do. This is frequently the case with papers that students write for introductory college courses, when the purpose in writing is generally more to demonstrate a grasp of the subject than to offer the reader new information. If you're writing an anthropology paper about the Shaker community, for example, chances are pretty good that the professor who assigned the paper already knows a great deal about the subject, especially if it's been a central topic of reading assignments and class lectures. Your paper, then, probably won't need to explain everything about the Shakers. You might mention that the group was originally an offshoot of the Quakers and was led for a time by Mother Ann Lee, but you wouldn't have to explain who the Quakers were or why Lee was called "Mother."

Partially Informed Readers

Partially informed readers know something about the subject, but probably not as much as you if you've studied the subject carefully. You aren't writing to show them what you know; rather, you're writing to help them understand the subject as well as you do. Suppose that you and some other students in your anthropology class form a study group and divide up the work of researching particular subjects. If you are reporting on the Shakers for your study group, you can assume that they'll be partially informed but not experts. Perhaps they know that the Shakers were a religious community, that their members advocated celibacy and pacifism, and that they were known as fine craftspeople; but perhaps they won't know how the sect was founded, when it flourished, or its specific religious practices.

Uninformed Readers

Uninformed readers know very little about the subject, so you'll have to explain even more to them. If you were writing a letter about your college classes to a friend who's moved away, for example, you might have to assume that he or she knows almost nothing about the Shakers and start from the beginning, even explaining that it was a religious sect.

INDIVIDUAL ACTIVITY

Look back at what you wrote about your community for the Before We Start activity at the beginning of this chapter. Rather than an uninformed reader, suppose that you are writing for a well-informed reader. Come up with four or five more statements about things you've noticed that other members of the community might not have noticed.

Thinking about Audience

When you consider your audience, take these sorts of things into account to be sure that your essay meets your readers' needs.

- What is the aim of your essay? What are you trying to accomplish?
- How many details should you include, and what kinds?
- What kind of evidence should you include, and how much?
- How many facts would be useful? Where should you get them?
- How large a role should opinion play in your essay?

R E A D I N G S

In the three following selections, the writers characterize cultures in very different ways. Jenny Vogt attempts to undermine some common stereotypes about Arabic people by giving several specific details about their culture. James Fallows concentrates mainly on his own reaction to a specific Japanese practice to show us what it's like. And Loretta Ilodibe recalls a festival in her home village in Nigeria. As you read, make some notes on ways in which you can characterize your culture.

PREREADING EXERCISE

Before you read each selection, look it over using one of the prereading exercises that you think works well for you. Also, make notes to yourself in the margin as you read.

THE ARAB PUZZLE
Jenny Vogt

This essay, which first appeared in the Palm Beach Post *(Fla.) in 1991, opens by presenting some stereotypes of Arabs, then goes on to talk more realistically about the Arab world. Before you begin reading, think about your own stereotypes of Arabs. What do you think of when you hear that someone is an Arab?*

1   The stereotypical Arab is a hawk-nosed man with an evil eye who is garbed in a flowing headdress and robe.

2   This "demonization" of Arabs, says Samir Abed-Rabbo, a director of the Brattleboro, Vt.–based Arab Council for Change, an Arab-American think tank, began with the Crusades in 1095 A.D. and has continued through the ages.

3   "The picture is of filthy oil-rich sheiks or sex-crazed maniacal individuals or terrorists," said Abed-Rabbo, a Palestinian with a doctorate in international law from the University of Miami. "We are told usually that Arabs are different, but I've yet to find an Arab with a tail."

4   Few Arabs fit such stereotypes. But some generalizations can be drawn of the Arab world, nevertheless.

5   Generally, it might be said that the typical Arab is family-oriented and God-fearing, following a strict code of conduct as set forth in the Koran, the book of Moslem beliefs. Arab experts agree. They also warn there are many exceptions to any generalizations that can be made about 21 Arab countries.

6   "The degree to which the individual subordinates himself to his family or clan or tribe is much greater in the Arab world than most Americans are used to," said Arthur Goldschmidt Jr., a professor of Middle East history at Penn State University. "But to say there's really one Arab mind-set would be like saying blacks have one mind-set. . . . Islam is probably the greatest influence, but Islam is also very complicated."

7   Islam requires a high degree of discipline, calling Moslems to prayer five times a day. Moslems are also required to fast from sunrise to sunset for a month each year and to abstain from sex during this time.

8   "Islam is not only a spiritual code, but is a way of life that structures the way a Moslem should behave in all aspects of life," Abed-Rabbo said. Most Moslems, he and Goldschmidt agree, however, adhere fairly strictly to Islamic teachings—probably more than Westerners generally adhere to their religions.

9   To get an idea of what it means to be a typical Arab, we've pulled together some Moslem customs and traditions, many of which grew out of the holy Koran. These rules are generally followed, although there are exceptions to all of them.

> Are you underlining and making notes in the margin about anything you find especially surprising or interesting in this article?

10   ▪ In the Moslem world, followers pray aloud—even outside the holy mosques.

11   "Parents are always invoking the name of God in public," Goldschmidt said. "It's like asking someone on the street . . . What bus should I take to the post office, my God? It's like saying please in the West."

12   ▪ In the Mideast, people tend to stand closer together, and men are commonly seen holding hands in the streets.

13   "They practically breathe into each person's mouth," Goldschmidt said. "I don't think that's religion. I think it's more a custom . . . and it really makes some sense [for men] to hold hands in crowded streets."

14   ▪ In Islamic culture, it is not considered respectful to call someone you do not know by [his or her] first name.

15   "If you don't know them, say 'brother' for a man or 'sister' for a female," Abed-Rabbo explained.

16   ▪ Gossip is frowned upon in Arab culture. If, for example, a man spreads the tale of a woman's alleged sexual exploits, he can be severely punished by the woman's family if he is unable to produce witnesses to the event, Abed-Rabbo said.

17   "It is probably the worst thing you could commit," he said. "It might lead to his death." Other transgressions that can lead to death include stealing, drug use and incest.

18   ▪ Settling disputes is best achieved between families in Islamic culture.

19   This typically means that a representative of the wronged party seeks the advice of a community leader, explaining their predicament, Abed-Rabbo said. If the leader agrees it is possible the party was wronged, he or she will visit the family of the accused to set a date for a meeting between the two sides.

20   If the two sides cannot amicably settle the dispute—often with punishment of the wrongdoer—the courts may then be drawn into the battle, he added.

21   ▪ In Islamic countries, there are few if any drinking establishments.

22   "I think it's safe to say that in most of the Arab world it [drinking alcohol] does not exist," Abed-Rabbo said.

23   ▪ Courting occurs in a highly structured, formal format. Divorce is possible, but easier for men to initiate. Premarital sex can result in death under certain circumstances.

24   "This is like an affront to the family's pride and their dignity," Abed-Rabbo said.

25   ▪ In Moslem countries, mothers are customarily paid more respect than in Western countries, Abed-Rabbo said.

26   The Koran states that heaven is "under the feet of mothers," meaning those who do not respect their mothers cannot hope to gain admission, he said, adding that all women demand similar respect.

27   Goldschmidt, however, noted that Moslem women are expected to boss only the household while Moslem men boss all matters outside the home.

28   ▪ The practice of veiling oneself can be found in many ancient cultures. The Koran states simply that people should be modest and that women should not display their "treasures" to strange men, Goldschmidt said.

29   "Many Moslems interpreted this to mean that women should not reveal bodily contours and should wear loose garments and a veil," he said.

30   ▪ On issues of hospitality, the elderly are always deferred to above everyone else in Moslem society. For instance, when serving food in a home, the eldest person is served first, whether . . . a man or a woman, Abed-Rabbo said.

31   It is also highly improper to rebuff offers of food if you are a guest in someone's home, he said.

32   "The best thing to do if they give you something to eat is to take a little bit to taste," he said. "Breaking the bread is a very important symbol in our culture."

33   Additionally, to present one's left hand in greeting is a major insult. Goldschmidt said the practice of extending one's right hand only in greet-

ing goes back to ancient Arab culture when one used the left hand strictly for cleaning oneself (before toilet paper) and the right strictly for eating.

POSTREADING EXERCISE

Reread "The Arab Puzzle," looking particularly at paragraphs 9–33. Here Vogt divides her article into several distinct sections, each focusing on a particular aspect of the Arab culture and community. Draw lines to mark off each of these sections, and note in the margins the topic covered in each. How does Vogt develop each topic?

LAND OF PLENTY
James Fallows

In this essay, from the June 1989 Atlantic *magazine, the author tells about his introduction to a Japanese practice very different from what he and his family were used to. As you read this essay, consider what you would have done in his situation.*

1   On *sodai gomi* nights in Japan we learn what kind of people we are. *Sodai gomi,* which rhymes with "oh my homey," means "bulky garbage." It's sometimes used colloquially to describe husbands who have retired from the salaryman life and now spend their time around the house. That *sodai gomi* problem may be a strain on Japanese families, but *sodai gomi* in its literal sense is a more serious trial for my family.

2   Three nights a week the residents of our neighborhood in Yokohama deposit their household trash at specified areas on the street corners. It's wrapped in neat bundles, it looks like gifts, it disappears at dawn. For two or three nights near the end of each month they bring out the *sodai gomi.* These are articles no longer wanted around the house and too big for normal trash collection. Big garbage can really be big: I've seen sofas, refrigerators, bookcases, chairs, bed frames, vacuum cleaners, an acetylene welding tank, a motorcycle, and numerous television sets.

3   *Sodai gomi* exists for two reasons. One is the small size of the typical Japanese house, with its lack of attic, cellar, garage, or spare room. When a new TV comes in, the old one must go out. (This also applies to cars. To buy a new one, you have to prove to the government that you have a place to park it, which for most people means getting rid of the old car. I can't figure out what happens to the old cars: they're certainly not on the roads, and so far I haven't seen one in a *sodai gomi* pile.)

4   The other reason is the Japanese desire for freshness and purity. No one here really enjoys using something that has passed through other people's hands. My Japanese friends seem to feel about buying a second-

hand radio, lamp, or table the way I'd feel about buying someone else's socks. There is a "recycle shop" in our neighborhood that sells used clothes and toys at cut rates. Presumably someone must buy there, since it's still in business, but usually shoppers seem to scoot by in embarrassment, as if it were a Frederick's of Hollywood shop. Whenever I'm listening to the Far East Network, the U.S. military's radio station, and hear an ad for a garage sale, I realize that the American soldiers are unusual not just because they have garages but also because they can sell their old possessions rather than throw them out.

5   Our first *sodai gomi* night came shortly after we moved into our current house. It cut into our hearts in a way none of our neighbors could have known. For one thing, we had no furniture, silverware, or other household belongings, because everything except the clothes in our suitcases was making a five-week sea journey up from our last house, in Malaysia. We had also just come from a culture with a wholly different approach to used goods. Malaysia is a land of tropical abundance, but no one throws anything away. Just before leaving we had auctioned off every spare item in the house, from frying pans and mosquito nets to half-used rolls of Scotch tape. Several customers were enthusiastically bidding for the shirts my sons had on. It was painful to go from that world to one in which we didn't have any household goods, couldn't bring ourselves to buy the overpriced new ones in the store—and then saw heaps of clean, new-looking merchandise just sitting on the street.

6   You can see where I am leading. It was not in us to resist. We had quickly tired of eating, sitting, relaxing, studying, and performing all other indoor activities on the floor, without tables or chairs, while waiting for our ship to come in. "Set the floor, please, boys," my wife would call at dinner time. I lay sprawled on my stomach in front of my computer keyboard, attempting to type while resting my weight on my elbows, trying to cheer myself with mental images of Abe Lincoln sprawled before the fire as a boy. Then one evening, as we trudged home at twilight from the train station, we saw two replenished-looking *sodai gomi* piles. In one was a perfectly nice plastic lawn chair, in the other an ordinary low Japanese tea table. You couldn't use both of these at the same time—if you sat in the lawn chair, you'd be too high to reach down to the table comfortably. But if we had the table we could at least eat without bending over to reach plates of food on the floor, which made me feel like a husky eating its chow.

7   We were in a crowd, of course, when we first saw the *sodai gomi*. We were too confused and timid to grab anything from the pile just then. But that

Remember the critical reading strategies we discussed earlier. Make notes in the margin about anything in the essay you're interested in or don't quite understand.

night I sat in our kitchen, peering through our window toward the *sodai gomi* at the end of the street. The door to a juku, or cram school, was near the piles. The last group of teenage students left there around eleven. After midnight the trains from Tokyo become much less frequent: I could depend on intervals of fifteen or twenty minutes between clumps of salarymen teetering drunkenly from the station toward home. The street looked bare at 12:30, so I made my move. The next morning we placed our breakfast dishes on our table, and I read the morning paper while luxuriating in my full-length lawn chair.

8   It was two more days before the *sodai gomi* collectors came. In those two nights we laid in as many provisions as we decently could. A shiny new bell for one son's bicycle, a small but attractive wooden cupboard, a complete set of wrenches and screwdrivers in a metal toolbox, a Naugahyde-covered barstool, a lacquer serving tray. If I didn't already know English, I would probably have taken the four large boxes containing four dozen tape cassettes from the Advanced Conversational English series. My son walked in the door one day, said "Guess what?" and presented a black-and-white TV. In self-defense I should point out that everything except a few rusty wrenches looked perfectly clean, whole, and serviceable. In any other culture you'd never believe these things were being thrown out.

9   That was last summer; we've learned a lot since then. We realize that *sodai gomi* is part of a larger cycle, in which it's important to give as well as receive. So when our household shipment arrived, we gave the lawn chair back to the pile—and later we bought a new color TV and gave back the black-and-white one. We've learned that we're not alone in our secret practice. Last month I met an American writer who lives on the outskirts of Tokyo. I admired the leather notebook he was carrying and asked him where he got it. "You'll never believe this . . . ," he said. We've learned that some Japanese, too, overcome their squeamishness about secondhand material. When I'm up late at night, I sometimes catch a glimpse of the *soadi gomi* area—a more disinterested glimpse, now that our house is furnished—and see a van cruising back and forth, checking it out. In the morning the choicest items are gone.

10   And I've learned where I'll draw the line. As the only foreigners in our neighborhood, we are laughably conspicuous. People must know that we're skimming the *sodai gomi,* but if we do our best to be discreet about it, operating in the dead of night, everyone can pretend not to notice and we bring no shame upon our kind. Late one night, on the way home from the train station, I saw two handsome wooden bookcases sitting by a lamppost. I thought of the books piled on our floor, I looked around me quickly, and I happily picked up one bookcase with both arms.

11   It was fifteen minutes before I could get back for the other—only to find that it wasn't there. Twenty yards down the street I saw a hunched, shuffling figure. An old wino in a filthy overcoat, with a crippled left leg, was laboriously dragging the bookcase away toward his lair. Within seconds I was heading home again, looking as if I'd never dream of wrestling a bum for a bookcase. But I know what first flashed through my mind when I saw my treasure disappear: "I can take this guy!"

POSTREADING EXERCISE

In the first reading in this chapter, Jenny Vogt looked at several different aspects of the Arab community. In "Land of Plenty," James Fallows focuses on just one aspect of Japanese life: the *sodai gomi.*

Reread "Land of Plenty," underlining the sentences and sections that best help you understand the custom and how Fallows and his family participated in it. What makes these parts of the article especially interesting for you?

THE YAM FESTIVAL
Loretta Ilodibe

Loretta Ilodibe, a native of Nigeria, came to the United States to attend school. In the following brief essay, she recalls one of her village's traditions, an annual harvest celebration.

1   Yam Festival takes place in my village, Nnewi, in the Anambra state of Nigeria. This festival occurs every October to mark the new yam harvest season. As the festival approaches, every family in the village contributes money to buy a cow for the feast. The cow is killed and butchered two days before New Yam Day and the meat is distributed door to door for every family to use in their New Yam meals.

2   People of all ages take part in the festival. Because there are over 2,000 people in my village, the festival takes place in a very big open market place. Every family will bring their own pots and firewood for cooking, along with some of the yams that they have just harvested. Cooking the food takes about three hours, so everyone starts to gather in the market place at 9:00 in the morning. At exactly noon, the ruler of the village, known as the Obi of Nnewi, comes out and addresses the whole crowd, telling them how much he appreciates their participation in the New Yam Festival. Then he says a short prayer thanking God for guiding and protecting us and asking that we continue to be guided and protected so we can witness the New Yam Festival again next year.

3   After he's finished, palm wine, beer, and soda are served to every

family, and people start bringing out the food they've prepared. The whole festival is like a big American pot-luck dinner; families often try each other's food and share what they brought.

4   After the eating and drinking is over, the traditional entertainment starts. First, the women, wearing wraparound skirts with matching scarves and lace blouses, dance barefoot. They perform a native dance called the Igba Eze. Following this, the men will present their dance, a masquerade. There are usually twenty masqueraders, ranging in age from twelve to thirty-five. The masqueraders dance around the market square with whips in their hands and chase the people. Everyone has a lot of fun, but the masquerade lasts for about three hours, so we're all pretty tired when it's over. When it's done, everyone comes together again in the marketplace where the Obi gives a closing speech thanking everyone for coming to the festival, and the oldest person in the village prays and breaks a kolanut for good luck and blessing.

5   The Yam Festival is a unique celebration in my village because it's the only one used to usher in blessing and prosperity for the following year. Moreover, it fosters unity among the sons and daughters of the village and the surrounding areas by bringing us all together to celebrate our harvest and each other's company.

POSTREADING EXERCISE

Loretta Ilodibe describes how a major holiday is celebrated in her community. Look back at her essay, noticing how she begins and ends and what comes in between. How is Ilodibe's essay organized? Does this seem like a good way to organize a description of how a holiday or other occasion is celebrated?

INDIVIDUAL ACTIVITY

Think again about the community you have written about for activities earlier in this chapter. Then do some more preliminary writing based on the following suggestions:

1. Write a few sentences about any stereotypes that others have of your community, as Vogt did. Then write a few more sentences to provide examples from real life that show that those stereotypes are misleading.

2. Think of some activity that everyone in your community would be familiar with but that outsiders might find unusual or surprising, as James Fallows found the Japanese *sodai gomi* surprising. Write a few sentences naming and defining that activity as well as giving some examples of it.

3. Think of a major holiday or another occasion for celebration in your community. Write a few sentences exploring why a detailed description of that celebration might be interesting to readers and what sorts of readers would probably find such an essay most interesting.

WRITING EFFECTIVE OPENINGS

We saw how important opening paragraphs are when you wrote your character sketch for Chapter 2. You know that you need to get your readers' attention at the outset if you expect them to read on. And you also know that you have to give them some idea of what your paper is about so that they'll know what to look for as they read on. There are many ways to create an effective opening for your paper. Here are a few of the most common techniques.

Offer Some Striking Details

We discussed the use of striking details in introductions in Chapter 2 on the character sketch. Keep in mind that you can select striking details for the openings of other kinds of papers as well.

See pages 42–44 for examples of using striking details at the opening of a character sketch.

Set Up a Contrast

You may remember that Jenny Vogt begins her article on Arab culture with a contrast: first she describes some stereotypes of the Arab community; then she states that such stereotypes are incorrect, the idea she will develop in the rest of her article:

The stereotypical Arab is a hawk-nosed man with an evil eye who is garbed in a flowing headdress and robe.

This "demonization" of Arabs, says Samir Abed-Rabbo, a director of the Brattleboro, Vt.–based Arab Council for Change, an Arab-American think tank, began with the Crusades in 1095 A.D. and has continued through the ages.

"The picture is of filthy oil-rich sheiks or sex-crazed maniacal individuals or terrorists," said Abed-Rabbo, a Palestinian with a doctorate in international law from the University of Miami. "We are told usually that Arabs are different, but I've yet to find an Arab with a tail."

Few Arabs fit such stereotypes. But some generalizations can be drawn of the Arab world, nevertheless.

Openings like this are especially effective if you're trying to demonstrate that some widely accepted ideas are really incorrect.

State Your Thesis

In his article about an unusual Japanese custom, James Fallows begins by stating specifically the point he is going to make in the rest of the article:

> On *sodai gomi* nights in Japan we learn what kind of people we are.

Such a statement is often called the *thesis* of an essay; many writers like to include such a statement in the opening paragraph because it clearly indicates what their essay will be about. It's also the kind of straightforward, no-nonsense approach that appeals to many teachers who want their students to get right to the point.

Similarly, you can begin with a general statement and work your way to a more specific thesis statement at the end of the first paragraph. Such an introduction can be especially effective if you're trying to show how your topic fits within some larger context. Student Krista Muller uses such an introduction in her paper on TV advertising in Chapter 4:

> People complain a lot because there are so many TV commercials that interrupt shows. But my complaint about commercials is that they are really unrealistic. The products and the lifestyle they show are very different from the way things really are. The media try to make you think that their products are going to change your life. But all they want to do is to make you buy what they're selling. When I look at most commercials, all I can think is, "That's not how things are in my world."

Begin with an Anecdote or Example

Brief narratives that illustrate your main point can also be effective openings, especially if they are unusual or controversial. Student Chi Nguyen uses this kind of introduction for her essay on teen suicide in Chapter 3:

> In 1989, one of my closest friends thought that her life was useless, that it had no meaning, so she killed herself. While her parents were away for the weekend, she locked herself in the garage and started the engine of her father's station wagon. She sat in the car and inhaled the carbon monoxide fumes. She fell asleep shortly afterward. The police found her there, after the neighbors heard the loud noises the car was making and went to investigate. Her parents did not know until they came back on Monday that their daughter had taken her own life. It was a great shock not just to them, but to all her friends and classmates, because she seemed like the kind of person that people think have it all; we never thought she was the kind who would do anything like that.

WRITING EFFECTIVE CONCLUSIONS

You might expect that after spending so much effort on organizing and developing your ideas effectively, just adding a conclusion would be the easy part. But it's not. Sometimes concluding an essay can be even harder than getting started or working through your ideas, no matter how time-consuming or frustrating the earlier processes may be. So if you get stuck on endings, don't worry: it's a common problem.

Just as there are many effective ways to begin an essay, there are also lots of ways to conclude one skillfully, depending on how you've organized your ideas, what you're trying to say, how long your essay is, and similar considerations. Let's look at some ways to conclude an essay.

Summarize Your Essay's Main Idea

A common way of concluding an essay is to provide a summary of its main point or main idea. This does not mean simply restating what you have already said in the same words or repeating the focusing sentences from your supporting paragraphs. Rather, you should try to leave your reader with a statement that explains the main point that all your preceding details are intended to support.

For example, in an essay earlier in this chapter, Loretta Ilodibe describes the Yam Festival celebrated yearly in her Nigerian village. In her conclusion she summarizes the special meaning of the festival:

> The Yam Festival is a unique celebration in my village because it's the only one used to usher in blessing and prosperity for the following year. Moreover, it fosters unity among the sons and daughters of the village and the surrounding areas by bringing us all together to celebrate our harvest and each other's company.

Similarly, in the conclusion to an essay in Chapter 5 about feeling left out when one is not fully comfortable with another language, Eleni Soekadis summarizes the main point that her preceding examples have been leading to:

> Basically, what it comes down to is remembering that people know different things and if you want them to feel included and understand what you're saying, you have to speak their language or help them learn yours.

Reiterate Your Thesis

Although you should not usually simply restate your thesis or main idea in the conclusion, it can be effective to reemphasize that idea for your reader—particularly if your essay is fairly long or complicated. But be careful when reiterating your thesis not to repeat the same words you used to introduce it. Doing so can make it seem that your essay has gone nowhere, that our understanding at the end is the same as it was at the beginning.

Look at the opening and concluding paragraphs of Iris C. Rotberg's essay on the use of standardized test scores to rate the performance of American students (presented in its entirety in Chapter 7). Here's her introduction:

> In a recent op-ed piece on the quality of U.S. education, Diane Ravitch suggests that "the greatest obstacle to those who hope to reform American education is complacency." I agree. As a nation, we are too complacent about the large proportion of our students who are in poverty, about the vast disparities in educational expenditures between rich and poor school districts, about the rising costs of higher education and what it does to student motivation. But these serious problems will not be addressed by international test comparisons that are seriously flawed and, in fact, irrelevant.

Rotberg says that in evaluating academic performance, we can't simply compare the test scores of American and foreign students. Her thesis is that improving our schools has nothing to do with international tests and will require that we not be complacent about the real problems our students face. Her conclusion reiterates this thesis to emphasize its importance:

> These issues will not be addressed by yet another round of international tests. Nor will test comparisons provide a better education for low-income students who attend schools with inadequate resources. These are the real problems we should not be complacent about. Let's focus our attention on the difficult public policy issues to be addressed rather than on spurious comparisons and rankings.

Connect the Ending to the Beginning

Another effective way to conclude is to refer to an anecdote or example that you used at the beginning of your essay to create interest for your readers. Connecting the beginning and ending in this way is sometimes called *framing* because the technique "surrounds" an essay as a picture frame surrounds a photograph or painting.

Chi Nguyen does this in her essay on teen suicide in Chapter 3. In the first paragraph she cites the example of her friend whose suicide came as a complete shock (see page 108). After listing a variety of causes for teen suicide and offering some suggestions for its prevention, Nguyen concludes by returning to the example of her friend:

> I wish that I had known what to do when my friend was in danger. I wish other people had known, too. We couldn't see the signs that she gave us then, and now it's too late. But maybe we can save someone else if we'll just pay attention.

Note that Nguyen also points to the future in her conclusion, suggesting her hopes about a change for the better. Looking to the future is a good way to end an essay that has the purpose of getting people to do something or make a change in their lives.

End with a Provocative Idea

Sometimes a good way to conclude an essay can be to leave your readers with something to think about, an idea that they may not have thought of before. Of course, this idea must be clearly related to the rest of the essay and must grow out of the details provided in it. But it can go beyond a summary or reiteration of the thesis.

In an essay on the lack of reality in television commercials (Chapter 4), Krista Muller uses the body of her essay to give a number of specific examples. She then ends not by summarizing these examples but by suggesting a reason television viewers—who recognize the lack of reality in commercials—respond to the messages of the commercials anyway:

> Everybody eats, and most people drive. We all know that commercials about food and cars are very unrealistic, but we continue to buy these products anyway. Why do we do it? Maybe it's because we wish that instead of living in our world, we lived in the happy, carefree world shown in TV commercials.

What to Avoid in Conclusions

It is as important to know what to avoid in conclusions as it is to recognize effective concluding strategies. The conclusion is the last part of your essay that your readers will see, so you want to be sure to leave them with a good impression. Last impressions are at least as important as first impressions. Here are a few things to avoid when you're writing a conclusion.

1. *Don't introduce new facts or ideas in your conclusion.* Sometimes beginning writers, thinking that they should save the most important points for last, introduce completely new ideas in the conclusion. That's really not effective. If the ideas are truly important, they should be introduced and developed in the body of your essay, not simply mentioned in the final paragraph.

2. *Don't just say what you've accomplished in your essay.* Your readers should be able to figure out what you've accomplished—and you have to trust your own abilities as a writer and their abilities as readers. If you find yourself starting your concluding paragraph with something like "In this essay I have shown that . . . ," it's time to consider a new approach to ending the essay.

3. *Don't apologize.* If you've thought about your essay and how well it communicates your ideas to your intended readers, there's no need for a conclusion like this: "Although I don't know a lot about many different high schools, I think that some of my ideas are still valid." If you've done your job, there's no need to apologize. If you feel you haven't quite communicated your ideas, look again at how you've presented them—the evidence you've chosen, the way you've organized that evidence, the vocabulary and sentence structure you've used—and how well the language reaches your audience.

INDIVIDUAL ACTIVITY

Select one of the papers you wrote earlier in the course, and draft a new conclusion for it in which you either summarize the main idea, reiterate your thesis, connect the ending to the beginning, or end with a provocative idea. Compare this new conclusion with the original. Which is better? Why? Are there other ways you could conclude the essay?

WRITING ASSIGNMENT: AN ESSAY ON YOUR COMMUNITY

In this chapter you've read articles in which writers have looked at the cultures and customs of particular communities in three different ways. Jenny Vogt described various aspects of Arab culture that differ in significant ways from many people's stereotypes of that culture. James Fallows detailed a specific practice common to Japanese culture and how he and his family participated in it. Loretta Ilodibe explained a particular holiday as it is celebrated in her Nigerian home village.

In your essay you will describe something about your own community that will be of interest to readers who are unfamiliar with it. You may choose as your audience people who are unfamiliar with the United States and would like to know what life is like here. Or, depending on the specific community you choose to write about, your audience may instead be people who live in the United States—even your classmates, perhaps—who know little about that community.

Keep in mind that you have to define the community you will be focusing on. It may be your school or workplace, your neighborhood or region, your city or state, even the United States as a whole. It may be your ethnic community, your religious community, or a particular social community you belong to.

You have various options for developing this essay, but any of the three readings in this chapter provide good examples: you might, like Vogt, point out some stereotypes about your culture and give examples to contradict them; you might, like Fallows, explain one particular aspect of your community and describe how different members participate in and respond to it; or, like Ilodibe, you could describe in detail a particular holiday celebration, game, or ritual that is typical of your culture.

Summary of Steps

Here's a summary of steps to take in completing this assignment. Check off each step after you've completed it.

_____ Brainstorm to decide just what facet of your culture and community you're going to write about. Be sure to consider these aspects:

- how you will narrow your topic
- what examples you'll use
- whether your tone should be formal or informal, serious or light-hearted

_____ Determine what main points you want to use to illustrate what your culture is like.

_____ Write down some specific information about your readers. What are your readers likely to know or not know about your community or culture? Are they well informed, partially informed, or uninformed?

_____ Group the examples and details you plan to use so that similar ones are together.

_____ Organize your points so that your readers can follow your ideas clearly.

_____ Be sure that your introduction clearly indicates your point of view and that each paragraph supports that view. Try to make your introduction capture your readers' attention.

_____ Make sure that your conclusion reinforces the main idea of your essay without simply restating it.

Student Sample

In this essay, student Terri Nelson focuses on just a small part of her community, using it to demonstrate why she likes her new home and how she came to appreciate it.

THE ZOO
Terri Nelson

1   Emporia, Kansas, is a really small town. When we moved here from St. Louis two years ago, it seemed to me that Emporia was just a stretch of road with the Iowa Beef Processing plant at one end and the Bunge Pet Food soybean towers at the other--and nothing to do in between. I wondered how I'd ever get along in a small town, and I really resented having to move from St. Louis. There's nothing to do, and the people are typical small-towners-- they're dull and boring, and they never get excited about anything. At least that's the way I saw them.

2   Now that I've lived here awhile, though, I've come to appreciate what this particular small town

has to offer. I still miss lots of things about St. Louis, but I've also found some favorite spots in Emporia, places I think even people just passing through would like to visit. My favorite place is the zoo.

3   That's right. Emporia, with just 26,000 people, actually has its very own zoo. In fact, it's the smallest accredited zoo in the United States. But that doesn't mean it isn't a nice place.

4   When we lived in St. Louis, I used to go to the zoo a lot. I liked to see the elephants and the bears, the kangaroos and lions, and the hundreds of birds in the outdoor aviary built for the 1900 World's Fair. I still go to the zoo, but now I have to be satisfied with a wallaby rather than a herd of kangaroos, a bobcat rather than lions and tigers, a pair of ring-tailed lemurs rather than a whole island of monkeys, lots of native Kansas ducks, a prairie dog village, and the biggest snapping turtle I've ever seen. Like the St. Louis zoo, the Emporia zoo also has an aviary, but you can't walk through it. It only has about twenty birds--some herons, egrets, ibises, and spoonbills. But it's so peaceful and quiet at the zoo that these birds actually nest there, and you can hear the young birds squawking for food and watch the parents feed them. There are also a couple of cinereous vultures, huge birds with tufted white heads, hooked beaks, razor-sharp claws, and a six-foot wingspan. And they've built a nest, too.

5   Best of all, though, there are no crowds to drown out the calls of the birds or to push you away from the two mule deer that want to lick your fin- gertips through the chain-link fence. If other peo- ple are watching the deer, they'll stand back and give you a chance to have your fingers licked, too. I guess that's what I really like about the zoo and why I think it best represents what I've come to think of as "my town." No crowds, nice people. In St. Louis, you have to drive miles to the zoo, duel with other drivers for parking spaces, stand in long

```
lines just to get a Coke, and be jostled by crowds
of impolite, rushing people everywhere in the park,
even to get a glimpse of the animals. As much as I
enjoyed the zoo there, I always came home exhausted
and tense. Eventually I realized that I loved the
zoo but hated the trip and the crowds. But now I can
bike or jog to the zoo; it's less than five miles
away, even from clear over on the other side of
town. And when I'm there I can relax completely and
really enjoy the animals. But mostly I can enjoy the
sense of peace and solitude.
```

```
6          Most important, though, going to the zoo has
taught me that people in my town aren't boring after
all. They're nice, and they're polite. At the zoo
everyone speaks in low tones, almost like they're in
a church or a museum. They all seem to recognize
that the zoo is a special place and that we all have
a right to enjoy it in our own way. They've helped
me realize that being in a small town isn't so bad
after all.
```

Peer Review

Once you have completed your discovery draft, you're ready to start peer reviews. Here's a recap of what you need to do.

- Exchange papers with a classmate.
- Be alert to what the writer both succeeds at doing and is having trouble doing.
- Write your peer review, using one of the forms on pages 245–46 and 247–48.
- Talk over your review with the writer for a few minutes.
- Go through the whole process with another classmate.
- After reading the peer reviews of your own draft, complete the Writer's Response to Peer Review forms that follow the Peer Review forms.

Revising Your Discovery Draft

By now you should have a small stack of paper: your notes, your completed discovery draft, and peer reviews written by two of your classmates. With these you can start revising the discovery draft into the final version of your paper, the one that you're actually going to turn in. Here's the process for revising.

- Reread your draft.
- Reread your peer reviews, noting what the reviewers found effective and what they suggested to improve the draft.
- Decide which of the comments you agree with and which you disagree with. (Remember, you don't have to agree with or make the changes your reviewers suggest; you have the final responsibility for your essay.)
- Look for places where the examples and details may not be appropriate for the intended audience. Should these be expanded? Deleted?
- Analyze each paragraph. Is each in the most effective form?
- Look at your introduction. Will it catch your readers' attention and make them want to read on? Does it help readers grasp what your essay is about?
- Look at your conclusion. Does it effectively reinforce the main idea without merely restating it?
- Look for places where you may have used several long or short sentences in a row. Do you need to vary sentence length to eliminate such a problem? Would sentence combining help?
- After you have written a second draft, reread your revised version. Do you find that your essay gives a better view of your community, making interesting use of examples and details and providing a clear description of what the community is like? If you are still not completely satisfied, you might wish to have another class member read your draft and do another peer review for you.
- Once you are satisfied with the organization, detail, and opening and conclusion of your essay, you're ready to do the final editing.

Editing Your Draft

Once you've gone over your peer reviews and revised your discovery draft, you're ready to edit your draft based on what you've learned in earlier chapters. As you edit, also consider your use of transitions and apostrophes.

Using Transitions between Paragraphs

You already know how important it is to plan the order of ideas in your essay. In earlier chapters we talked about getting your ideas in an order that makes it easy for your readers to follow. Once you've got them in the arrangement that you think is most effective, there is one more thing that you can do to help your readers follow what you're saying: add transitions.

The most common way to link paragraphs is to use transitional words or phrases. For example, when you have a series of reasons or examples to support a point, you can start one paragraph with "First, . . . ," the next

A *transition* is a word or phrase, even a whole sentence, that you use to link one paragraph to another and to show the relationship between ideas in those paragraphs.

with "Second, . . . ," and the following with "Third, . . ." If you want to show that

a paragraph adds further information to the one that precedes it, you might begin with "Furthermore" or "In addition." If you want to indicate a contrast with the previous paragraph, you might begin with something like "On the other hand" or "However."

In narratives, transitions often refer to relationships in time. For example, when Loretta Ilodibe relates how the Yam Festival is celebrated in her village, she uses a number of transitions that show how events follow one another in time:

> As the festival approaches . . . (paragraph 1)
>
> At exactly noon . . . (2)
>
> After he's finished . . . (3)
>
> After the eating and drinking is over . . . (4)

James Fallows uses similar transitions in relating how his family learned to borrow from the *sodai gomi:*

> It was two more days before . . . (8)
>
> That was last summer . . . (9)
>
> Late one night . . . (10)
>
> It was fifteen minutes before . . . (11)

The important point is that each transition should serve as a guidepost to help your readers follow what you're saying.

Transitions usually form a link between the last sentence of one paragraph and the first sentence of the next, but that's not always the case. In the following paragraphs from an essay in Chapter 8, Maria Muniz links the first sentence of one paragraph with the first sentence of the preceding paragraph to provide the transition.

> I recently had a conversation with a man who generally sympathizes with the Castro regime. We talked of Cuban politics and although the discussion was very casual, I felt an old anger welling inside. After 16 years of living an "American" life, I am still unable to view the revolution with detachment or objectivity. I cannot interpret its results in social, political, or economic terms. Too many memories stand in my way.
>
> And as I listened to this man talk of the Cuban situation, I began to remember how as a little girl I would wake up crying because I had dreamed of my aunts and grandmothers and I missed them. I remembered my mother's trembling voice and the sad look on her face whenever she spoke to her mother over the phone. I thought of the many letters and photographs that somehow were always lost in transit. And as the conversation continued, I began to remember how difficult it often was to grow up Latina in an American world.

Muniz could have started the second paragraph with "I remember how as a little girl . . . ," a transition that would tie in nicely with the last sentence of the first paragraph. But by taking us back to the man she talked with, she reminds us of the situation that started her thinking about her past, her conversation with a man whose political views intensified Muniz's sense of isolation.

In order for your transitions to be effective, your paragraphs have to be in a logical order. Think of transitions as road signs to help your readers follow where you're going from paragraph to paragraph. If your paragraphs don't follow logically from one to the next, no amount of transitional devices will make them successful.

Common Transitional Words and Phrases

*K*eep in mind that you can't just choose a transitional word or phrase from this partial list and insert it into your essay. To be effective, each transition must fit naturally in the context of your essay.

immediately	eventually
afterward	finally
next	before
following	after
simultaneously	

To indicate addition or similarity:

also	in addition
besides	moreover
equally important	similarly
furthermore	too

To indicate contrast:

but	on the contrary
yet	however
on the other hand	nevertheless

To indicate time:

meanwhile	at the same time
later	

To indicate sequence or level of importance:

first, second	finally
last	next

To indicate result or cause:

therefore	thus
accordingly	so
consequently	because

To indicate an example or detail:

for example	specifically
for instance	that is
in other words	

GROUP ACTIVITY

Working together, read through one of the essays in Chapter 7, looking particularly at the beginning of each paragraph. Circle each use of a transitional word or phrase. How do these words and phrases connect the new paragraph to the preceding one?

INDIVIDUAL ACTIVITY

Reread your draft, underlining the transitions that you have used at the beginnings of paragraphs and within paragraphs. Does each transition clearly express the relationship between ideas that you intend? Are there places where the addition of transitional words or phrases would make it easier for your readers to follow what you are trying to say?

Using Apostrophes Appropriately

Of all the marks of punctuation, apostrophes are probably the easiest to use incorrectly. Whether it's the lack of an apostrophe where it's needed or the use of an apostrophe where it isn't needed, the result can be very confusing for readers. Apostrophes are used primarily to indicate (1) the possessive form of nouns (indicating ownership) and (2) contractions (indicating the omission of letters).

There are four rules to keep in mind in deciding whether or not an apostrophe is needed.

1. *Always* use an apostrophe to indicate that a noun is possessive (that is, that it "owns" the word that follows). To form the possessive of singular nouns, add -'s:

   a singer's voice (the voice *of a singer*)

   Fred's books (the books *of Fred*)

   the boss's office (the office *of the boss*)

   For plural nouns that end in *s* add only an apostrophe to form the possessive:

   the singers' voices (the voices *of the singers*)
   the bosses' offices (the offices *of the bosses*)

   Plural nouns that do not end in *s* form the possessive as singular nouns do, by adding -'s:

men's ties (ties *for men*)
children's books (books *for children*)

Note that *mens'* and *childrens'* are incorrect.

2. *Always* use an apostrophe to indicate that letters have been left out in a contraction:

do not = *don't*   I have = *I've*

it is = *it's*   they are = *they're*

3. *Never* use an apostrophe to indicate the possessive form of a personal pronoun:

my, mine	your, yours	their, theirs
his	her, hers	its

Note particularly that *it's* (contraction: *it is*) and *its* (possessive: *belonging to it*) are often confused, as are *they're (they are)* and *their (belonging to them)* and *you're (you are)* and *your (belonging to you)*. Check carefully to see that you've always used apostrophes appropriately with these words.

4. *Never* use apostrophes with verbs or with nouns that are not possessive:

My grandmother loves (not *love's*) eggs and yams (not *egg's* or *yam's*).

INDIVIDUAL ACTIVITY

Check to see that apostrophes have been used appropriately in the following sentences. Add any that are necessary, and delete any that are unnecessary.

1. "They practically breathe into each persons mouth," Goldschmidt said. "I dont think that's a religion. I think its more a custom."

2. If a man spreads the tale of a womans' alleged sexual exploits, he can be severely punished by the woman's family.

3. Those who do not respect they're mothers cannot hope to gain admission to heaven.

4. To present ones left hand in greeting is a major insult. The practice of extending ones right hand only in greeting goes back to ancient Arab culture's.

5. Its highly improper to rebuff offers' of food if your a guest in someone's home.

METAESSAY

The writing process for this essay involved several parts:

- brainstorming and selecting some ideas relating to your culture or community
- selecting appropriate examples and details
- identifying your audience
- arranging the examples and details
- writing a discovery draft
- making suggestions in peer reviews
- revising with special attention to your introduction and conclusion

Which parts of the writing process were especially easy or difficult for you? In a brief essay, discuss the one most difficult part of the process and explain how you tried to overcome that difficulty.

PEER REVIEW FORM 1: AN ESSAY ON YOUR COMMUNITY

Writer's Name: _____

Reviewer's Name: _____

First number the paragraphs of the paper you are reviewing. Then write out your answer to each of the following questions. Use the paragraph numbers for reference, and use the back of this page if you need more space. When you have completed this review, tear out this page and give it to the writer.

1. What is the main element of his or her community or culture that the writer focuses on?

_____

_____

_____

_____

2. Are the examples and details that the writer provides clear? Which ones give you a good idea of what the culture or community is like?

_____

_____

_____

_____

3. What additional examples or details would help the writer convey his or her ideas more effectively?

_____

_____

_____

_____

4. Is the essay organized effectively, with adequate transitions linking the paragraphs? If not, suggest some transitions that would be useful.

_____

_____

_____

_____

5. Are there sentences that would benefit from being combined? If so, put brackets around the sentences that could go together, and explain why you think so.

_____

_____

_____

_____

6. Do all of the subjects and verbs agree? Circle any verbs that you think don't agree with their subjects, and explain why you think so. (See the subject-verb checklist on pages 75–76.)

_____

_____

_____

_____

7. Do all of the pronouns have clear antecedents? Are all of the pronouns in the correct person, number, and case? Circle any pronouns that you think might be incorrect, and explain why you think so. (See the pronoun checklist on page 162).

_____

_____

_____

_____

PEER REVIEW FORM 2: AN ESSAY ON YOUR COMMUNITY

Writer's Name: _____

Reviewer's Name: _____

First number the paragraphs of the paper you are reviewing. Then write out your answer to each of the following questions. Use the paragraph numbers for reference, and use the back of this page if you need more space. When you have completed this review, tear out this page and give it to the writer.

1. What is the main element of his or her community or culture that the writer focuses on?

_____

_____

_____

_____

2. Are the examples and details that the writer provides clear? Which ones give you a good idea of what the culture or community is like?

_____

_____

_____

_____

3. What additional examples or details would help the writer convey his or her ideas more effectively?

_____

_____

_____

_____

4. Is the essay organized effectively, with adequate transitions linking the paragraphs? If not, suggest some transitions that would be useful.

_____

_____

_____

_____

5. Are there sentences that would benefit from being combined? If so, put brackets around the sentences that could go together, and explain why you think so.

_____

_____

_____

_____

6. Do all of the subjects and verbs agree? Circle any verbs that you think don't agree with their subjects, and explain why you think so. (See the subject-verb checklist on pages 75–76.)

_____

_____

_____

_____

7. Do all of the pronouns have clear antecedents? Are all of the pronouns in the correct person, number, and case? Circle any pronouns that you think might be incorrect, and explain why you think so. (See the pronoun checklist on page 162).

_____

_____

_____

_____

WRITER'S RESPONSE TO PEER REVIEW 1

> *Read the peer reviews you received from two members of your group; then fill out one of these forms for each one. (This exercise will help you decide how you want to follow your reviewers' suggestions when you revise your discovery draft. It will help your reviewers understand how they can provide the most effective information for you.)*

Writer's Name: _____

Reviewer's Name: _____

1. Did this reviewer's comments help you see the strengths and weaknesses of your discovery draft? If they were not helpful, what kinds of information and suggestions were you hoping to get?

_____

_____

_____

_____

_____

2. Based on this review, in what ways do you plan to revise your discovery draft?

_____

_____

_____

_____

_____

3. Which of the reviewer's comments and suggestions did you find most helpful? Why?

_____

_____

_____

_____

_____

4. Which of the reviewer's comments and suggestions do you disagree with? Why?

_____

_____

_____

_____

_____

WRITER'S RESPONSE TO PEER REVIEW 2

Read the peer reviews you received from two members of your group; then fill out one of these forms for each one. (This exercise will help you decide how you want to follow your reviewers' suggestions when you revise your discovery draft. It will help your reviewers understand how they can provide the most effective information for you.)

Writer's Name: _____

Reviewer's Name: _____

1. Did this reviewer's comments help you see the strengths and weaknesses of your discovery draft? If they were not helpful, what kinds of information and suggestions were you hoping to get?

_____

_____

_____

_____

_____

2. Based on this review, in what ways do you plan to revise your discovery draft?

_____

_____

_____

_____

_____

3. Which of the reviewer's comments and suggestions did you find most helpful? Why?

_____

_____

_____

_____

_____

4. Which of the reviewer's comments and suggestions do you disagree with? Why?

_____

_____

_____

_____

_____

SELF-EVALUATION FORM: AN ESSAY ON YOUR COMMUNITY

Complete this evaluation and turn it in with your essay.

Name: _____

Essay Title: _____

Date: _____

1. How much time did you spend on this paper? What did you spend most of your time on (getting started, drafting, revising, something else)? Do you think you needed to spend more time or less time on some of these parts of the writing process?

_____

_____

_____

_____

_____

2. What do you like best about your paper?

_____

_____

_____

_____

_____

3. What changes have you made in your paper since the peer review?

_____

_____

_____

_____

_____

4. If you had an additional day to work on your paper, what other changes would you make?

_____

_____

_____

_____

_____

5. What things would you like your instructor to give you special help with when reading and commenting on this paper?

_____

_____

_____

_____

_____

WRITING FOR AN ACADEMIC AUDIENCE

An Essay on American Schools

GOALS

To help you write an essay on American schools, we'll concentrate on the following goals in this chapter:

- Finding and maintaining a tone appropriate to your audience and your topic.

- Choosing words carefully and effectively so that both their denotation and their connotation are appropriate.

- Combining sentences using prepositions.

- Using hyphens, dashes, and parentheses effectively.

Writing Preview

Using what you've learned in this and earlier chapters, you'll write an essay about how American schools can be improved, drawing on your own experiences as well as on evidence from the essays in this chapter.

BEFORE WE START . . .

Think about your own experiences in high school or the experiences of someone close to you. Recall some of the high and low points in those experiences, things you liked or disliked very much. These might include experiences with teachers, classes, extracurricular activities, or friends. Which one stands out for you as the best experience? Which stands out as the worst?

Take about fifteen minutes to write a paragraph in which you discuss your one best and your one worst high school experience, explaining why you think they were best and worst.

Once you have finished writing about your best and worst experiences in high school, read what you have written to the other members of your group or class. Do you all share some of the same kinds of experiences? Do many of you remember the same kinds of things as especially good or bad experiences?

FINDING AN APPROPRIATE TONE

You already know that the tone of voice you use when you're speaking helps determine how people react, both to what you're saying and to you. Even children recognize this fact: when a parent says, "Don't you use that tone of voice when you speak to me," they know they're in trouble. We respond to a speaker's tone in many ways, distinguishing the sincere from the sarcastic, the sympathetic from the hostile, the friendly from the formal. Tone is crucial to spoken communication because it reflects the speaker's attitude and influences the response of listeners.

For example, if you say to your history professor something like "Yo, Prof! How ya 'spect us to get everythin' else done if you keep assignin' so much work for class?" is the professor likely to respond to you as a serious, hardworking student who is genuinely concerned with doing the best possible job? Or is she more likely to think that you don't take the course as seriously as you should and that you're looking for ways to get out of work? If you are asking for an extension on your term paper, chances are you'd want to adopt a more serious, formal tone, perhaps indicating both in what you say and the way you say it that you respect your professor and are asking for a favor rather than making a demand.

The same applies to the tone you adopt in your writing for college and on the job. In most cases you will want to avoid an overly informal tone and be

> For information on identifying your audience, see Chapter 6.

careful not to shift between a formal and an informal tone within a given piece of writing.

Levels of Formality

The tone and level of formality of a piece of writing are determined by several factors, including the words used (called *diction*), the length of sentences, the complexity of sentence structure, and the kind of information and examples included. Slang, short and simple sentences, and many references to the first person (I), for example, create a very informal tone, as in the following:

> Some people are saying we should dump summer vacations. Not according to my friends. I think it's stupid to think that kids in America shouldn't get a summer vacation. We need that break to get our heads together. Then we can get back in the groove in the fall. And some kids have to work too. So maybe kids do forget some stuff over the summer. Well, it probably wasn't that important anyway. I say keep the summer vacation!

A tone this informal is not appropriate for most academic writing situations. It is also possible, though, for one's tone in writing to be *too* formal, with many obscure words and phrases, overly complicated sentences, and a sense of distance from the subject matter:

> A number of respected commentators on the American educational system have maintained that a three-month summer hiatus is highly detrimental to the intellectual development of the country's student populace. This is an essentially fallacious notion based on the premise that youngsters cannot recall previously learned material when classes resume in the fall. In point of fact, the break provides an opportunity for students to refresh their mental energies in preparation for a return to the ongoing learning situation. Moreover, there exist students for whom the break is an economic necessity. The abolition of summer vacations is unwarranted according to any standard of judgment.

Students sometimes try to adopt such an overly formal tone because they believe it will make them sound more impressive. Almost always, however, such writing sounds stilted and, more important, is unclear and hard to follow.

It's much better to try for a tone that lies between these two extremes, using familiar words (but not slang expressions or colloquialisms), a variety of sentence lengths and structures, and a clear presentation of evidence:

> Critics argue that long summer vacations are one of the many problems of the U.S. educational system. They say that after a summer break—which may be as long as three months—students have trouble picking up where they left off so that the whole process of education suffers. Yet the experience of actual students contradicts this argument. Students I surveyed all said that summer break helped them rest, relax, and prepare for fall classes. Many also said that the money they earned from summer jobs allowed them to stay in school. My evidence shows that summer vacation is more beneficial than detrimental for most students.

Contractions

Writing that uses many contractions (don't, wouldn't, he'll) seems more informal than writing that uses none. (In fact, we've chosen to use contractions throughout this book to help keep the tone from seeming too stuffy or formal.) Some instructors, though, believe that contractions are too informal and should not be used in academic writing. If you're not sure, it's probably best to avoid contractions.

Contractions are usually acceptable in most business writing as long as they are not overused because the purpose of much business writing is to make close, immediate contact with the reader.

The tone of this passage would be appropriate for most academic and professional writing situations.

Some instructors—particularly in writing assignments that are based mostly on personal experiences—are willing to accept a certain degree of informality. But as you continue to practice academic writing, it's a good idea to develop a tone that is more formal than conversational. Keep your tone in mind, particularly as you revise and edit, and try to make sure that it is not too informal. And don't strain to sound so formal that your writing gets confusing and hard for readers to follow.

GROUP ACTIVITY

The preceding discussion contains three paragraphs as examples of informal tone, overly formal tone, and the tone appropriate for most academic writing situations. Each of the paragraphs actually conveys basically the same information. Compare the three paragraphs sentence by sentence, noting how different words are used to make the same point. Note, for example, in the third paragraph the words that are used instead of the slang expressions in the first paragraph and the difficult or obscure words in the second. Why do you think the final example is the most appropriate for academic writing?

Slang and Colloquial Language

Slang is very informal language, often developed and used within a particular group. Students have their own slang (zoned, all-nighter, no-brainer), as do computer hackers, musicians, and many other groups, including

Continued

Continued

ethnic and racial ones. Sometimes slang is limited to a group so that outsiders may not understand what it means. At other times slang expressions become quite widespread through the media so that they are familiar to many people. Most slang expressions become dated within a few months or a year.

Colloquial language *is also informal. In fact, some colloquialisms originated as slang terms that ultimately become part of our informal spoken language. They include words like* super *(to mean "good"),* nuts *(to mean "insane"),* guy *(to mean "man"), and* to crash *(to mean "rest").*

Because of their informality, slang and colloquial language should be avoided in almost all academic and professional writing. (Don't try to make such words acceptable by putting them in quotation marks: You have to be "nuts" to work and go to school full time. *You'll only draw attention to the language and make it seem awkward.)*

Generally, it's easy to recognize that a word or phrase is too informal: if you hear it spoken but never see it in writing except perhaps in advertising and the popular press, then it's probably too informal for academic writing. If you're still not certain, check a dictionary; most will indicate if a word is colloquial or slang, and slang expressions often may not appear at all.

GROUP ACTIVITY

Here's a chance to turn some formal dialogue into slang. On page 260 is a conversation between two people. The language we've used for this conversation is far more formal than we'd really expect two people who know each other at all to use. Working with your group, turn the formal language into slang by filling in the blank balloons.

INDIVIDUAL ACTIVITY

Look back at what you wrote about your best and worst high school experiences for the Before We Start activity at the beginning of this chapter. Rewrite it to raise its level of formality—substituting other words for any slang or colloquial language, combining sentences to show relationships, eliminating contractions, and expanding on descriptions to make them fuller and clearer.

Have a friend or a member of your writing group compare the two versions and decide which is more appropriate for a college writing assignment.

OK, now you try it. Working with your group, use slang to fill in the balloons so they say the same thing.

Consistent Tone

Once you've determined the tone that is most appropriate for your audience, it's important that you maintain that tone consistently and avoid tone shifts.

At a job interview you might explain your interest by saying, "I want to do something productive with my summer and earn some money for school," but in a conversation with a close friend you might say, "I don't want to vegetate around the house all day, and besides, I don't want to be so broke that I can't hang with my friends next year at school." Both of these responses are appropriate to the audience and situation, and the tone for each is consistent. But what would happen if you mixed the tones? A prospective employer would probably not respond positively to an applicant who said, "I want to do something productive with my summer, and besides, I don't want to be so broke that I can't hang with my friends next year at school."

Tone shifts often result from using a word or phrase that doesn't fit the situation. Obviously, the more words you have at your disposal, the more easily you'll be able to control the consistency of your tone. If you're going to pick the most effective word to fit your tone and message, it's important to work on increasing your vocabulary. As we've suggested in earlier chapters, the best way to do that is by looking up unfamiliar words as you encounter them in your reading to help you understand how other writers use them. That will ensure that the words you use are not limited to a vocabulary that may not always be appropriate for an academic audience.

INDIVIDUAL ACTIVITY

Underline any shifts from an appropriate academic tone in the following passage. Then revise the passage to make it consistent in tone throughout.

In some public schools the quality of the teachers is not very high. There are, of course, some caring and committed professionals who are able to excite students and get the best from them. But there are also the losers who just sit on their behinds and read aloud from the textbook and the jerks who spend their time putting students down and making them feel like scum. It is no wonder that the dropout rate is so high. When students feel that most of their teachers could give a damn about their learning experience, they just say to heck with it and figure they might as well just find a job. They are defeated by an educational system that doesn't respond to their needs.

READINGS

The three readings that follow all focus on the quality of public schools in the United States and on educational reform. The first two look specifically at standardized test scores that show a decline in the performance of U.S. students and that suggest students in this country are not as well prepared as their foreign counterparts. The third attempts to put the problem into historical perspective and to raise questions about what can be done to improve American schools.

PREREADING EXERCISE

The following three readings are all more formal and more academic in tone than most of the readings in earlier chapters. They include many statistics, which may make them more difficult to read. Before reading each, skim through it and mark passages where statistics are presented. In the margin, make notes to yourself explaining in your own words what the statistics mean.

U.S. SCHOOLS
THE BAD NEWS IS RIGHT
Diane Ravitch

Diane Ravitch is a historian who has written extensively about American education. She also served in the U.S. Department of Education under Presidents Reagan and Bush and has often been critical of what might be called "liberal" trends in public education. In this piece, which originally appeared on the opinion page of the Washington Post, *she argues that the poor performance of American students on standardized tests means that we need to develop tougher educational standards.*

Complacency Is the Enemy of Better Education

1   The greatest obstacle to those who hope to reform American education is complacency. Most people believe that the schools were good enough when they were children and that they are good enough now.

2   But the dynamic growth of our system of education has spawned serious problems of educational quality. When you succeed at keeping almost everyone in school, you must figure out ways to educate everyone you keep in school.

3   Recently several researchers have nevertheless asserted that concern about the quality of American education is vastly overstated. Gerald Bracey, formerly of the National Education Association, argues that public schools in the United States have never been better. A group from the Sandia National Laboratories in Albuquerque asserts that all is well except for the schools in inner cities. Iris Rotberg of the National Science Foundation (not speaking for that agency, which does not endorse her views) claims that the international assessments on which our students perform so poorly are invalid measures.

4   If the bearers of good news were right, we could all sit back and relax. Unfortunately, they are not.

5   Claiming that "achievement in American schools is as high as it has ever been," Bracey insists that there has been no SAT score decline. But there has been an SAT score decline, especially on verbal aptitude, during the past 20 years. In 1972, the SAT verbal average was 453, and the SAT math average was 484. In 1991, the SAT verbal reached a historic low of 422, while the SAT math leveled off at 474.

6   Both Bracey and Sandia hold that any apparent decline in the SAT score can be attributed to the addition of low-scoring minorities to the pool of test-takers. It is true that the per-

> This is a fairly complicated essay. Are you taking time to underline and make notes about the points that you think are most important and to explain any statistics in your own words?

centage of minorities who take the test has grown from 16 percent in 1977 to 28 percent in 1991, and it is also true that the average scores of minority test-takers are lower than the average scores of whites. But it is not true that this demographic change alone has dragged down the scores, because the white average fell by 10 points since 1976, the first year scores were available by ethnic group.

7   The SAT is a measure of developed ability, developed largely in school. The rising scores of black students (up by 19 points on the SAT verbal and by 31 points on the SAT math since 1976) demonstrate that the schools can, through deliberate policies, improve student achievement on the SAT and other tests.

8   Surely the addition of minority students is not the cause of the sharp drop-off of high-scoring students on the SAT verbal during the past 20 years. In 1972, 116,630 students scored higher than 600; by 1991, that number had fallen by 35 percent to 74,836. The high-scoring students were 11.4 percent of the test-takers in 1972, but only 7.2 percent in 1991. If this decline in verbal scores were attributable to more minority students taking the SAT, we would expect a similar decline in math scores. Yet during the same period, the number of high-scoring students in math remained stable.

9   Many studies have found that during this period, schools assigned less homework, textbooks contained easier vocabulary, required courses were often replaced by nonacademic electives, and grades were inflated. Are we to believe that these trends had no effect on student achievement?

10   Sandia and Rotberg belittle the importance of international assessments of mathematics and science, on which our students' performance has been lamentable. They claim that comparing our students with their counterparts in other countries is like comparing apples and oranges.

11   "We educate everyone," say the critics, "while they educate only their elites." This is not true for Japan, which retains even more students in high school than we do, and Japanese students consistently outperform

ours. In fact, the designers of international assessments have taken care to point out what percentage of the age cohort is in school. In most cases, the comparison is clearly between oranges and oranges. . . .

12   Critics decry these international comparisons because, they say, our culture is different from that of other countries. They say it is not fair to compare ourselves to countries like Japan and Korea because they value education and we do not. But that misses the point. We should not be willing to accept current attitudes toward education as part of our culture. We must learn to place a higher value on education.

13   Or, say the critics, the international assessments are unfair because, students in nations like Japan and Korea have a better curriculum than ours; their students get a steady dose of math and science from kindergarten through 12th grade. But that is an accurate description of the kind of change we must make to prepare our students for the 21st century.

14   Why do Asian students perform so much better than our own? According to Harold Stevenson of the University of Michigan, who has studied schools in the United States, Japan and China for more than a decade, the difference lies partly with the schools and partly with parental attitudes. In his studies of elementary school mathematics, Stevenson found that the highest-scoring American school ranked below the lowest-scoring Asian schools.

15   Asian schools expect more of students than ours do; there is more time for learning, and it is time better spent. Asian parents stress their children's effort, not their innate ability; American parents are more complacent, more easily satisfied than Asian parents, regardless of their children's performance in school.

16   It is possible to recognize the great successes of our schools in extending educational opportunity while acknowledging that we must improve the quality of education. We should not write off the poor performance of a large proportion of our children and attribute it to their race, gender or social class. We should not cry "unfair" when we don't like the results of international comparisons. We must be prepared to learn from others, and we should not be satisfied until we can provide an education of quality for all of our children. Opportunity without quality is an empty promise.

POSTREADING EXERCISE

1. What does Ravitch mean by "complacency" (paragraph 1)? Do you think most students and parents are complacent about American schools?

2. Ravitch says that overall SAT scores

have declined while the scores of black students have risen (5–7). How does Ravitch explain this? What do you think of her explanation?

3. Do you think it makes sense to com-

pare the performance of American students with the performance of, for example, Asian students (12–15)? Can we learn how to improve our schools by studying what other countries do, or are the problems of U.S. schools unique?

WHAT TEST SCORES DON'T MEASURE
Iris C. Rotberg

In the following piece, published in the Washington Post *several days after the essay by Diane Ravitch, Iris Rotberg, a member of the National Science Foundation, responds to Ravitch's claims. According to Rotberg, we should pay little attention to tests that compare American students with their counterparts in other countries "because it is virtually impossible to control for the major societal differences among nations" and for factors such as who takes the tests and what kinds of courses are required.*

1   In a recent op-ed piece on the quality of U.S. education, Diane Ravitch suggests that "the greatest obstacle to those who hope to reform American education is complacency." I agree. As a nation, we are too complacent about the large proportion of our students who are in poverty, about the vast disparities in educational expenditures between rich and poor school districts, about the rising costs of higher education and what it does to student motivation. But these serious problems will not be addressed by international test comparisons that are seriously flawed and, in fact, irrelevant.

2   Ever since international comparisons of science and mathematics test scores began in the 1960s, Americans have believed the myth that U.S. students are outclassed by those in other nations. Yet, after almost three decades of apparent failures on international tests, we have maintained a level of productivity in science and engineering that is overwhelming. The fact is that international comparisons of test scores are highly misleading indicators of the quality of a nation's education system or the expertise of its future scientists and engineers.

3   The rankings of nations in international test comparisons are meaningless because it is virtually impossible to control for the major societal differences among nations. For example, attendance rates in the final years of high school are much higher in the United States than in most other countries. Indeed, the first international assessments compared the average score of more than 75 percent of the age group in the United States with the average score of the top 9 percent of the students in West Germany, the top 13 percent in the Netherlands and the top 45 percent in Sweden. The more students who take the test, the lower will be the average score. That score has little to do with the quality of education in any country. . . .

4   It is not just a matter of student attendance rates. For example, it has been observed that in a recent mathematics assessment of 13-year-olds in six countries, 99 percent of the age group attended school. What isn't stated is that the samples of children actually tested were not representative of the entire country. Thus the entire United States was compared with only selected Canadian provinces. Only the largest of several language groups in Spain participated in the comparisons. The Inner London Educational Authority chose not to participate in the assessment.

5   Moreover, some countries exclude from the testing significant numbers of low-achieving schools and schools in which the curriculum is considered inade-

> Be sure to underline and make notes about any passages that you agree or disagree with, as well as any passages that you have difficulty understanding.

quate. Several use the track system, separating students according to ability as early as 11 years of age. We do not know which students are represented in test comparisons.

6   In other countries, students take courses almost exclusively in their fields of specialization after age 16. Thus high school students who are tested in science and mathematics have studied essentially only science and mathematics from age 16 on. . . .

7   Differences in the incidence of poverty among students taking the test also affect the rankings. Countries with substantial proportions of low-income students taking the test tend to score lower than countries with less poverty or than those whose low-income students are not tested simply because they are not in school.

8   In addition, curriculum differences from nation to nation affect test results. For example, advanced mathematics students in the United States are more likely to defer calculus until college than are their counterparts in many other countries. While there is room for debate about whether a higher proportion of U.S. high school students should take calculus, this issue cannot be resolved on the basis of test scores of students who have never taken the subject.

9   But there is a more fundamental issue. Even if the test results accurately portrayed the relative "rankings" of participating countries, we are still left with the matter of whether test scores are a useful measure of those things that are most important.

10   The fact is that the quality of our scientific output and the skills of our science and engineering majors are extremely high. While our success in turning research into marketable products is questionable, our international competitiveness relates less to weakness in science education or international test comparisons than to far more subtle factors: the lack of incentives for industry to invest in long-term product develop-

ment, financial incentives that lead to offshore manufacturing, licensing practices and the emphasis placed on military at the expense of civilian research.

11   These issues will not be addressed by yet another round of international tests. Nor will test comparisons provide a better education for low-income students who attend schools with inadequate resources. These are the real problems we should not be complacent about. Let's focus our attention on the difficult public policy issues to be addressed rather than on spurious comparisons and rankings.

POSTREADING EXERCISING

1. Rotberg says she agrees with Ravitch that "the greatest obstacle to those who hope to reform American education is complacency" (paragraph 1). What does she think Americans are too complacent about? How does this differ from what Ravitch thinks?

2. Rotberg believes that it is wrong to blame the quality of science education in the United States on the fact that we are less effective than other countries at "turning research into marketable products" (10). Where does she lay the blame for America's lack of competitiveness?

3. What do you think are the biggest problems facing American schools?

A PRIORITY FOR THE TWENTY-FIRST CENTURY
Gerald Leinwand

The following selection is from Chapter 1 of Gerald Leinwand's study of U.S. education, Public Education. *Here Leinwand lists some of the problems of American education, compares present-day complaints about American education with those of earlier eras, and raises some fundamental questions about improving the quality of education in the United States.*

1   During the 1980s, the state of public education in America was the subject of front-page newspaper headlines, feature magazine articles and countless television programs. These popular, and often dramatic, accounts of the shortcomings in the nation's schools were based on a series of alarming reports of studies conducted by distinguished educators. Their conclusion: American education needs improvement.

2   Let's take a closer look at these problems.

A Nation at Risk

3   In the report of the National Commission on Excellence in Education titled *A Nation at Risk* (1983), the investigators wrote:

. . . While we can take justifiable pride in what our schools and colleges have historically accomplished and contributed to the United States and the well-being of its people, the educational foundations of our society are presently being eroded by a rising tide of mediocrity that threatens our very future as a nation and a people. What was unimaginable a generation ago has begun to occur—others are matching and surpassing our educational attainments.

If an unfriendly foreign power had attempted to impose on America the mediocre educational performance that exists today, we might well have viewed it as an act of war. As it stands we have allowed this to happen to ourselves.

4   The realities of the current state of America's public schools and their students continue to disturb the American people:

■ Every eight seconds of the school day, an American child drops out of school (552,000 in the 1987–88 school year).

■ Every school day, an estimated 135,000 American children bring guns to school.

■ Among six industrialized countries (France, England, Wales, Canada, the Netherlands and the United States), the United States had the highest teen pregnancy rate.

■ American schoolchildren know less geography than schoolchildren in Iran, less math than schoolchildren in Japan and less science than schoolchildren in Spain.

■ The United States makes a proportionally smaller investment in education than the five other industrialized nations mentioned above.

■ American students' test scores are lower than those of students in Japan, Hungary, England and other countries.

■ Between 1979 and 1986, federal assistance in education dropped 22.4%.

■ In other countries, young men and women of about high school age spend more days in school than those in the United States. While American students spend about 180 days in school, pupils in Japan attend for 243 days, those in the Soviet Union attend for 208, Hong Kong pupils spend 195 days in school, and British and Canadians spend 192 and 186, respectively.

■ Seventy-three percent of American 13-year-olds watch television three or more hours a day. The number of children who watch TV for a similar amount of time in other countries: Britain, 72%; Canada, 65%; Ireland, 55%; Spain, 54%; and South Korea, 51%.

■ Only 27% of American students spend two or more hours a day on homework. Compare the percentage of 13-year-olds who spend two or more hours a day on homework in some other countries: Spain, 59%; Britain, 35%; South Korea, 28%; and English-speaking Canada, 25%.

5   Will America's youth be educated enough to serve themselves and their country in the next century? When more than half of the new jobs will require education beyond high school, how will the next generation compete? It is no exaggeration to say that the future of the nation rests upon the answers to these questions.

A Golden Age?

6   . . . There is a tendency to view the past as a "golden age." When we probe, however, for a "golden age" of American education, we find this era difficult to identify. What years were really golden when compared to the others? What made them so golden? For one thing, in the past there were smaller numbers of children and youth attending school. Those who went to school for any length of time tended to be intellectually and/or economically privileged. Most students who were not of a privileged background left school early, even though universal education was set forth as a goal in the United States.

7   Current judgments of school success or failure are made on the basis of a host of statistical data not available until relatively recently. Would Americans take a favorable view of their schools during the "golden age" had statistics about achievement levels in reading, arithmetic, writing or dropout rates existed 75 years ago? Prior to World War I, whatever success was attributed to the public schools was done so on the basis of intuition or perception rather than statistical measurement of educational accomplishment.

> Do any of the facts in this essay surprise you or remind you of your own experiences? Remember to make notes in the margins about your responses.

8   In other words, we can really only guess at how "good" the educational system was of even the most recent past. Our knowledge is grounded on opinions and guesses, and, over the years, memories and recollections become less and less reliable. . . .

9   In 1909, a systematic study was attempted to find out why children drop out of school. The conclusion is as valid today as it was then. Children drop out of school because they are failing. Lack of success was and remains the most common reason for leaving school prematurely. By this measure, it was concluded that the elementary schools of the earlier 20th century were failing the children and were in urgent need of reform; if children felt they were achieving some success by being in school, they would stay.

10   Between 1911 and 1913, in its Final Report, the Committee on

School Inquiry startled the nation by reporting that "illiteracy in the United States is fifty times greater than that of Germany, Norway, Sweden or Denmark." In fact, during World War I, the military turned away thousands of potential soldiers because they were illiterate.

11   During the years after World War I, the following complaints were heard about the public schools:

■ In 1929, educators were worried about the "large number of pupils playing hookey."

■ In 1938, the Regents of New York State reported that in their state, "the boys and girls who leave high school without graduating outnumber the graduates nearly two to one."

■ The public became ever more aware of reading problems during the early 1940s as the nation sought to induct draftees for military service in World War II. About 200,000 men were barred because of illiteracy.

■ In February 1947, Benjamin Fine, education editor for the *New York Times,* wrote a series of articles demonstrating what he called the American public school system's "most serious crisis in history." In a six-month investigation of the nation's schools, he reported that since 1940, 350,000 teachers left the schools to serve in military or civilian capacities in World War II. One in every seven remaining teachers had a substandard, emergency, teaching certificate. There were 125,000 new and inexperienced teachers. About 60,000 teachers had only a high school education; 6,000 schools closed because of a shortage of teachers. The average teacher's salary of $37 per week was lower than that of the average truck driver, garbage collector or bartender.

Gross inequities existed. In some classroom units as much as $6,000 was spent per unit while others spent as little as $100. School buildings stood in deplorable condition while both the Soviet Union and Great Britain spent more of their national income on schools.

■ In 1955, Rudolf Flesch's book *Why Johnny Can't Read* became a bestseller as more Americans began to fear their children were not reading as well as they should. Parents felt that America's teaching methods were faulty.

■ In 1957, the Soviet satellite *Sputnik* was launched into space, giving the Soviets a head start over the United States in the race to conquer space. Americans worried about falling behind in science and technology, areas in which the nation felt a great deal of pride in accomplishment. As a consequence, the merits of the American school system were called into serious question.

■ In the late 1950s, a journalist for the *World Telegram and Sun* took a teaching job in a New York City junior high school. From this vantage point, he reported on the assaults, brawls, disruptions and violence rampant in the schools.

■ In 1958, the *New York Times* reported nearly 40,000 pupils were left back that year, most often for reading problems, and some because of "general neglect of studies, especially in math."

■ In 1961, the superintendent of New York City schools announced one-third of all junior high school students were more than two years behind in reading, and 10,000 seventh-graders were reading four years below level.

12   Although this historic overview places current problems in context, they are no less daunting: As the 20th century draws to a close, illiteracy is a growing problem. A new term, "innumeracy," has been coined to draw attention to a national deficiency in the mastery of basic skills in mathematics. There is increased concern that our current system of education is not giving its students the tools they need to compete successfully in the new global marketplace. Can the schools be fixed? If so, how? By whom? If more money is needed, who pays? If schools cannot be fixed, what should replace them?

POSTREADING EXERCISE

1. Leinwand begins with a list of disturbing facts about American schools (paragraph 4). Which do you find most disturbing? Can you think of ways to overcome this problem?

2. In the section titled "A Golden Age?" (6–11), Leinwand discusses some of the problems of American schools in the past.

What are a few of these? How similar are they to problems facing American schools today? Why do you think Leinwand spends so much time describing them?

3. List one or two facts in this reading and in those by Ravitch and Rotberg that you think are most important in considering the real problems facing American schools.

GROUP ACTIVITY

The tone of the three preceding readings is what we described earlier as appropriate for most academic writing. Choose a passage from each essay to read aloud to other members of your group. Then discuss whether the tone is consistent. Does any of the language seem too informal or overly formal for an educated audience?

INDIVIDUAL ACTIVITY

Look at Leinwand's list of problems in paragraph 4. Come up with your own list of problems based on your experiences as a student in American schools or as a parent of American school students. Alternatively, you might list some of the strengths of the schools you're familiar with. (If you never attended American schools prior to college, list the qualities of the schools you attended and compare them with those of American schools as described by the writers in this chapter and by your American friends.)

CHOOSING WORDS CAREFULLY

As we said earlier, one way you can help control the tone of what you write is by your choice of words, your diction. Choosing words carefully helps you convey a positive image to your reader and also makes your writing clearer. To help ensure that your diction is as effective as possible, you first need to work to expand your vocabulary. We've already suggested one way to do this: take note of unfamiliar words as you read, try to define these words from the surrounding context, and then check the definition in a dictionary. You can even keep a list of words that strike you as particularly interesting and potentially useful for your own writing.

Don't be afraid to use words in your writing that are not part of your normal speaking vocabulary. But when you do, be careful that the words actually mean what you intend. It's a good idea to check a dictionary for the exact definition of any word you're not absolutely sure of.

Denotation and Connotation

In finding the right word, you also need to think about *denotation* and *connotation.* A word's denotation is its most specific and narrow meaning, what you find when you look up the word in a dictionary. But many words also have connotations— implied, often emotional associations that are just as important as the denotation.

To see the importance of connotation, think about the words *overweight, fat,* and *plump.* The denotation of each of these words is essentially the same; in the most specific and narrowest sense, each means "heavier than the average or the ideal." But we don't use the words interchangeably because they have different connotations, both positive and negative. *Overweight,* everyone would probably agree, is the most neutral of the three, simply stating a condition without implying a strong judgment: *fat,* on the other hand, has definite negative associations, while *plump* has much more positive ones. So when a company wants to say that its brand of hot dog is bigger than the competition, it is more likely to call it "plump" than "fat," while people unhappy about their weight are more likely to say "these pants make me look fat" than "they make me look plump." And a doctor talking to a patient is more likely to say "overweight" than either "fat" or "plump."

You are already doubtless aware of the connotations of a great many words and use them appropriately for your intended meaning without having to think twice. But you need to be careful when using less familiar words that they don't have connotations you don't intend. For example, Iris Rotberg refers to comparisons between the test scores of American students and students elsewhere as "spurious." If you checked the meaning of *spurious* in a dictionary, you would find that its denotative meaning is "false." Still, it cannot be used wherever you would use *false* because its connotations are so much more negative: *spurious* suggests a high degree of deceit and even an

Avoiding Sexist Language

In writing for academic and professional audiences, you should avoid language that denigrates or implicitly excludes women. Referring to women as girls *may have been acceptable at one time, but a great many readers today—both men and women—find such language inaccurate and even offensive. Likewise, try to find substitutes for gender-based terms:* mail carrier *(for* mailman*),* chair *or* chairperson *(for* chairman*),* firefighter *(for* fireman*),* people *(for* man *or* mankind*), and so on.*

Also try to avoid the pronoun he *or* his *unless the reference is clearly to a male. For example, the sentence "Every teacher should respect his students" can* be revised in at least two ways to eliminate this unwarranted use of *his:*

> Every teacher should respect *his or her* students.
> All teachers should respect *their* students.

Notice that "Every teacher should respect their *students" is not correct because* every teacher *is singular but* their *is plural. Even though this usage is heard increasingly in spoken English, it isn't acceptable in careful academic writing. (See pages 160–61 and 343–44 for more on pronoun agreement.)*

intent to cause harm. So to say, for example, "Half of the statements on the test were true and half were spurious" is not really to say what you mean.

When you discover new words in your reading, the context can often help you recognize their connotations. Be sure you understand those connotations before using such words in your writing.

Words That Sound Alike

Many times a wrong word is used in writing because it sounds like the right word but is spelled differently: *to/too/two; accept/except; affect/effect.* The same thing may also happen when words are spelled as they are pronounced in casual conversation; for example, the verb phrase *could have* is incorrectly written *could of,* and the phrase *used to* is incorrectly written *use to.*

Keep a list of any problems that your instructor points out in your use of such sound-alike words. As you edit your final drafts, look carefully for the words on your list, and make sure you have used them correctly.

GROUP ACTIVITY

Individually, underline any words in the following passage that seem to you to be misused. Some may have the wrong denotation, some may have the wrong connotation, and some may sound like the right word but be spelled differently. Also underline any examples of sexist language. As a group, discuss your choices. Did you identify the same problems? Can you explain any differences in what you noted and what others in your group found?

One of the biggest complaints about American schools is that they are unsafe. In many schools gangs intimate innocuous students who are trying to avoid trouble. Gang members lug guns in there pockets and even threaten teachers. In years past authorities were aloud to use capital punishment to discipline ruthless students. Today the worst punishment a principle can afflict on a student is to expel him. Allowing paddles back in the classroom may not be the resolution to the problem of disciplining students, but educators must detect ways to protect students and school personal from harm.

WRITING ASSIGNMENT: AN ESSAY ON AMERICAN SCHOOLS

What can be done to improve our schools? Even if you don't believe that U.S. schools are inferior to those in other countries, you'll still surely have some ideas about how they can be made more effective. Write an essay in which you draw on your own experience with U.S. schools—those you've attended along with those attended by your friends, your siblings, your children—to describe one or more ways of improving American schools. You may also draw on your knowledge of schools in other countries, based on your own experience or the readings in this chapter. (If your experience with American schools is very limited, you might focus on the strengths and weaknesses of the schools you attended elsewhere and what these examples might suggest for improving other schools.)

Your essay should be directed to an academic audience of professionals interested in improving American schools, and your tone should be appropriate for that audience.

Summary of Steps

Here's a summary of steps to take in completing this assignment. Check off each step after you've completed it.

_____ Brainstorm about some problems you've experienced in schools that you or others you know have attended. Then brainstorm some specific solutions to each of these problems.

_____ Choose one or two ideas from your brainstorming list that you feel most strongly about and that you think would make the most difference in improving schools.

_____ Make a list of experiences—your own, your friends', your family's—that help explain the problem and support your suggestions for improvement.

_____ Consider whether any of the facts and examples from the essays in this chapter could help support your ideas.

_____ Write down some specific information about your audience. What information do your readers probably know or probably not know about U.S. education?

_____ Look through your list of experiences concerning education and any information you've noted from readings in this chapter. Pick out those items that you feel would be most understandable and effective for your readers.

_____ Arrange your evidence—your experiences and the facts and examples from the readings—in the order in which you want to present it in your essay.

_____ Make sure your introduction indicates your view on improving U.S. schools in a way that captures the readers' attention.

_____ Make sure your conclusion reinforces the main idea of your essay without simply restating it.

_____ Consider the relationship between the ideas in your paragraphs, and use appropriate transitional words, phrases, or sentences to help your readers follow your ideas.

_____ Make sure your tone is consistent and appropriate for an academic audience.

Student Sample

In the following essay, student Dionne Stoneham remembers her high school both for its beauty and for its problems. Using her own experience as the primary basis of her discussion, she makes some suggestions about how American schools can be improved.

THE LONG HALLWAYS
Dionne Stoneham

1   The long, endless hallways--that's what I remember. The long orange hallways that strayed into classrooms and labs, but always ended at a window--a tall window that allowed me to see miles and miles of sky. I always thought my high school was very

beautiful, with its spacious classrooms and colorful walls, but those windows were what made it special because for four years I could look out and think about the future.

2   I miss them now, but time away from that picture has allowed me to see some of the negative things that went on in those hallways as well. My situation wasn't much different from the one Gerald Leinwand describes. There were drugs; there was violence. I wondered how such a beautiful school could hold such violent people. There were constant fights, and we were not allowed to carry back packs for fear of concealed weapons being smuggled in. On the last few days of school I remember being stopped at the entrance of the building and having all of my property searched. These were only a few of the atrocities that went on, not to mention the drug dealing, alcohol abuse, and babies being made or had. Why, one may ask, was this happening to a good school in a middle-class school district?

3   These days there is only so much that a teacher or a principal can do to a make a misbehaving student follow the rules. Suspension is the ultimate threat, but even that doesn't really do the job. No matter how severe the problems the student causes, in the end the punishment is given to the local neighborhood, because the menace to the school is turned out to roam the streets and be a menace to society. Maybe Leinwand is right; maybe things weren't much worse in "the old days." Still, in the days of corporal punishment students came to associate mischief with pain. Paint graffiti on the wall, face the paddle at school and the belt at home. To put it crudely, fear kept them straight. Nowadays, when the worst punishment isn't really so bad, what's to keep students from painting that wall? Suspension? That's probably just what they want.

4   Sadly, the students are not the only ones to blame. Teachers as well as parents also play a large part in the destruction of youthful morals. When I walked into the high school my senior year, whose

face greeted me at the door? Not the frowning forehead of Mrs. Lister or the cheerful smile of Mrs. Jay. It was some woman only a couple of years older than I was. She was unsure and unfamiliar, so it was hard for us to respect her. High school kids can't learn anything from someone they don't respect. Students need experienced, hardworking teachers, but as the students get more obnoxious, these teachers move away and are replaced by young, eager, twenty-somethings who don't have the experience to deal with 17-, 18-, or 19-year olds who have children, jobs, and guns. As times change, so must the schools.

5   At home the student is more often than not missing a parent or simply missing supervision. The parents have to be able to instill moral fiber into their children so when it comes time for them to leave home, the parents' teaching will always be with the child.

6   No blame, of course, is to be taken away from the students themselves. I refer to these people as students, not children, because 15- to 19-year olds are not children. They are thinking, capable people, and they know right from wrong. It does not matter if a 17-year-old boy is raised on the street and never goes to school. He still knows that murder is wrong. He knows that dealing drugs is wrong. More than anyone, students are responsible for the conditions of their high schools. When they start to care about their futures and education, things will improve, and not one second before.

Peer Review

Once you have your complete discovery draft, you're ready to start peer reviews. Here's a recap of what you need to do.

- Exchange papers with a classmate.
- Be alert to what the writer both succeeds at doing and is having trouble doing.
- Write your peer review, using one of the forms on pages 285–86 and 287–88.

- Talk over your review with the writer for a few minutes.
- Go through the whole process with another classmate.
- After reading the peer reviews of your own draft, complete the Writer's Response to Peer Review forms that follow the Peer Review Forms.

Revising Your Discovery Draft

By now you should have a small stack of paper: your notes, your completed discovery draft, and peer evaluations written by two of your classmates. With these you can start revising the discovery draft into the final version of your paper, the one that you're actually going to turn in. Here's the process for revising.

- Reread your draft.
- Reread your peer reviews, noting what the reviewers found effective and what they suggested to improve the draft.
- Decide which of the comments you agree with and which you disagree with. (Remember, you don't have to agree with or make the changes your reviewers suggest; you have the final responsibility for your essay.)
- Consider whether the evidence you provide communicates your ideas about U.S. schools effectively to your intended audience.
- Consider whether your tone is appropriate for an academic audience and is consistent throughout the paper.
- Consider your diction. Is it appropriate for an academic audience, with no slang or colloquial language? Are you sure you've used the right words for your intended meaning and avoided sexist language?
- Analyze each paragraph. Is each in the most effective form?
- Look at your introduction. Is it interesting and clear? Will it make your readers want to read on? Does it help readers know what your essay is about?
- Look at your conclusion. Does it reinforce the main idea without merely restating it?
- Look for places where you may have used several long or short sentences in a row. Do you need to vary sentence length to eliminate such a problem? Would sentence combining help?
- After you have written a second draft, reread your revised version. Does your essay explain clearly your ideas about solving a problem in American schools? Are your ideas supported by relevant and well-founded evidence? If you are still not completely satisfied, you might wish to have another class member read your draft and do another peer review for you.

■ Once you are satisfied with the organization, level of detail and evidence, and tone in your essay, you're ready to do the final editing. First, go over your draft carefully to make sure that all the subjects and verbs agree (see the checklist on pages 75–76), that you've avoided sentence fragments, that the pronouns are used appropriately (see the checklist on page 162), and that you've looked for any other editing problems that turn up in your writing consistently. Then read the following section for more advice on ways to make your sentences as effective as possible.

Editing Your Draft

As you edit your final draft for elements covered in earlier chapters, consider also whether any sentences can be combined by using prepositions and whether you have used hyphens, dashes, and parentheses properly.

Combining Sentences with Prepositions

In earlier chapters, we looked at several ways of combining sentences: with coordinating conjunctions, with subordinating conjunctions, with modifiers, and with verbals. In this section we're going to look at combining sentences with prepositions. Look at this paragraph made up of several short sentences:

The car approached the railroad crossing. The driver was distracted. A cow was distracting him. The cow was black. It had white spots. The train was coming fast. The driver didn't see the train. The crossing bell rang. The bell got the driver's attention. He slammed on the brakes. He was saved. The bell saved him.

Read through the paragraph again, and try to combine as many of the sentences in it as you can.

Chances are you included at least one of the following phrases in your version of the paragraph:

distracted by a (black) cow

with white spots

saved by the bell

Phrases like these, formed by a preposition and a noun or pronoun that follows, are called prepositional phrases, and we use them all the time.

Prepositions indicate the relationship between a noun or pronoun and another word in a sentence. Many prepositions express relationships of time or space. One

Some Common Prepositions

about	as	between	inside	out	toward
above	at	by	into	outside	under
across	because of	down	like	over	until
after	before	during	near	past	up
against	behind	except	of	since	upon
along	below	for	off	through	with
among	beneath	from	on	throughout	within
around	beside	in	onto	to	without

way to tell if a word is a preposition is to use it before either *the trees* or *the day* in a sentence. If one of the phrases makes sense, chances are the word is a preposition.

Here's a paragraph with several prepositional phrases:

> <u>Before first period</u> I was <u>in homeroom</u> <u>for twenty minutes</u>. <u>During first period</u> I sat <u>in study hall</u> <u>for an hour</u>. <u>Between classes</u> we had another fifteen minutes <u>of free time</u>. Many <u>of the seniors</u> had another free period <u>as hall monitors</u>. I think one problem <u>with American schools</u> is the little amount <u>of time</u> students spend learning.

As you can see, almost any sentence you write might include a prepositional phrase.

INDIVIDUAL ACTIVITY

Read through an earlier draft of the essay you're working on now, and circle every prepositional phrase. Are you surprised at the number you find?

Combining sentences by using prepositions is not as common as the other methods we've discussed. There are times, however, when combining two sentences with a preposition can help eliminate unnecessary words. Look at the following two sentences:

> There are many problems with American schools. Some of these are grade inflation, lower standards, and burned-out teachers.

In these sentences, the words *there are* and *some of these* don't contribute much. The sentences can be combined into one smoother sentence with the preposition *among:*

> *Among* the many problems with American schools are grade inflation, lower standards, and burned-out teachers.

Here's another example of sentence combining with a preposition:

> Diane Ravitch and Iris Rotberg disagree. They see American schools in two different ways.

> Diane Ravitch and Iris Rotberg disagree *about* American schools.

INDIVIDUAL ACTIVITY

Read through your draft. Do you find any repetitive sentences that could be combined using a preposition?

Using Hyphens, Dashes, and Parentheses

Three marks of punctuation that you may want to try using when you write for an academic audience are the hyphen, the dash, and parentheses.

Hyphens

The most common use of the hyphen is to link the parts of a compound adjective. When two or more words form a single adjective, you should join those words with hyphens. Look at the way Iris Rotberg uses hyphens in this sentence:

> For example, in the international mathematics assessment of 1988, our 13-year-old students were compared with their counterparts in Ireland, Korea, the United Kingdom, and Spain.

The expression "13-year-old" consists of three words, but they are used as a single adjective modifying *students,* so they're linked with

> An adjective modifies a noun or pronoun. For more on adjectives, see pages 154–56.

hyphens. Here are two more examples of compound adjectives linked by hyphens:

> In his studies of elementary school mathematics, Stevenson found that the *highest-scoring* American school ranked below the *lowest-scoring* Asian schools.

You should also use a hyphen when you have to break a word at the end of a line, like the break of *adjective* in the first line following the head "Hyphen" on page 281. Because the word *adjective* will not all fit on one line, it is "broken" between syllables, and the hyphen is used to indicate the break. Whenever you break a word at the end of a line like this, though, be sure to make the break only between syllables. If you're not sure of where the syllable breaks occur, check your dictionary. It will indicate the proper breaking points.

Dashes

Dashes are used to set off phrases within a sentence so that they get special emphasis. Look, for example, at this sentence from Gerald Leinwand's *Public Education:*

> Perhaps no other institution in American society—from defense to big business to medicine—is understood to be as vital to the country's future as the American school.

Compound Adjectives Linked by Hyphens

Here are some examples of compound adjectives linked by hyphens.

high-scoring students	ten-year study	over-the-counter medications	middle-class values
		low-income families	African-American studies

By setting off the phrase "from defense to big business to medicine" with dashes, Leinwand is able to put special emphasis on it, pointing out how important these institutions are.

Keep in mind that you should only use dashes for emphasis; consequently, you should use them sparingly, or they will lose their special effect.

When using a typewriter, computer, or word processor, you can indicate a dash by typing two unspaced hyphens (--).

Parentheses

Use parentheses to enclose explanations that give additional information and are not essential to the meaning of the sentence. In the following paragraph, columnist James J. Kilpatrick uses parentheses to provide information to help readers compare the American and English school systems:

> In England, by way of example, all 16-year-olds (our 10th graders) take a general examination on their academic achievements. Then about half of them begin a two-year college-preparatory program (the equivalent of our 11th and 12th grades) leading to a second examination when the students are 18.

These parenthetical phrases are not absolutely necessary; the sentences would still be grammatically correct and make sense if they were dropped. But they add information that many readers will find helpful.

INDIVIDUAL ACTIVITY

Read through your draft, making sure that you have used hyphens with any compound adjectives. Also consider whether you might revise any sentences using dashes to set off phrases for special emphasis and whether there are places where you could insert additional explanatory information using parentheses.

METAESSAY

The writing process for this essay involved several parts:

- Brainstorming and selecting a problem to write about
- Listing appropriate personal experiences and facts from the readings
- Analyzing the audience and selecting details with that audience in mind
- Arranging the evidence
- Writing a discovery draft with an effective introduction and conclusion
- Making suggestions in peer reviews
- Revising with an eye to your tone and diction

Which of these parts of the writing process were especially easy or difficult for you? In a brief essay, discuss the one most difficult part of the process and explain how you tried to overcome that difficulty.

PEER REVIEW FORM 1: AN ESSAY ON AMERICAN SCHOOLS

Writer's Name: _____

Reviewer's Name: _____

First number the paragraphs of the paper you are reviewing. Then write out your answer to each of the following questions. Use the paragraph numbers for reference, and use the back of this page if you need more space. When you have completed this review, tear out this page and give it to the writer.

1. What problem does the writer identify, and what is his or her main suggestion for improving U.S. schools?

_____

_____

_____

_____

2. Do the personal experiences and facts and examples from the readings used by the writer convince you that the writer's views are correct? If so, why? If not, why not?

_____

_____

_____

_____

3. What additional evidence would help support the writer's analysis?

_____

_____

_____

_____

4. Does the conclusion reinforce the main idea without simply restating it?

_____

_____

_____

_____

5. Is the essay effectively organized, with adequate transitions linking the paragraphs? If not, suggest some transitions that would be useful.

_____

_____

_____

_____

6. Are there sentences that would benefit from being combined? If so, put brackets around the sentences that could go together, and explain why you think so.

_____

_____

_____

_____

7. Do all of the subjects and verbs agree? Circle any verbs that you think don't agree with their subjects, and explain why you think so. (See the subject-verb checklist on pages 75–76.)

_____

_____

_____

_____

8. Do all of the pronouns have clear antecedents? Are all of the pronouns in the correct person, number, and case? Circle any pronouns that you think might be incorrect, and explain why you think so. (See the pronoun checklist on page 162.)

_____

_____

_____

_____

9. Are the tone and diction appropriate for an academic audience? Are they consistent throughout the paper? Suggest some changes that might help the writer improve his or her tone.

_____

_____

_____

_____

PEER REVIEW FORM 2: AN ESSAY ON AMERICAN SCHOOLS

Writer's Name: _____

Reviewer's Name: _____

First number the paragraphs of the paper you are reviewing. Then write out your answer to each of the following questions. Use the paragraph numbers for reference, and use the back of this page if you need more space. When you have completed this review, tear out this page and give it to the writer.

1. What problem does the writer identify, and what is his or her main suggestion for improving U.S. schools?

_____

_____

_____

_____

2. Do the personal experiences and facts and examples from the readings used by the writer convince you that the writer's views are correct? If so, why? If not, why not?

_____

_____

_____

_____

3. What additional evidence would help support the writer's analysis?

_____

_____

_____

_____

4. Does the conclusion reinforce the main idea without simply restating it?

_____

_____

_____

_____

5. Is the essay effectively organized, with adequate transitions linking the paragraphs? If not, suggest some transitions that would be useful.

_____

_____

_____

_____

6. Are there sentences that would benefit from being combined? If so, put brackets around the sentences that could go together, and explain why you think so.

_____

_____

_____

_____

7. Do all of the subjects and verbs agree? Circle any verbs that you think don't agree with their subjects, and explain why you think so. (See the subject-verb checklist on pages 75–76.)

_____

_____

_____

_____

8. Do all of the pronouns have clear antecedents? Are all of the pronouns in the correct person, number, and case? Circle any pronouns that you think might be incorrect, and explain why you think so. (See the pronoun checklist on page 162.)

_____

_____

_____

_____

9. Are the tone and diction appropriate for an academic audience? Are they consistent throughout the paper? Suggest some changes that might help the writer improve his or her tone.

_____

_____

_____

_____

WRITER'S RESPONSE TO PEER REVIEW 1

> *Read the peer reviews you received from the members of your group; then fill out one of these forms for each one. (This exercise will help you decide how you want to follow your reviewers' suggestions when you revise your discovery draft. It will also help your reviewers understand how they can provide the most effective information for you.)*

Writer's Name: _____

Reviewer's Name: _____

1. Did this reviewer's comments help you see the strengths and weaknesses of your discovery draft? If they were not helpful, what kinds of information and suggestions were you hoping to get?

_____

_____

_____

_____

_____

2. Based on this review, in what ways do you plan to revise your discovery draft?

_____

_____

_____

_____

_____

3. Which of the reviewer's comments and suggestions did you find most helpful? Why?

_____

_____

_____

_____

4. Which of the reviewer's comments and suggestions do you disagree with? Why?

_____

_____

_____

_____

_____

WRITER'S RESPONSE TO PEER REVIEW 2

Read the peer reviews you received from the members of your group; then fill out one of these forms for each one. (This exercise will help you decide how you want to follow your reviewers' suggestions when you revise your discovery draft. It will also help your reviewers understand how they can provide the most effective information for you.)

Writer's Name: _____

Reviewer's Name: _____

1. Did this reviewer's comments help you see the strengths and weaknesses of your discovery draft? If they were not helpful, what kinds of information and suggestions were you hoping to get?

_____

_____

_____

_____

_____

2. Based on this review, in what ways do you plan to revise your discovery draft?

_____

_____

_____

_____

_____

3. Which of the reviewer's comments and suggestions did you find most helpful? Why?

_____

_____

_____

_____

_____

4. Which of the reviewer's comments and suggestions do you disagree with? Why?

_____

_____

_____

_____

_____

SELF-EVALUATION FORM: AN ESSAY ON AMERICAN SCHOOLS

Complete this evaluation and turn it in with your essay.

Name: _____

Essay Title: _____

Date: _____

1. How much time did you spend on this paper? What did you spend most of your time on (getting started, drafting, revising, something else)? Do you think you needed to spend more time or less time on some of these parts of the writing process?

_____

_____

_____

_____

_____

2. What do you like best about your paper?

_____

_____

_____

_____

_____

3. What changes have you made in your paper since the peer review?

_____

_____

_____

_____

_____

4. If you had an additional day to work on your paper, what other changes would you make?

_____

_____

_____

_____

_____

5. What things would you like your instructor to give you special help with when reading and commenting on this paper?

_____

_____

_____

_____

_____

READING INTO WRITING

An Essay on Education and Identity

GOALS

To help you write an essay on the role of education in shaping personal identity, we'll concentrate on the following goals in this chapter:

- Using other writers' words and ideas in your own essay by

    summarizing

    paraphrasing

    quoting

- Acknowledging your use of other writers' words and ideas.

- Using quotation marks and underlining.

Writing Preview

After reading about the educational experiences of three writers, you'll write your own essay about the ways in which education often changes people's lives, supporting your ideas with information from the published essays (through paraphrase and quotation) as well as from your own memories and earlier experiences with education.

BEFORE WE START . . .

In Chapter 5 we saw that not speaking a language can make people feel isolated. But language barriers aren't the only causes of isolation. Most of us have at one time or another had the feeling that we didn't quite fit in, especially in a new situation such as the first days at a new school or a new job. Sometimes, however, these feelings can be triggered by our own families or a circle of old friends after an experience, such as going away to school or learning an important lesson, has changed us in some way.

Think about your own experiences as a student. Take ten minutes to write about a time when you felt out of place because of your education. This might have been because of something that happened in school, perhaps even in this writing class. Or it might have been due to a personal change related to school that made you feel isolated from people you'd known for years. What specific things made you feel out of place? Did you overcome the feeling? If so, how? If not, have your feelings changed over time?

When you've finished writing, share what you have written with the members of your group or class. Have other people had similar experiences or very different ones?

USING OTHER WRITERS' IDEAS IN YOUR OWN WRITING

Much of the writing you'll do for your college courses will require that you consult written sources. This means more than just copying an article out of an encyclopedia or writing an essay and throwing in a couple of quotations and endnotes. You have to understand your source materials thoroughly, determine how well they support your own views, and integrate the other writers' ideas into your own essay through careful use of summary, paraphrase, and quotation. And, of course, you must acknowledge your use of other writers' ideas in detail so that your readers can find the original sources if they want to.

You've already had some practice in using sources. In Chapter 2, for example, when you wrote a character sketch, you interviewed a person and then used information provided by that person as the basis of your sketch. You were using a source—an oral source. In other chapters we've suggested that you might include some points from the readings in the chapter to support ideas you advanced in your essay. Now we're going to show you some specific methods for using written sources in your own writing and give you some practice in doing so.

Before you can use a source in your writing, you have to be sure that you understand clearly what the writer is saying. The critical reading skills you've developed so far as you've practiced prereading strategies and noted your views or questions in the margins as you read can help you understand a writer's ideas. If you jot down your thoughts and questions as you read potential sources, you should be able to identify the most important ideas in them fairly easily.

Obviously, you can't use *everything* another writer says on your subject—any essay you write should consist primarily of your own ideas. So

For some help with reading critically and keeping notes, see pages 135–36 in Chapter 4.

you have to select carefully from other writers—sometimes from several writers—the ideas that relate best to your own. Once you have understood a writer's ideas and have determined how they relate to your own views, you're ready to use those ideas in your writing.

Three techniques permit you to insert other writers' ideas into your own writing: *summary, paraphrase,* and *quotation.* When you summarize what another writer says, you reduce a whole essay, article, or chapter to just a paragraph or boil a paragraph down to just a sentence written in your own words. A paraphrase is more explicit: when you paraphrase a sentence or a paragraph, you include virtually all the details of the original, but you express them in your own words. Quotation is even more exact: If what another writer says seems particularly striking or important, you may choose to quote the writer directly in your own writing, using the other writer's exact words (and indicating clearly that you are doing so).

In the next sections we'll look at these three ways of incorporating other writers' ideas into your writing, using the following paragraph from Maria Muniz's "Back, but Not Home" as our sample source:

> I came to the United States with my parents when I was almost five years old. We left behind grandparents, aunts, uncles, and several cousins. I grew up in a very middle-class neighborhood in Brooklyn. With one exception, all my friends were Americans. Outside of my family, I do not know many Cubans. I often feel awkward visiting relatives in Miami because it is such a different world. The way of life in Cuban Miami seems very strange to me, and I am accused of being too "Americanized." Yet, although I am now an American citizen, whenever anyone has asked my nationality, I have always and unhesitatingly replied, "Cuban."

Summarizing

A summary is a distillation of the main ideas of another writer's material, expressed in your own words. In Chapter 5 we concentrated on using summarizing as a means of understanding someone's writing or keeping notes on the writer's ideas. Here we'll concentrate on using summaries as part of your own writing.

Whenever you summarize another writer's work as part of your essay, it's important that the main focus still be on your own ideas. So you have to make it clear to your readers why you're including the summary and

For more on summarizing, see pages 189–90. And don't forget about the importance of evidence—see pages 176–79.

how it supports your point. Keep in mind that a summary should serve as a piece of the evidence that you provide to explain your ideas; you should not rely on it as the focus of your essay.

Suppose that you wanted to explain your own sense of isolation from family members by comparing your experience to Muniz's. You don't have to quote her or restate everything she says to make your point, but you could summarize just a bit of her experience:

> My sense of isolation isn't as bad as Maria Muniz's, but it's similar. *In "Back, but Not Home," Muniz says she feels out of place around her Cuban relatives because their lives are so different.* In a similar way, I feel out of place around my northern cousins. My family sees me as too much like a native Georgian, even though I was born in Minnesota. Every time I go back up North, my cousins make fun of the way I talk and try to imitate the way I say "y'all."

The writer here doesn't use everything Muniz writes about; this writer summarizes one of Muniz's ideas—that she feels out of place among her Cuban relatives. Note that the writer doesn't include any of the details about when Muniz came to the United States, who was left behind, or the kind of neighborhood Muniz grew up in. Those details aren't relevant to the writer's purpose here, so there's no point to mentioning them, no matter how important they might be for Muniz.

Look, too, at the way the writer introduces the summary. The introductory sentence lays out the relationship between her experience and Muniz's: "My sense of isolation isn't as bad as Maria Muniz's, but it's similar." That first sentence lets the reader know exactly why the summary that follows is included: The writer is comparing a personal experience to Muniz's, noting similarities. When you introduce a summary in such an explicit way, readers know exactly why you're using the summary and what you expect them to understand from it.

Paraphrasing

A paraphrase is a restatement in your own words of everything another writer says that is pertinent to your point. It is quite different from a summary. When you summarize, you reduce the length of the original considerably, leaving out many details and focusing on the writer's main idea or a single relevant point. A paraphrase, by contrast, can be just as long as the original because all the information in the original is included—expressed in your own words. Obviously, you're not likely to paraphrase a whole book or even a whole essay or other piece of writing. More likely, you'll paraphrase just a sentence or two—perhaps, on rare occasions, an entire paragraph.

Why paraphrase when you're trying to say everything that another writer said? Often your intent will be to simplify information for your readers. Sometimes you'll merely want to make the information fit the style of your essay. Here is a paraphrase of two sentences from Muniz's essay.

Original

I often feel awkward visiting relatives in Miami because it is such a different world. The way of life in Cuban Miami seems very strange to me, and I am accused of being too "Americanized." Yet, although I am now an American citizen, whenever anyone has asked my nationality, I have always and unhesitatingly replied, "Cuban."

Paraphrase

Maria Muniz says she feels out of place when she visits her friends in Florida because life in the Cuban sections of Miami is very different from what she's used to. Her relatives think that she's too American, but she still thinks of herself as Cuban.

Here are the paraphrased sentences in a whole paragraph.

My sense of isolation isn't as bad as Maria Muniz's, but it's still similar. *In "Back, but Not Home," she says she feels out of place when she visits her friends in Florida because life in the Cuban sections of Miami is very different from what she's used to. Her relatives think that she's too American, but she still thinks of herself as Cuban.* I have the same kind of problem. My family sees me as too much like a native Georgian, even though I was born in Minnesota. Every time I go back up north, my cousins make fun of the way I talk, but when I'm in Georgia, my friends all call me "Yankee," and I still think of myself as a northerner.

The paraphrase is not much shorter than the original version, nor is it any less complex, and it presents all of the information found in the original. But the language is more like that in the rest of the writer's paragraph, so the paraphrase fits better than quoting the original material directly would. Once again, note that the writer introduces the paraphrase so that readers understand its purpose in the context of the writer's own point.

It is important to keep in mind that a paraphrase should be in your own words. If you compare the paraphrase of the Muniz sentences with the original, you'll see that the writer of the paraphrase has used different words and different sentence structures to restate Muniz's ideas. If you want to include a phrase or special words directly from the original in your paragraphs, you need to enclose those words in quotation marks to show that they are not your own. For example, you might paraphrase one of Muniz's points like this:

Muniz says she feels out of place when she visits relatives in Florida "because it is such a different world." Her relatives think that she's too American, but she still thinks of herself as Cuban.

If you use a writer's original language without quotation marks, you could be accused of plagiarism.

Quoting

A quotation is a word-for-word reproduction of the original material. When you quote, you copy your source material directly, being very careful not to make any changes. Sometimes it's very useful to quote directly from material you've read in order to support one of your points. You may already have used direct quotation in your character sketch or your essays on language on American schools, and you'll be expected to use supporting quotations in most college writing.

It's important to understand that there's more to quoting than just using quotation marks and identifying your sources. Too often, student writers don't choose their quotations carefully and quote too much. Avoid the temptation to quote a whole paragraph unless you're writing an essay of more than six or seven pages. In fact, you should think carefully before quoting full sentences. Often quoting just a short phrase or two from your source will provide all the support you need:

My sense of isolation isn't as bad as Maria Muniz's, but it's still similar. In "Back, but Not Home," she says she feels "awkward visiting relatives in Miami," just as

Guidelines for Using Quotations

- Be sure to enclose the quotation in quotation marks (see pages 322–24).

- Identify the original writer or speaker. Your readers will find it useful to know not only the speaker or writer's name but also something about him or her. For example, you might introduce a quotation with something like this:

Maxine Hong Kingston, a Chinese-American writer, says, . . .

- Document your source. The easiest way is to do so right in the text (see pages 316–18).

It's crucial that you remember to use quotation marks and to document your quotations. If you don't, you could be accused of plagiarism.

I feel awkward visiting my relatives in Minnesota. She says that her family accuses her of being "too 'Americanized,'" and mine accuses me of being too southern.

The writer doesn't quote Muniz's complete sentences, just phrases from them. By selecting carefully from Muniz's paragraph, she helps emphasize how similar her situation is to Muniz's.

Tips for Effective Quotation

■ *Quote sparingly.* When you quote, select phrases or sentences because they say something especially important in an unusually effective way.

■ *Quote fairly.* We've probably all read movie ads that take a movie critic's words out of context. A critic may say, "This movie is the most stupendous bomb that the director has ever made, a disaster of epic proportions," while the movie ad quotes "stupendous . . . epic proportions." Don't try to deceive readers in this way when you quote.

■ *Quote accurately.* The movie ad we cited may not be fair, but at least it uses the critic's actual words. If the ad had said, "Famous New York critic Theodore Steinway calls this 'a major movie of epic proportions,'" then it would have been both unfair and inaccurate, since the critic didn't write all those words. Use the exact words your source used, and don't add or change any words in a quotation.

■ *Connect quotations to your own point with a clear introduction.* To make sure that your reader understands how a quotation helps support the point that you are trying to make, be sure to introduce it carefully. Notice how the introduction to the quotation from Muniz's essay in the following paragraph supports the point the writer is trying to make:

Many times people who have lived in the United States for a number of years feel great pride in their national heritage. My mother, for instance, has been in this country since she was a small child, yet she still feels pride in being Swedish. Maria Muniz has the same sort of feeling. She says, "Although I am now an American citizen, whenever anyone has asked my nationality, I have always and unhesitatingly replied, 'Cuban'" (paragraph 2).

GROUP ACTIVITY

First read the following paragraph from Maria Muniz's "Back, but Not Home." Then follow the instructions.

> When I try to review my life during the past 16 years, I almost feel as if I've walked into a theater right in the middle of a movie. And I'm afraid I won't fully understand or enjoy the rest of the movie unless I can see and understand the beginning. And for me, the beginning is Cuba. I don't want to go "home" again; the life and home we left behind are long gone. My home is here and I am happy. But I need to talk to my family still in Cuba.

1. Summarize the paragraph. Then compare your summary with those of other members of your group or class. Did you all say the same thing, or do some summaries differ from others?

2. Paraphrase this paragraph. Then compare your paraphrase with those of other members of your group or class. Did you all select the same material to include in the paraphrase, or do some of you disagree about what the important material is?

3. Write a sentence of your own in which you quote part of this paragraph. Then compare your sentence with those of other members of your group or class. Notice how many different ways there are of selecting and introducing quotations.

READINGS

As we noted at the beginning of the chapter, the process of education can significantly affect how we view ourselves. When we find ourselves in a world of new ideas, new ways of thinking, and new ways of communicating, we may at first feel out of place and isolated; we may doubt our own abilities. But as we become more comfortable in this new world, our self-image can change. We may then feel that we're losing touch in some ways with the world we lived in up until then.

The authors of the readings in this chapter have experienced similar changes and feelings. Maria Muniz suffered as a young girl in American schools because it was assumed that a Cuban immigrant could not do as well as native-born students; ironically, as an adult she feels more comfortable with non-Cuban Americans than with her Cuban relatives. Mike Rose was mistakenly placed in his high school's vocational track, and because students "will float to the mark you set," he believed that was where he belonged; yet when the mistake was discovered and he was transferred to the college prep program, his self-image changed completely, and he became an ambitious and hardworking student. And when Peter Rondinone started college under an open admissions program, he felt isolated both from his family and friends—who didn't understand why he wanted an education—and from the college world, where he struggled with a "sense of inadequacy."

As you read these essays don't forget to look up the definitions of any words you can't understand from the context.

For some tips on carrying on a dialogue with the writer, see pages 135–136.

Most important, take time to write notes in the margin about points you agree or disagree with, questions you have about anything the writer says, experiences the writer describes with which you can sympathize, and other thoughts that cross your mind. You'll be using these three essays when you write your own essay on education, so these marginal annotations will come in handy as you plan your discovery draft.

PREREADING EXERCISE

Before you read the following essays, skim each of them very quickly. Don't try to read all the sentences; just look over the pages, briefly noting some of the background incidents and ideas that the writers use. As you skim, jot down four or five words or phrases that catch your attention in each essay. Next write a paragraph in which you explain what these words or phrases lead you to expect from each essay.

BACK, BUT NOT HOME
Maria Muniz

This essay, written in 1979, details one young woman's early feelings of loneliness and loss as a recent Cuban immigrant in an American school. In building a new life in the United States, she and her family struggled, but for Muniz the new world became "home."

1   With all the talk about resuming diplomatic relations with Cuba, and with the increasing number of Cuban exiles returning to visit friends and relatives, I am constantly being asked, "Would you ever go back?" In turn, I have asked myself, "Is there any reason for me to go?" I have had to think long and hard before finding my answer. Yes.

2   I came to the United States with my parents when I was almost five years old. We left behind grandparents, aunts, uncles, and several cousins. I grew up in a very middle-class neighborhood in Brooklyn. With one exception, all my friends were Americans. Outside of my family, I do not know many Cubans. I often feel awkward visiting relatives in Miami because it is such a different world. The way of life in Cuban Miami seems very strange to me, and I am accused of being too "Americanized." Yet, although I am now an American citizen, whenever anyone has asked my nationality, I have always and unhesitatingly replied, "Cuban."

3   Outside American, inside Cuban.

4   I recently had a conversation with a man who generally sympathizes

with the Castro regime. We talked of Cuban politics, and although the discussion was very casual, I felt an old anger welling inside. After 16 years of living an "American" life, I am still unable to view the revolution with detachment or objectivity. I cannot interpret its results in social, political, or economic terms. Too many memories stand in my way.

5   And as I listened to this man talk of the Cuban situation, I began to remember how as a little girl I would wake up crying because I had dreamed of my aunts and grandmothers and I missed them. I remembered my mother's trembling voice and the sad look on her face whenever she spoke to her mother over the phone. I thought of the many letters and photographs that somehow were always lost in transit. And as the conversation continued, I began to remember how difficult it often was to grow up Latina in an American world.

6   It meant going to kindergarten knowing little English. I'd been in this country only a few months, and although I understood a good deal of what was said to me, I could not express myself very well. On the first day of school I remember one little girl's saying to the teacher: "But how can we play with her? She's so stupid she can't even talk!" I felt so helpless because inside I was crying, "Don't you know I can understand everything you're saying?" But I did not have words for my thoughts, and my inability to communicate terrified me.

7   As I grew a little older, Latina meant being automatically relegated to the slowest reading classes in school. By now my English was fluent, but the teachers would always assume I was somewhat illiterate or slow. I recall one teacher's amazement at discovering I could read and write just as well as her American pupils. Her incredulity astounded me. As a child, I began to realize that Latina would always mean proving I was as good as the others. As I grew older, it became a matter of pride to prove I was better than the others.

> Are you carrying on your dialogue with the writer?

8   As an adult I have come to terms with these memories and they don't hurt as much. I don't look or sound very Cuban. I don't speak with an accent, and my English is far better than my Spanish. I am beginning my career and look forward to the many possibilities ahead of me.

9   But a persistent little voice is constantly saying, "There's something missing. It's not enough." And this is why when I am now asked, "Do you want to go back?" I say "yes" with conviction.

10   I do not say to Cubans, "It is time to lay aside the hurt and forgive and forget." It is impossible to forget an event that has altered and scarred all our lives so profoundly. But I find I am beginning to care less and less about politics. And I am beginning to remember and care more about the

child (and how many others like her) who left her grandma behind. I have to return to Cuba one day because I want to know that little girl better.

11   When I try to review my life during the past 16 years, I almost feel as if I've walked into a theater right in the middle of a movie. And I'm afraid I won't fully understand or enjoy the rest of the movie unless I can see and understand the beginning. And for me, the beginning is Cuba. I don't want to go "home" again; the life and home we all left behind are long gone. My home is here, and I am happy. But I need to talk to my family still in Cuba.

12   Like all immigrants, my family and I have had to build a new life from almost nothing. It was often difficult, but I believe the struggle made us strong. Most of my memories are good ones.

13   But I want to preserve and renew my cultural heritage. I want to keep "la Cubana" within me alive. I want to return because the journey back will also mean a journey within. Only then will I see the missing piece.

POSTREADING EXERCISE

Select one paragraph or idea from Muniz's essay that you think you might be able to use in your own essay on education. Spend a few minutes writing a summary of that paragraph or idea; then write an introductory statement to go with it.

I JUST WANNA BE AVERAGE
Mike Rose

Growing up in a poor section of Los Angeles, Mike Rose was not expected to be a success in school, particularly when because of a mistake in his high school placement record, he was assigned to vocational classes. The following selection from his book Lives on the Boundary, *shows his feelings of isolation at Our Lady of Mercy High School and how he eventually found his place there. As you read, don't forget to make notes about passages and ideas you think you might be able to use in your own essay on education.*

1   Entrance to school brings with it forms and releases and assessments. Mercy relied on a series of tests, mostly the Stanford-Binet, for placement, and somehow the results of my tests got confused with those of another student named Rose. The other Rose apparently didn't do very well, for I was placed in the vocational track, a euphemism for the bottom level. Neither I nor my parents realized what this meant. We had no sense

that Business Math, Typing, and English–Level D were dead ends. The current spate of reports on the schools criticizes parents for not involving themselves in the education of their children. But how would someone like Tommy Rose, with his two years of Italian schooling, know what to ask? And what sort of pressure could an exhausted waitress apply? The error went undetected, and I remained in the vocational track for two years. What a place. . . .

2   Students will float to the mark you set. I and the others in the vocational classes were bobbing in pretty shallow water.

> This is a long essay, so remember to make notes as you read.

Vocational education was aimed at increasing the economic opportunities of students who do not do well in our schools. Some serious programs succeed in doing that. . . . The vocational track, however, is most often a place for those who are just not making it, a dumping ground for the disaffected. There were a few teachers who worked hard at education; young Brother Slattery, for example, combined a stern voice with weekly quizzes to try to pass along to us a skeletal outline of world history. But mostly the teachers had no idea of how to engage the imaginations of us kids who were scuttling along at the bottom of the pond.

3   And the teachers would have needed some inventiveness, for none of us was groomed for the classroom. It wasn't just that I didn't know things—didn't know how to simplify algebraic fractions, couldn't identify different kinds of clauses, bungled Spanish translations— but that I had developed various faulty and inadequate ways of doing algebra and making sense of Spanish. Worse yet, the years of defensive tuning out in elementary school had given me a way to escape quickly while seeming at least half alert. During my time in Voc. Ed., I developed further into a mediocre student and a somnambulant problem solver, and that affected the subjects I did have the wherewithal to handle: I detested Shakespeare; I got bored with history. My attention flitted here and there. I fooled around in class and read my books indifferently—the intellectual equivalent of playing with your food. I did what I had to do to get by, and I did it with half a mind. . . .

4   One day in religion class, [another student] said the sentence that turned out to be one of the most memorable of the hundreds of thousands I heard in those Voc. Ed. years. We were talking about the parable of the talents, about achievement, working hard, doing the best you can do, blah-blah-blah, when the teacher called on the restive Ken Harvey for an opinion. Ken thought about it, but just for a second, and said (with studied, minimal affect), "I just wanna be average." That woke me up. Average? Who wants to be average? Then the athletes chimed in with the clichés

that make you want to laryngectomize them, and the exchange became a platitudinous melee. At the time, I thought Ken's assertion was stupid, and I wrote him off. But his sentence has stayed with me all these years, and I think I am finally coming to understand it.

5   Ken Harvey was gasping for air. School can be a tremendously disorienting place. No matter how bad the school, you're going to encounter notions that don't fit with the assumptions and beliefs that you grew up with—maybe you'll hear these dissonant notions from teachers, maybe from the other students, and maybe you'll read them. You'll also be thrown in with all kinds of kids from all kinds of backgrounds, and that can be unsettling—this is especially true in places of rich ethnic and linguistic mix, like the L.A. basin. You'll see a handful of students far excel you in courses that sound exotic and that are only in the curriculum of the elite: French, physics, trigonometry. And all this is happening while you're trying to shape an identity, your body is changing, and your emotions are running wild. If you're a working-class kid in the vocational track, the options you'll have to deal with this will be constrained in certain ways: you're defined by your school as "slow"; you're placed in a curriculum that isn't designed to liberate you but to occupy you, or, if you're lucky, train you, though the training is for work the society does not esteem; other students are picking up the cues from your school and your curriculum and interacting with you in particular ways. . . . What Ken and so many others do is protect themselves from such suffocating madness by taking on with a vengeance the identity implied in the vocational track. Reject the confusion and frustration by openly defining yourself as the Common Joe. Champion the average. Rely on your own good sense. . . . [Ignore] everything you—and the others— fear is beyond you: books, essays, tests, academic scrambling, complexity, scientific reasoning, philosophical inquiry.

6   The tragedy is that you have to twist the knife in your own gray matter to make this defense work. You'll have to shut down, have to reject intellectual stimuli or diffuse them with sarcasm, have to cultivate stupidity, have to convert boredom from a malady into a way of confronting the world. Keep your vocabulary simple, act stoned when you're not or act more stoned than you are, flaunt ignorance, materialize your dreams. It is a powerful and effective defense—it neutralizes the insult and the frustration of being a vocational kid and, when perfected, it drives teachers up the wall, a delightful secondary effect. But like all strong magic, it exacts a price.

> Are you looking up any words you aren't familiar with?

7   My own deliverance from the Voc. Ed. world began with sophomore

biology. Every student, college prep to vocational, had to take biology, and unlike the other courses, the same person taught all sections. When teaching the vocational group, Brother Clint probably slowed down a bit or omitted a little of the fundamental biochemistry, but he used the same book and more or less the same syllabus across the board. If one class got tough, he could get tougher. He was young and powerful and very handsome, and looks and physical strength were high currency. No one gave him any trouble.

8   I was pretty bad at the dissecting table, but the lectures and the textbook were interesting: plastic overlays that, with each turned page, peeled away skin, then veins and muscle, then organs, down to the very bones that Brother Clint, pointer in hand, would tap out on our hanging skeleton. Dave Snyder was in big trouble, for the study of life—versus the living of it—was sticking in his craw. We worked out a code for our multiple-choice exams. He'd poke me in the back: once for the answer under A, twice for B, and so on; and when he'd hit the right one, I'd look up to the ceiling as though I were lost in thought. Poke: cytoplasm. Poke, poke: methane. Poke, poke, poke: William Harvey. Poke, poke, poke, poke: islets of Langerhans. This didn't work out perfectly, but Dave passed the course, and I mastered the dreamy look of a guy on a record jacket. And something else happened. Brother Clint puzzled over this Voc. Ed. kid who was racking up 98s and 99s on his tests. He checked the school's records and discovered the error. He recommended that I begin my junior year in the College Prep program. . . .

9   Switching to College Prep was a mixed blessing. I was an erratic student. I was undisciplined. And I hadn't caught on to the rules of the game: Why work hard in a class that didn't grab my fancy? I was also hopelessly behind in math . . . , and physical sciences were simply beyond me. I had a miserable quantitative background and ended up copying some assignments and finessing the rest as best I could. Let me try to explain how it feels to see again and again material you should once have learned but didn't.

10   You are given a problem. It requires you to simplify algebraic fractions or to multiply expressions containing square roots. You know this is pretty basic material because you've seen it for years. Once a teacher took some time with you, and you learned how to carry out these operations. Simple versions, anyway. But that was a year or two or more in the past, and these are more complex versions, and now you're not sure. And this, you keep telling yourself, is ninth- or even eighth-grade stuff.

11   Next it's a word problem. This is also old hat. The basic elements are as familiar as story characters: trains speeding so many miles per hour or

shadows of buildings angling so many degrees. Maybe you know enough, have sat through enough explanations, to be able to begin setting up the problem: "If one train is going this fast . . ." or "This shadow is really one line of a triangle . . ." Then: "Let's see . . ." "How did Jones do this?" "Hmmmm." "No." "No, that won't work." Your attention wavers. You wonder about other things: a football game, a dance, that cute new checker at the market. You try to focus on the problem again. You scribble on paper for awhile, but the tension wins out and your attention flits elsewhere. You crumple the paper and begin daydreaming to ease the frustration.

12   The particulars will vary, but in essence this is what a number of students go through, especially those in so-called remedial classes. They open their textbooks and see once again the familiar and impenetrable formulas and diagrams and terms that have stumped them for years. There is no excitement here. No excitement. Regardless of what the teacher says, this is not a new challenge. There is rather, embarrassment and frustration and, not surprisingly, some anger in being reminded once again of long-standing inadequacies. No wonder so many students finally attribute their difficulties to something inborn, organic: "That part of my brain just doesn't work." Given the troubling histories many of these students have, it's miraculous that any of them can lift the shroud of hopelessness sufficiently to make deliverance from these classes possible. . . .

13   Jack MacFarland couldn't have come into my life at a better time. . . . Mr. MacFarland had a master's degree from Columbia and decided, at twenty-six, to find a little school and teach his heart out. He never took any credentialing courses, couldn't bear to he said, so he had to find employment in a private system. He ended up at Our Lady of Mercy teaching five sections of senior English. He was a beatnik who was born too late. His teeth were stained, he tucked his sorry tie in between the third and fourth buttons of his shirt, and his pants were chronically wrinkled. At first, we couldn't believe this guy, thought he slept in his car. But within no time, he had us so startled with work that we didn't much worry about where he slept or if he slept at all. We wrote three or four essays a month. We read a book every two to three weeks, starting with the *Iliad* and ending up with Hemingway. He gave us a quiz on the reading every other day. He brought a prep school curriculum to Mercy High.

14   MacFarland's lectures were crafted, and as he delivered them he would pace the room jiggling a piece of chalk in his cupped hand, using it to scribble on the board the names of all the writers and philosophers and plays and novels he was weaving into his discussion. He asked questions

often, raised everything from Zeno's paradox to the repeated last line of Frost's "Stopping by Woods on a Snowy Evening." He slowly and carefully built up our knowledge of Western intellectual history—with facts, with connections, with speculations. We learned about Greek philosophy, about Dante, the Elizabethan worldview, the Age of Reason, existentialism. He analyzed poems with us, had us reading sections from John Ciardi's *How Does a Poem Mean?*—making a potentially difficult book accessible with his own explanations. We gave oral reports on poems Ciardi didn't cover. We imitated the styles of Conrad, Hemingway, and *Time* magazine. We wrote and talked, wrote and talked. The man immersed us in language. . . .

15 There were some lives that were already beyond Jack MacFarland's ministrations, but mine was not. I started reading again as I hadn't since elementary school. I would go into our gloomy little bedroom or sit at the dinner table while, on the television, Danny McShane was paralyzing Mr. Moto with the atomic drop, and work slowly back through *Heart of Darkness,* trying to catch the words in Conrad's sentences. I certainly was not MacFarland's best student; most of the other guys in College Prep, even my fellow slackers, had better backgrounds than I did. But I worked very hard, for MacFarland had hooked me. He tapped my old interest in reading and creating stories. He gave me a way to feel special by using my mind. And he provided a role model that wasn't shaped on physical prowess alone, and something inside me that I wasn't quite aware of responded to that. . . .

16 There's been a good deal of research and speculation suggesting that the acknowledgment of school performance with extrinsic rewards—smiling faces, stars, numbers, grades—diminishes the intrinsic satisfaction children experience by engaging in reading or writing or problem solving. While it's certainly true that we've created an educational system that encourages our best and brightest to become cynical grade collectors and, in general, have developed an obsession with evaluation and assessment, I must tell you that venal though it may have been, I loved getting good grades from MacFarland. I now know how subjective grades can be, but then they came tucked in the back of essays like bits of scientific data, some sort of spectroscopic readout that said, objectively and publicly, that I had made something of value. I suppose I'd been mediocre for too long and enjoyed a public redefinition. And I suppose the workings of my mind, such as they were, had been private for too long. My linguistic play moved into the world; . . . these papers with their circled red B-pluses and A-minuses linked my mind to something outside it. I carried them around like a club emblem.

POSTREADING EXERCISE

Select one paragraph from Rose's essay that you think you might be able to use in your own essay on education. Spend a few minutes writing a paraphrase of that paragraph; then write an introductory statement to go with it.

OPEN ADMISSIONS AND THE INWARD "I"

Peter J. Rondinone

Peter Rondinone grew up in a tough Bronx neighborhood during the 1960s and 1970s. For him high school was a waste of time, a place where he learned little. Even though he felt comfortable with his high school friends, Rondinone sensed a growing rift when be began college as part of an open admissions program and they did not. His goals and knowledge set him apart not only from them but also from his family. As you read, remember to carry on your dialogue with the writer so you keep notes on ideas and passages you might be able to use in your own essay.

1   The fact is, I didn't learn much in high school. I spent my time on the front steps of the building, smoking grass with the dudes from the dean's squad. For kicks we'd grab a freshman, tell him we were undercover cops, handcuff him to a banister, and take his money. Then we'd go to the back of the building, cop some "downs," and nod away the day behind the steps in the lobby. The classrooms were overcrowded anyhow, and the teachers knew it. They also knew where to find me when they wanted to make weird deals. If I agreed to read a book and do an oral report, they'd pass me. So I did it and graduated with a "general" diploma. I was a New York City public school kid.

2   I hung out on a Bronx streetcorner with a group of guys who called themselves "the Davidson Boys" and sang songs like "Daddy-lo-lo." Everything we did could be summed up with the word "snap." That's a "snap." She's a "snap." We had a "snap." Friday nights we'd paint ourselves green and run through the street swinging baseball bats. Or we'd get into a little rap in the park. It was all very perilous. Even though I'd seen a friend stabbed for wearing the wrong colors and another blown away with a shotgun for "messin'" with some dude's woman, I was too young to realize that my life too might be headed toward a violent end.

3   Then one night I swallowed a dozen Tuminols and downed two quarts of beer at a bar in Manhattan. I passed out in the gutter. I puked and rolled under a parked car. Two girlfriends found me and carried me home. My overprotective brother answered the door. When he saw me—

eyes rolling toward the back of my skull like rubber—he pushed me down a flight of stairs. My skull hit the edge of a marble step with a thud. The girls screamed. My parents came to the door and there I was: a high school graduate, a failure, curled in a ball in a pool of blood.

4   The next day I woke up with dried blood on my face. I had no idea what had happened. My sister told me. I couldn't believe it. Crying, my mother confirmed the story. I had almost died! That scared hell out of me. I knew I had to do something. I didn't know what. But pills and violence didn't promise much of a future.

5   I went back to a high school counselor for advice. He suggested I go to college.

6   I wasn't aware of it, but it seems that in May 1969 a group of dissident students from the black and Puerto Rican communities took over the south campus of the City College of New York (CCNY). They demanded that the Board of Higher Education and the City of New York adopt an open-admission policy that would make it possible for anybody to go to CCNY without [meeting] the existing requirements: SATs and a high school average of 85. This demand was justified on the premise that college had always been for the privileged few and excluded minorities. As it turned out, in the fall of 1970 the City University's 189 campuses admitted massive numbers of students—15,000—with high school averages below 85. By 1972, I was one of them.

7   On the day I received my letter of acceptance, I waited until dinner to tell my folks. I was proud.

8   "Check out where I'm going," I said. I passed the letter to my father. He looked at it.

9   "You jerk!" he said. "You wanna sell ties?" My mother grabbed the letter.

10   "God," she said. "Why don't you go to work already? Like other people."

11   "Later for that," I said. "You should be proud." . . .

12   I spent that summer alone, reading books like *How to Succeed in College* and *30 Days to a More Powerful Vocabulary*. My vocabulary was limited to a few choice phrases like "Move over, Rover, and let Petey take over." When my friends did call for me, I hid behind the curtains. I knew that if I was going to make it, I'd have to push these guys out of my consciousness as if I were doing the breaststroke in a sea of logs. I had work to do, and people were time-consuming. As it happened, all my heavy preparations didn't amount to much.

13   On the day of the placement exams I went paranoid. Somehow I got the idea that my admission to college was some ugly practical joke that I wasn't prepared for. So I copped some downs and took the test nodding. The words floated on the page like flies on a crock of cream.

14   That made freshman year difficult. The administration had placed me in all three remedial programs: basic writing, college skills, and math. I was shocked. I had always thought of myself as smart. I was the only one in the neighborhood who read books. So I gave up the pills and pushed aside another log.

15   The night before the first day of school, my brother walked into my room and threw a briefcase on my desk. "Good luck, Joe College," he said. He smacked me in the back of the head. Surprised, I went to bed early.

16   I arrived on campus ahead of time with a map in my pocket. I wanted enough time, in case I got lost, to get to my first class. But after wandering around the corridors of one building for what seemed like a long time and hearing the sounds of classes in session, the scrape of chalk, and muted discussions, I suddenly wondered if I was in the right place. So I stopped a student and pointed to a dot on my map.

> This is another long essay. If you keep your "dialogue" notes as you're reading, it'll be easier to use when you write your own essay.

17   "Look." He pointed to the dot. "Now look." He pointed to an inscription on the front of the building. I was in the right place. "Can't you read?" he said. Then he joined some friends. As he walked off I heard someone say, "What do you expect from open admissions?"

18   I had no idea that there were a lot of students who resented people like me, who felt I was jeopardizing standards, destroying their institution. I had no idea. I just wanted to go to class.

19   In Basic Writing I, the instructor, Regina Sackmary, chalked her name in bold letters on the blackboard. I sat in the front row and reviewed my *How to Succeed* lessons: Sit in front/don't let eyes wander to cracks on ceilings/take notes on a legal pad/make note of all unfamiliar words and books/listen for key phrases like "remember this"—they are a professor's signals. The other students didn't know what to expect. We were public school kids from lousy neighborhoods, and we knew that some of us didn't have a chance; but we were ready to work hard.

20   Before class we had rapped about our reasons for going to college. Some said they wanted to be the first in the history of their families to have a college education—they said their parents never went to college because they couldn't afford it or because their parents' parents were too poor—and they said open admissions and free tuition ($65 per semester) was a chance to change that history. Others said they wanted to be educated so they could return to their neighborhoods to help "the people"; they were the idealists. Some foreigners said they wanted to return to their own countries and start schools. And I said I wanted to escape the boredom and pain I had known as a kid on the streets. But none of them

said they expected a job. Or if they did they were reminded that there were no jobs.

21   Ms. Sackmary told us that Basic Writing I was part of a three-part program. Part one would instruct us in the fundamentals of composition: sentence structure, grammar, and paragraphing; part two, the outline and essay; and part three, the term paper. She also explained that we weren't in basic writing because there was something wrong with us—we just needed to learn the basics, she said. Somehow I didn't believe her. After class I went to her office. She gave me a quick test. I couldn't write a coherent sentence or construct a paragraph. So we made an agreement: I'd write an essay a day in addition to my regular classwork. Also, I'd do a few term papers. She had this idea that learning to write was like learning to play a musical instrument—it takes practice, everyday practice.

22   In math, I was in this remedial program for algebra, geometry, and trigonometry. But unlike high school math, which I thought was devised to boggle the mind for the sake of boggling, in this course I found I could make a connection between different mathematical principles and my life. For instance, there were certain basics I had to learn—call them 1, 2, and 3—and unless they added up to 6 I'd probably be a failure. I also got a sense of how math related to the world at large: Unless the sum of the parts of a society equaled the whole, there would be chaos. And these insights jammed my head and made me feel like a kid on a Ferris wheel looking at the world for the first time. Everything amazed me!

23   Like biology. In high school I associated this science with stabbing pins in the hearts of frogs for fun. Or getting high snorting small doses of the chloroform used for experiments on fruit flies. But in college biology I began to learn and appreciate not only how my own life processes functioned but how there were thousands of other life processes I'd never known existed. And this gave me a sense of power, because I could deal with questions like Why do plants grow? not as I had before, with a simple spill of words: "'Cause of the sun, man." I could actually explain that there was a plant cycle and cycles within the plant cycle. You know how the saying goes—a little knowledge is dangerous. Well, the more I learned, the more I ran my mouth off, especially with people who didn't know as much as I did. . . .

24   To deal with the heavy workload from all my classes, I needed a study schedule, so I referred to my *How to Succeed* book. I gave myself an hour for lunch and reserved the rest of the time between classes and evenings for homework and research. All this left me very little time for friendships. But I stuck to my schedule and by the middle of the first year I was getting straight A's. Nothing else mattered. Not even my family.

25   One night my sister pulled me from my desk by the collar. She sat

me on the edge of the bed. "Mom and Dad bust their ass to keep you in school. They feed you. Give you a roof. And this is how you pay them back?" She was referring to my habit of locking myself in my room.

26   "What am I supposed to do?" I said.

27   "Little things. Like take down the garbage."

28   "Come on. Mom and Dad need me for that?"

29   "You know Dad has arthritis. His feet hurt. You want him to take it down?" My sister can be melodramatic.

30   "Let Mom do it," I said. "Or do her feet hurt too?"

31   "You bastard," she said. "You selfish bastard. The only thing you care about is your books."

32   She was right. I was selfish. But she couldn't understand that in many ways college had become a substitute for my family because what I needed I couldn't get at home. Nobody's fault. She cried. . . .

33   I had learned a vital lesson from these countless hours of work in isolation: my whole experience from the day I received my letter of acceptance enabled me to understand how in high school my sense of self-importance came from being one of the boys, a member of the pack, while in college the opposite was true. In order to survive, I had to curb my herd instinct.

34   Nobody, nobody could give me what I needed to overcome my sense of inadequacy. That was a struggle I had to work at on my own. It could never be a group project. In the end, though people could point out what I had to learn and where to learn it, I was always the one who did the work; and what I learned I earned. And that made me feel as good as being one of the boys. In short, college taught me to appreciate the importance of being alone. I found it was the only way I could get my serious work done.

35   But those days of trial and uncertainty are over, and the open-admissions policy has been eliminated. Anybody who enters the City University's senior colleges must now have an 80 percent high school average. And I am one of those fortunate individuals who in a unique period of American education was given a chance to attend college. But I wonder what will happen to those people who can learn but whose potential doesn't show in their high school average; who might get into street crime if not given a chance to do something constructive? I wonder because if it weren't for open admissions, the likelihood is I would still be swinging baseball bats on the streets on Friday nights.

POSTREADING EXERCISE

Select one paragraph from Rondinone's essay that you think you might be able to use in your own essay on education.

Spend a few minutes writing two or three sentences in which you quote from that paragraph.

Now that you have read the essays by Maria Muniz, Mike Rose, and Peter Rondinone, take fifteen minutes to write about which writer's experiences you have most in common with and which you have least in common with. Then read your comments to the other members of your group or class. Do you all share similar experiences, or do other students have more in common with a different writer than you do?

ACKNOWLEDGING SOURCES

In future writing courses and in your courses in other subject areas, you will probably be assigned research papers requiring you to acknowledge and document sources according to the strict conventions of the particular discipline. Then, you will need to consult a detailed handbook that shows the preferred formats for citing different kinds of works. Here we'll just provide a basic strategy for acknowledging sources that will be all you'll need when you refer to the readings in this text for the following Writing Assignment.

The basic strategy is this: In your introduction to the summary, paraphrase, or quotation, include the *original writer's name;* the first time you refer to the writer's work, you may also want to mention the *title of the essay or book.* At the end of the summary, paraphrase, or quotation, put the *number of the page on which the original material appeared.* The page number goes *in parentheses.* Here are two examples:

Reasons to Acknowledge Sources

- It is only fair to give other writers credit when you use their ideas in your work.
- Your readers may be interested in following up on your source to check the original wording, to find more information, even to read the whole article or book for themselves. When you acknowledge the source, you give them the information they need to do so.

- If you don't get into the habit of acknowledging other writers' words and ideas whenever you use them in your own writing, you might make the mistake of plagiarizing—making it look as if another writer's words and ideas are your own. Whether intentional or accidental, plagiarism can result in a student's failing a course or even being expelled from school.

Quotation: First Reference

In his essay "I Just Wanna Be Average," Mike Rose says, "Students will float to the mark you set" (306).

Paraphrase: Later Reference

Rondinone believes that the open admissions policy at City University rescued him from a life on the streets, and he feels that other young people like himself will suffer because open admissions no longer exists (315).

Note that in both cases, the page numbers in parentheses come before the period at the end of the sentence; with quotations, they come after the closing quotation marks.

This basic method of acknowledging sources is probably all you'll need when your sources are from an assigned textbook in your class. Your readers will already know where you found the essay you are citing, and in fact, some instructors may not even require that you include page numbers.

Keep in mind, however, that if you quote or paraphrase an outside source, you should provide more detailed information about it so that your readers will be able to track it down if they wish. Check with your instructor before using any outside sources.

Checklist for Using Written Sources

- When you summarize a written source, be sure that you restate the main idea clearly in your own words.

- When you paraphrase a written source, be sure that you include all the ideas and supporting detail of the original *in your own words*. If you use special phrases or words from the original, put them in quotation marks.

- If you've quoted from your written source, be sure that you've

  carefully selected quotations so that they are relevant, accurate, and brief

  enclosed the quotations in quotation marks

  quoted fairly so you don't misrepresent your source

Continued

Continued

- Be sure that you've introduced your quotations, paraphrases, or summaries in such a way that your readers will clearly understand the point you are making.

- Be sure that you have acknowledged your sources as completely as necessary for your readers.

WRITING ASSIGNMENT: AN ESSAY ON EDUCATION AND IDENTITY

You've seen in this chapter how education can affect people's lives. It can make people feel like outsiders in some situations and insiders in others. It can change the way they feel about themselves and how they approach the world. Why do you think education has such a powerful effect on people? Use the essays by Muniz, Rose, and Rondinone as well as your own experience as evidence to help show some ways in which education affects how people define themselves. Then suggest some reasons that education affects people in these ways.

Summary of Steps

Here's a summary of steps to take in completing this assignment. Check off each step after you've completed it.

_____ Brainstorm to come up with as many examples as you can of ways in which education changes people's lives. Be sure to consider

- your own experience
- your classmates' experiences
- Muniz's, Rose's, and Rondinone's experiences

_____ Group these experiences so that similar ones are together (such as those that are positive, those that are negative, those that bring people closer to family and friends, and those that pull people apart from family and friends).

_____ Select the groups of experiences that you think you might use for your essay.

_____ Now brainstorm about why education might cause the effects that you've listed.

_____ From your lists, determine what main ideas you'll include in your essay.

_____ Organize your points so that your readers can follow your ideas clearly.

_____ Be sure the introduction clearly indicates your point of view and that each paragraph supports that view.

Student Sample

In the following essay, Jerrold Hawkins, a first-year college student, relates his experiences to those he read about in the essays by Muniz, Rose, and Rondinone.

THE BEGINNING OF LIFE
Jerrold Hawkins

1   What makes education so important? Perhaps it's important because it encompasses so many parts of life. There are not only issues of learning but of social growth as well. The combination of these two helps shape who we are and form what our lives are like.

2   The most difficult part of the education process is discovering where we fit in. Many kids who have early problems in school are labeled bad students. Unfortunately, many react to this and act as they have been labeled. For instance, Mike Rose was mistakenly labeled and placed in lower-level classes even though he was capable of being a good student. It was hard for him to overcome that label and reach his potential because he was bored by the low-level classes; he didn't pay much attention in school, and so he didn't learn much. As Rose says in his essay "I Just Wanna Be Average," "Students will float to the mark you set" (306). I understand what being constantly frustrated in a slow-moving lower-level class feels like because I was put in such classes until the ninth grade. I was bored, too, just like Rose, and so I didn't do well.

3   I also know what the reverse feels like, being in a higher-level class, because I was put in regular classes when I changed schools. I liked the idea of being in regular classes, but I was too far behind. Even though I really worked hard, my classes

were always intimidating for me. I spent most of the time confused, but I never wanted to ask questions to avoid being perceived as stupid. When Maria Muniz describes feeling like an outsider in "Back, but Not Home" (303), I know what she means. I was not in another country, but I still felt separation and confusion for the first couple of years in regular classes.

4   I learned a lot in those years, though. Learning is not always about books, but something much deeper and much more personal. Education goes way beyond grades and report cards. Somehow we must grow socially as well. In "Open Admissions," Peter Rondinone describes a young group that liked "hanging out" and did not care about school. He pretended not to care so he could be part of this group. Yet he wanted to be better and do more with his life (311). What is saddening is that many members of such groups are bright, smart people. However, they do not try in school so they can fit in with the crowd, even though they are capable of being excellent students.

5   I have always been a quiet person, and like many students, it took several years before I felt as though I fit in. I eventually became more comfortable with school and with myself. As a result, I became a better, more well-rounded student. I finally realized how important an education was and how I needed to focus my attention on it in order to be successful.

6   Many people do not realize how difficult going to school is. You must pass your classes, get the required number of credits, and keep your grade point average high. But most important, you must learn who you are and discover what you want to be. School is a small world that we all at one time must learn to survive in.

Peer Review

Once you have your complete discovery draft, you're ready to start peer reviews. Here's a recap of what you need to do.

- Exchange papers with a classmate.
- Be alert to what the writer both succeeds at doing and is having trouble doing.
- Write your peer review, using one of the forms on pages 325–26 and 327–28.
- Talk over your review with the writer for a few minutes.
- Go through the whole process with another classmate.
- After reading the peer reviews of your own draft, complete the Writer's Response to Peer Review forms that follow the Peer Review forms.

Revising Your Discovery Draft

By now you should have a small stack of paper: your notes, your completed discovery draft, and peer reviews written by two of your classmates. With these you can start revising the discovery draft into the final version of your paper, the one that you're actually going to turn in. Here's the process for revising.

- Reread your draft.
- Reread your peer reviews, noting what the reviewers found effective and what they suggested to improve the draft.
- Decide which of the comments you agree with and which you disagree with. (Remember you don't have to agree with or make the changes your reviewers suggest; you have the final responsibility for your essay.)
- Is your main point clear to your readers? If not, consider revising your introduction or your conclusion to make that point more direct.
- Should you add more examples or evidence to help support your ideas? If so, go back to your original brainstorming notes, or brainstorm to discover other experiences you might use. Also, look back at the readings to find evidence you could include from one of these writers that would support your ideas.
- Have you clearly acknowledged your sources, and will readers understand why you have included that source material? If not, add introductions to the source material that will help readers understand.
- Are the paragraphs all in the most effective form? Could some benefit from having a focusing sentence at the beginning or at the end? Can your reader easily determine the main idea of each paragraph? Are the paragraphs well developed and coherent?
- Have you used several long or short sentences in a row? Do you need to vary sentence length to eliminate such a problem? Would sentence combining help?
- After you have written a second draft, reread your revised version. Do you find that your essay is better supported by relevant and well-founded evidence? If

you are still not completely satisfied, you might wish to have another class member read your draft and do another peer review for you.

- Once you are satisfied with the organization, detail, and evidence in your essay, read it carefully to be sure that you've expressed your opinion clearly, that you've used relevant evidence from the readings in this chapter to support your views, and that you've acknowledged those sources appropriately.

- Now you're ready to do the final editing of your essay. First, go over your draft carefully to make sure that all the subjects and verbs agree (see the checklist on pages 75–76), that the pronouns are used appropriately (see the checklist on page 162), that you've avoided sentence fragments (see pages 111–113 and 336–38), and that you've used apostrophes correctly (see pages 242–43 and 351). Then read the following section for more advice on ways to make your sentences as effective as possible.

Editing Your Draft

In editing an essay that uses outside sources, you'll need to check your use of quotation marks and underlining.

Using Quotation Marks

Quotation marks have two major uses:

- To indicate a direct quotation
    from a written source
    in speech and dialogue
- To indicate titles of
    essays
    stories
    poems
    songs

We've shown several examples earlier in this chapter of using quotation marks to indicate quotations from written works. One thing to keep in mind is that in almost all cases, any punctuation should come inside the closing quotation marks:

Maria Muniz remembers "how difficult it often was to grow up Latina in an American world," and she says that as a child she realized that "Latina would always mean proving I was as good as the others."

Note in the following how Peter Rondinone uses quotation marks in a similar way to indicate direct quotation of spoken dialogue:

> "You bastard," she said. "You selfish bastard. The only thing you care about is your books."

We've also shown examples of using quotation marks around the titles of essays: "Back, but Not Home," by Maria Muniz. Use quotation marks in the same way for titles of other short works, such as stories, poems, and songs, as Peter Rondinone encloses a song title in quotation marks in his second paragraph:

> I hung out on a Bronx streetcorner with group of guys . . . and sang songs like "Daddy-lo-lo."

In addition to these general uses, quotation marks can be used to set off a particular word because it is unusual in context or to suggest that the writer is being ironic. Here are two examples from Peter Rondinone's essay:

> I'd seen a friend stabbed for wearing the wrong colors and another blown away with a shotgun for "messin'" with some dude's woman.

> So I did it and graduated with a "general" diploma. I was a New York public school kid.

In the first example, *messin'* is put in quotation marks to indicate that it is a slang term and not at the same level of diction as the rest of the essay. In the second, Rondinone's use of quotation marks indicates that a "general" diploma wasn't worth much.

Similarly, when Mike Rose puts the word *slow* in quotation marks in the following sentence, he indicates both that it is literally what the school thought and that he disagrees with the term:

If you're a working-class kid in the vocational track, the options you'll have to deal with this will be constrained in certain ways: you're defined by your school as "slow"; you're placed in a curriculum that isn't designed to liberate you but to occupy you . . .

Using Underlining and Italics

In handwritten and typed work, underlining serves the same purpose that italics do in word processed or printed work. You may notice that we've used italic type *(like this)* throughout this book to highlight important terms or information. Such extensive use of italics is common in textbooks, where it is important for students to be able to distinguish especially important material easily.

In most writing, however, such emphasis is required much less frequently. The main use of underlining or italics is to distinguish the titles of books, plays, movies, television series, newspapers, magazines, and any other long works or works that contain multiple selections or episodes. In the following example, Mike Rose uses italics for the title of a book and a magazine:

He analyzed poems with us, had us reading selections from John Ciardi's *How Does a Poem Mean?*—making a potentially difficult book accessible with his own explanations. We gave oral reports on poems Ciardi didn't cover. We imitated the styles of Conrad, Hemingway, and *Time* magazine.

METAESSAY

The writing process for this essay required you to do the following:

■ Focus your ideas about the ways education affects people and select evidence to support your ideas.

■ Group similar experiences and select the groups to write about.

■ Determine what causes the changes or effects you chose to consider.

■ Write a discovery draft in which you give examples of changes affected by education and explain why they occurred.

■ Review your classmate's papers and offer suggestions for improvement.

■ Revise your draft, giving special attention to the techniques of quotation, paraphrase, and summary.

Which parts of the writing process were especially easy or difficult for you? In a brief essay, discuss the one most difficult part of the process, and explain how you tried to overcome that difficulty.

PEER REVIEW FORM 1: AN ESSAY ON EDUCATION AND IDENTITY

Writer's Name: _____

Reviewer's Name: _____

First number the paragraphs of the paper you are reviewing. Then write out your answer to each of the following questions. Use the paragraph numbers for reference, and use another page if you need more space. When you have completed this review, tear out this page and give it to the writer.

1. What is the writer's main idea about why education affects people?

_____

_____

_____

_____

2. Does the writer use enough examples to convince you that education changes people's lives in the way he or she suggests? Which are the writer's best examples?

_____

_____

_____

_____

3. What additional evidence would help support the writer's analysis?

_____

_____

_____

_____

4. Note each use of summary, paraphrase, or quotation. Is it always clear why the source material was used? If not, point out any problems, and explain what is not clear.

_____

_____

_____

_____

5. Is the essay effectively organized with adequate transitions linking the paragraphs? If not, suggest some transitions that would be useful.

_____

_____

_____

_____

6. Are there sentences that would benefit from being combined? If so, put brackets around the sentences that could go together, and explain why you think so.

_____

_____

_____

_____

7. Do all the subjects and verbs agree? Circle any verbs that you think don't agree with their subjects, and explain why you think so. (See the subject-verb checklist on pages 75–76.)

_____

_____

_____

_____

8. Do all of the pronouns have clear antecedents? Are all of the pronouns in the correct person, number, and case? Circle any pronouns you think might be incorrect, and explain why you think so. (See the pronoun checklist on page 162.)

_____

_____

_____

_____

9. Are the paraphrases, summaries, and quotations adequately documented? Point out any that aren't, and explain why you think so. (See the Checklist for Using Written Sources on pages 317–18.)

_____

_____

_____

_____

PEER REVIEW FORM 2: AN ESSAY ON EDUCATION AND IDENTITY

Writer's Name: _____

Reviewer's Name: _____

First number the paragraphs of the paper you are reviewing. Then write out your answer to each of the following questions. Use the paragraph numbers for reference, and use another page if you need more space. When you have completed this review, tear out this page and give it to the writer.

1. What is the writer's main idea about why education affects people?

_____

_____

_____

_____

2. Does the writer use enough examples to convince you that education changes people's lives in the way he or she suggests? Which are the writer's best examples?

_____

_____

_____

_____

3. What additional evidence would help support the writer's analysis?

_____

_____

_____

_____

4. Note each use of summary, paraphrase, or quotation. Is it always clear why the source material was used? If not, point out any problems, and explain what is not clear.

_____

_____

_____

_____

5. Is the essay effectively organized with adequate transitions linking the paragraphs? If not, suggest some transitions that would be useful.

_____

_____

_____

_____

6. Are there sentences that would benefit from being combined? If so, put brackets around the sentences that could go together, and explain why you think so.

_____

_____

_____

_____

7. Do all the subjects and verbs agree? Circle any verbs that you think don't agree with their subjects, and explain why you think so. (See the subject-verb checklist on pages 75–76.)

_____

_____

_____

_____

8. Do all of the pronouns have clear antecedents? Are all of the pronouns in the correct person, number, and case? Circle any pronouns you think might be incorrect, and explain why you think so. (See the pronoun checklist on page 162.)

_____

_____

_____

_____

9. Are the paraphrases, summaries, and quotations adequately documented? Point out any that aren't, and explain why you think so. (See the Checklist for Using Written Sources on pages 317–18.)

_____

_____

_____

_____

WRITER'S RESPONSE TO PEER REVIEW 1

Read the peer reviews you received from the members of your group; then fill out one of these forms for each one. (This exercise will help you decide how you want to follow your reviewers' suggestions when you revise your discovery draft. It will also help your reviewers understand how they can provide the most effective information for you.)

Writer's Name: _____

Reviewer's Name: _____

1. Did this reviewer's comments help you see the strengths and weaknesses of your discovery draft? If they were not helpful, what kinds of information and suggestions were you hoping to get?

_____

_____

_____

_____

_____

2. Based on this review, in what ways do you plan to revise your discovery draft?

_____

_____

_____

_____

_____

3. Which of the reviewer's comments and suggestions did you find most helpful? Why?

_____

_____

_____

_____

_____

4. Which of the reviewer's comments and suggestions do you disagree with? Why?

_____

_____

_____

_____

_____

WRITER'S RESPONSE TO PEER REVIEW 2

Read the peer reviews you received from the members of your group; then fill out one of these forms for each one. (This exercise will help you decide how you want to follow your reviewers' suggestions when you revise your discovery draft. It will also help your reviewers understand how they can provide the most effective information for you.)

Writer's Name: _____

Reviewer's Name: _____

1. Did this reviewer's comments help you see the strengths and weaknesses of your discovery draft? If they were not helpful, what kinds of information and suggestions were you hoping to get?

_____

_____

_____

_____

_____

2. Based on this review, in what ways do you plan to revise your discovery draft?

_____

_____

_____

_____

3. Which of the reviewer's comments and suggestions did you find most helpful? Why?

_____

_____

_____

_____

4. Which of the reviewer's comments and suggestions do you disagree with? Why?

_____

_____

_____

_____

_____

SELF-EVALUATION FORM: AN ESSAY ON EDUCATION AND IDENTITY

Complete this evaluation and turn it in with your essay.

Name: _____

Essay Title: _____

Date: _____

1. How much time did you spend on this paper? What did you spend most of your time on (getting started, drafting, revising, something else)? Do you think you needed to spend more time or less time on some of these parts of the writing process?

_____

_____

_____

_____

_____

2. What do you like best about your paper?

_____

_____

_____

_____

_____

3. What changes have you made in your paper since the peer review?

_____

_____

_____

_____

_____

4. If you had an additional day to work on your paper, what other changes would you make?

_____

_____

_____

_____

_____

5. What things would you like your instructor to give you special help with when reading and commenting on this paper?

_____

_____

_____

_____

_____

A SURVIVOR'S GUIDE TO ENGLISH

Your academic and professional success will be enhanced by knowing how to communicate effectively. Part of effective communication involves correct usage because expressing yourself correctly reflects the care with which you present yourself.

It may seem at times as if there are an overwhelming number of usage rules; in fact, though, native speakers understand most of these instinctively. It might also help not to think of them as rules. We prefer to think of them as conventions, some of which may change over time but are for now the accepted ways educated people use language. As an example of a changing convention, consider *shall* and *will*. People used to distinguish between the two, using *shall* for the first person ("I shall wait") and *will* for all others, but now few people use *shall* at all, let alone make such a distinction.

Even though usage conventions change, you still need to be aware of them, and certain ones are too important to ignore. The usage conventions we present here are those that generally give students the most trouble. You'll need to follow them when you write in college or on the job and when you speak with your teachers or boss.

Many of the conventions we cover in this "Survivor's Guide" are summaries of issues we've covered elsewhere in the text. In such instances, we refer you to the fuller discussion so you can easily turn to that section to refresh your memory. As you continue your study of writing, you'll want to consult a fuller handbook of grammar and usage, but this guide contains the minimum you need to know about grammatical conventions.

SENTENCES

Several of the most important errors occur at the sentence level; these are also the errors that readers are most likely to notice first about your writing.

Sentence Fragment

A sentence fragment is part of a sentence (that is, a phrase or dependent clause—see pages 111–13 and 159) treated as if it's a complete sentence.

> *Fragment:* The bright red, expensive sports car.

This is a fragment because it has no main verb; it could be either a subject or an object, but it isn't a complete sentence.

To correct a sentence fragment, either combine it with another sentence, as we describe in the editing sections in Chapters 3, 4, 5, and 7), or rewrite it so it has both a subject and a main verb (see pages 71–76):

> The bright red, expensive sports car *sped around the corner.*

> *The police chased* the bright red, expensive sports car.

Fragments are also often the result of using a verbal as if it were the main verb of a sentence (see pages 197–98).

> *Fragment:* The bright red, expensive sports car *speeding* around the corner.

This problem can be corrected by substituting a true verb for the verbal:

> The bright red, expensive sports car *sped* around the corner.

You can also add a helping verb:

> The bright red, expensive sports car *was speeding* around the corner.

Another common sentence fragment is a dependent clause, punctuated as a complete sentence, following an independent clause to which it should be attached.

> *Independent clause and fragment:* I can usually finish some reading assignments on the bus. Even though commuting to school is mostly a pain.

> *Corrected:* Even though commuting to school is mostly a pain, I can usually finish some reading assignments on the bus.

INDIVIDUAL ACTIVITY

Underline any sentence fragments in the following passages. Then rewrite each passage to correct any fragments.

1. People don't always realize how much they can annoy someone. By saying things they think are funny. My brother, for example. He is six feet five inches tall, and strangers often say things like "How's the weather up there." Which he has heard probably a hundred times. He always nods his head and laughs a little, but he really finds such comments stupid. And annoying. He would rather people didn't make jokes about his height. Even if they aren't intended to be mean.

   _____

   _____

   _____

   _____

   _____

   _____

2. In Arabic, the word *Islam* means "submission to the will of God." Who is called *Allah* in Arabic. The prophet of Islam was Muhammad, who recorded the word of Allah in the Koran. The holy book of Islam. Muslims, the followers of Islam, today occupy much of North Africa and the Middle East. As well as Pakistan and Indonesia. Muslim states are generally very conservative. Civil law often being closely connected to religious law.

   _____

   _____

   _____

   _____

   _____

   _____

Comma Splice and Fused Sentence

A comma splice is two independent clauses (see pages 159 and 203) separated by only a comma.

Comma splice: The driver looked left, the car turned right.

A fused sentence resembles a comma splice: it also has two independent clauses but no punctuation between them.

Fused sentence: The driver looked left the car turned right.

You can correct a comma splice or fused sentence in three ways:

- by linking the two independent clauses with a conjunction (see pages 114–19):

  The driver looked *left, but* the car turned right.

- by separating the two independent clauses with a semicolon (see page 350):

  The driver looked *left; the* car turned right.

- by punctuating the two independent clauses as two separate sentences, each beginning with a capital letter and ending with a period, question mark, or exclamation point:

  The driver looked *left. The* car turned right.

INDIVIDUAL ACTIVITY

In the following passage, indicate in the blank following each sentence whether it is a comma splice (CS), a fused sentence (F), or correct (OK). Then make changes as necessary to correct any sentence errors.

Dream researchers have found that everyone dreams, even babies. _____ We may have as many as four or five dreams a night, we just don't remember our dreams when we wake up. _____ If we do remember them, we don't take them seriously. _____ However, many experts believe dreams are important they can provide us with insights into our feelings and thoughts. _____ We remember nightmares, for example, our subconscious is trying to get us to pay attention to a particular fear or emotional problem. _____ Some experts advise that we pay attention to as many of our dreams as we can. _____ To do that, we have to remember our dreams, it can help if we remind ourselves of this before we go to sleep. With paper and a pencil next to the bed, we can record a dream as soon as we wake up. _____ Then it is important to interpret the dream it may relate to one's current life or to the future in many different ways. _____

Mixed Constructions

A mixed construction is a shift from one type of sentence to another. Such errors most commonly occur when the writer shifts from making a statement to asking a question within the same sentence.

> *Mixed construction:* He asked me, was I going to the movies?

As this example indicates, shifts frequently result from using incomplete quotations or reported speech; the writer begins the sentence as a simple statement about something that happened but shifts at midsentence to an indirect quotation.

You can correct mixed constructions by keeping the declarative statement form:

> He asked me if I was going to the movies.

Or you can use an actual quotation as part of your own sentence:

> He asked me, "Are you going to the movies?"

Dangling and Misplaced Modifiers

Modifiers need to point very clearly to the words they modify. Writers sometimes place a modifier at the beginning of a sentence without providing a later noun that it can modify. This is called a dangling modifier.

Dangling modifier: Looking out the side window, the car crashed.

This sentence is complete—it has a subject and a predicate, after all—but there's no true indication of who or what was looking out the side window. Obviously, the car couldn't do the looking, yet that's what the structure of the sentence indicates. There's no other noun for *looking out the side window* to modify.

Dangling modifiers can be corrected by adding the noun or other term being modified:

While the driver was looking out the side window, the car crashed.

A modifier is misplaced when it appears to modify a noun other than the one the writer intended it to.

Misplaced modifier: Pulling into the station, the passengers were impatient to board the train.

Here the modifier *pulling into the station* seems to modify *passengers,* the closest noun. Misplaced modifiers can be corrected by placing them closer to the noun they actually modify:

The passengers were impatient to board the train pulling into the station.

INDIVIDUAL ACTIVITY

Rewrite each of the following sentences to correct any mixed constructions or misplaced modifiers.

1. Almost eight feet long and weighing over four hundred pounds, the park ranger was attacked by an alligator. _____

_____

2. Many students wonder, how can they afford a college education? _____

_____

_____

3. Working until midnight, the paper was finished. _____

_____

_____

4. Canceled because of snow, at the end of the semester students had to make

up classes. _____

_____

5. My boss asked me, did I finish totaling the receipts? _____

_____

_____

6. Swinging through the trees, the researcher watched the monkeys through

binoculars. _____

_____

_____

7. Impressed by my honesty, I was offered a reward when I returned the lost

watch. _____

_____

AGREEMENT

For a sentence to be both effective and correct, all of its parts must be in agreement. That is, verbs must agree with their subjects, and pronouns must agree with their antecedents, the nouns they refer to.

Subject-Verb Agreement

Verbs have to agree with their subjects. If the subject is singular, the verb must be singular; if the subject is plural, the verb must be plural.

Subject-verb agreement error: *She and I was* going to a street fair.
Corrected: *She and I were* going to a street fair.

See the editing guidelines in Chapter 2, especially the subject-verb checklist on pages 75–76 and the forms of *be, have,* and *do* on pages 73–74.

Noun-Pronoun Agreement

Each pronoun must have a clear antecedent (the noun to which it refers) and must agree with that antecedent in person, number, and case.

> *Noun-pronoun agreement error:* All of the equipment in the gym was expensive; *they* were almost brand new.

Because *equipment* is treated as a singular noun, even though it refers to more than one thing, the pronoun must also be singular:

> All of the equipment in the gym was expensive; *it* was almost brand new.

See the editing guidelines in Chapter 4 for more details, especially the pronoun checklist on page 162.

INDIVIDUAL ACTIVITY

Correct any errors of subject-verb or noun-pronoun agreement in the following sentences.

1. Everyone probably has their favorite movie monster. Mine happens to be the werewolf.
2. Werewolves has been part of European folklore for many years.
3. The first werewolf movie made in Hollywood was *Werewolf of London* in 1934. Then between 1941 and 1948 there was five popular movies starring Lon Chaney as the wolfman.
4. *Abbott and Costello Meet the Wolfman,* the last of the Lon Chaney movies, really takes the story to a ridiculous extreme, but there are people like myself who enjoys it anyway.
5. Each critic has their own opinion, but to me the worst of all the werewolf movies have to be *I Was a Teenage Werewolf.*
6. In terms of the transformation from man to wolf, the best special effects happens in *An American Werewolf in London.* People may find this surprising because it was created without the use of computer technology.
7. Jack Nicholson and Michelle Pfeiffer stars in a more recent werewolf movie, *Wolf,* which is more a psychological thriller than a true monster movie.

Don't use *me, him, her, us,* or *them* as subjects:

Incorrect: John and me are going out.

Incorrect: Laura and her are going with us.

Use *I, he,* or *she* instead:

Correct: John and I are going out.

Correct: She and Laura are going with us.

Articles

*I*n many sentences, the noun will be preceded by an article (*the, a,* or *an*). Generally, the *points out something specific:* "I saw the *dog*" (perhaps you mean the mangy schnauzer down the street that you've talked about earlier). A, on the other hand, is nonspecific: "I saw a dog" (just any dog, not one you expect your listener or reader to know about). An *is used instead of* a *before nouns that start with a vowel sound:* (a, e, i, o, *or* u): "The monkey ate an *orange,* an *apple, and* a *banana in less than* an *hour."*

Adverbs and Adjectives

Adverbs modify verbs, adjectives, or other adverbs; adjectives modify nouns or pronouns (see pages 154–56 and 159). A problem occurs when writers use an adverb where they should use an adjective, or vice versa.

Adjective used but adverb needed: The car sped by *quick.*

Corrected: The car sped by *quickly.*

While an error such as the one above is unlikely for most native speakers, there can be some confusion when the verb in the sentence can be taken to mean two different things. For example, in the sentence "The dog smelled *badly*," the adverb *badly* modifies the verb *smelled,* and the writer is indicating something about the dog's sense of smell. That makes sense if you are talking about an ATF drug-sniffing dog that had to be retired. But if you mean to indicate that the dog stinks, then the sentence should read "The dog smelled *bad,*" using the adjective *bad* to refer to the noun *dog.*

Double Subjects

Avoid using an unnecessary noun or pronoun that creates a double subject for your sentences.

> *Double subject: John and his brother, they* are really mean.
> *Corrected: John and his brother* are really mean.
> *Corrected: They* are really mean.

Sometimes writers will realize that a pronoun isn't clear and try to clarify it by using a noun in parentheses to explain what it refers to. That is another type of double subject.

> *Double subject: They (John and his brother)* are really mean.

If a pronoun isn't clear, don't use it.

> *Corrected: John and his brother* are really mean.

Double Negatives

Be sure that you don't use more than one negative with any single verb. This seems like a fairly minor point, since your meaning would probably be clear anyway; if you write, "I don't got no money," people will understand that you're broke. But it's not a minor error since most readers will see the use of double negatives as an absolutely unacceptable grammatical error, especially in college papers.

> *Double negative:* I *don't* go *nowhere* except to work.
>
> *Corrected:* I *don't* go anywhere except to work.
>
> *Corrected:* I go *nowhere* except to work.

CAPITALIZATION

While just about everyone knows that you should always start a sentence with a capital letter, there are some other uses of capitalization that often give writers trouble. Here are the most common places you need to use a capital letter:

- people's names: George, Bobbi
- titles used with people's names: Dr. Hinkel, Professor O'Brien, Ms. Lago, Prince Albert (But don't capitalize a title when it is used without a name: the doctor, the professor, the prince.)
- the names of companies: General Motors, Microsoft
- acronyms and official abbreviations of companies and other organizations: IBM, GM, NASA, USC
- nations: Nigeria, England
- languages: French, Spanish
- cities, states, and counties: Columbus, Ohio; Franklin County
- the titles of

    books: *Catch-22*

    plays: *Hamlet*

    movies: *The Terminator*

    television shows: *Saturday Night Live*

    short stories: "Young Goodman Brown"

    poems: "The Raven"

    (Don't capitalize articles or prepositions in titles unless they are the first word: *The Naked and the Dead.*)

- days of the week, holidays, and months: Tuesday, July 4, Independence Day
- the call letters of radio and television stations: WCBS, KDKA

PUNCTUATION

Improperly used or missing punctuation often distracts or even confuses readers, so it's important to know the correct use of the most common punctuation marks.

Comma

Use a comma for the following purposes:

- To separate three or more items in a series:

    The building was old, dirty, and deserted.

- To separate independent clauses linked with a conjunction:

    The building was deserted, but the rest of the neighborhood was attractive.

- To set off nonrestrictive elements (see box below):

    Carrie, who is usually so prompt, was late for class today.

Nonrestrictive elements are words, phrases, or clauses that describe rather than restrict or limit the words they modify. Restrictive elements, on the other hand, do restrict or limit the modified words. The following examples may help make this distinction clearer:

All students who have passed Calculus 201 are eligible for the engineering program.

Here the clause "who have passed Calculus 201" restricts the word it modifies—it tells which specific group of students is eligible for the engineering program. If we eliminated the modifying clause, then the meaning of the sentence would change significantly; it would say that all students (regardless of the courses they've passed) are eligible for the engineering program. Since the clause is restrictive, it's an integral part of the sentence and is not set off with commas.

Continued

Continued

Now look at a sentence with a nonrestrictive modifier:

> All students, who are usually happy when they finish finals, will begin their holiday break on December 17.

The clause "who are usually happy when they finish finals" gives some information about students in general, but it does not limit those whose break starts on December 17 to any particular subgroup. If it's dropped from the sentence, the basic information is still the same: break starts on December 17. This modifier, then, is nonrestrictive and is therefore set off with commas.

- To set off such interrupting elements as transitional terms and parenthetical phrases:

> Bill thought, on the other hand, that they should leave now.

- After a subordinate introductory word, phrase, or clause:

> On Tuesdays, I have my biology lab.

See pages 203–5 for more details on using commas.

When Not to Use a Comma

There are lots of times when you shouldn't use a comma, but the most common error with commas is to put one between a subject and its verb. This is especially common with compound subjects, like the following:

> Both Ralph and Martha, went to the movies.

If the subject (or part of it) is directly adjacent to the verb, don't stick a comma between them.

Continued

Continued

You also need to be careful not to use an unnecessary comma after the verb:

He decided, he would go along.

or at places where you might pause for emphasis in speaking:

He decided that, they would have to pay his way.

INDIVIDUAL ACTIVITY

Most of the commas have been deleted from the following two paragraphs, both from essays in Chapter 8 (pages 311 and 319). Add commas as necessary; then check your version against the original.

1. In math I was in this remedial program for algebra geometry and trigonometry. But unlike high school math which I thought was devised to boggle the mind for the sake of boggling, in this course I found I could make a connection between different mathematical principles and my life. For instance there were certain basics I had to learn—call them 1, 2, and 3—and unless they added up to 6 I'd probably be a failure. I also got a sense of how math related to the world at large: unless the sum of the parts of a society equaled the whole there would be chaos. And these insights jammed my head and made me feel like a kid on a Ferris wheel looking at the world for the first time. Everything amazed me!

Peter J. Rondinone,
"Open Admissions and the Inward 'I'"
(page 314, paragraph 22)

2. I also know what the reverse feels like being in a higher-level class because I was put in regular classes when I changed schools. I liked the idea of being in regular classes but I was too far behind. Even though I really worked hard my classes were always intimidating for me. I spent most of the time confused but I never wanted to ask questions to avoid being perceived as stupid. When Maria Muniz describes feeling like an outsider in "Back, but Not Home" I know what she means. I was not in another country but I still felt separation and confusion for the first couple of years in regular classes.

Jerrold Hawkins,
"The Beginning of Life"
(pages 319–20, paragraph 3)

Semicolon

Use a semicolon between two closely related independent clauses:

> They were late for class; the exam had already begun.

See page 339.

Colon

Use a colon after an independent clause introducing a list:

> There are three major highways near my house: US-59, I-35, and I-10.

Period

Use a period in the following instances:

- At the end of a sentence
- After an abbreviation that includes lowercase letters (*Ms., Mrs., St., Dr.*) (Abbreviations using all capital letters generally don't take a period.) The postal abbreviations for states, for example, don't take them: OH (Ohio), NE (Nebraska), nor do common acronyms like NASA (National Aeronautic and Space Administration), FBI (Federal Bureau of Investigation), or CIA (Culinary Institute of America or, if you prefer, Central Intelligence Agency).

Don't Abbrev.

While abbreviations can be very handy, especially when you're writing a discovery draft or taking notes, you should generally avoid them in more formal writing. You can abbreviate such common titles as Mr. *or* Dr. *when they're attached to a name:* Dr. Schwartz; Mr. Jones. *But don't abbreviate them when you're using them as a noun.*

> *Correct:* She went to the doctor.
> *Correct:* She went to Dr. Jones.
> *Incorrect:* She went to the Dr.

- After a person's initials: G. R. Kirk
- With dates and times: A.D. 1558; 2132 B.C.; 12:32 P.M., 9:50 A.M. (The use of periods with both dates and times is optional. You can use A.D. 1558 or AD 1558, and you can write 12:32 P.M. or 12:32 PM.)

Question Mark

Use a question mark to indicate an actual question ("Are you going to the store?") or to indicate a questionable date: "Edmund Spenser, 1552(?)–1599, was an English poet." In cases like the second, the question mark indicates that the date is not known by anyone. If you just haven't bothered to look up a date, you can't appropriately use the question mark to avoid your responsibility for being accurate.

Avoid using the question mark to indicate irony or sarcasm: "He is a very smart(?) person."

Exclamation Point

Use an exclamation point to indicate excitement or shouting:

"Help!" he cried out. "I've been shot!"

Unless you have a very specific reason for using it, though, you should generally avoid using the exclamation point in most college and business writing.

Apostrophe

Use an apostrophe in the following instances:

- To indicate that letters are missing in contractions: don't (do not), can't (cannot), wouldn't (would not).
- To indicate possessives: the boy's book, the horses' collars (As these examples indicate, if the word normally ends in *s,* you can use just the apostrophe, but if it ends in any other letter, you should use both the apostrophe and *s.*

See pages 242–43.

> Never use an apostrophe with a possessive pronoun: his book, her car, its collar. *It's* means "it is," not "belonging to it."

Use a hyphen for the following purposes:

- To join the individual words that make up a compound adjective before a noun or pronoun:

> It was a well-written paper.

Do not use the hyphen, though, if the words follow the noun or pronoun:

> The paper was well written.

- With fractions written out as words:

> one-half, three-quarters

- To break a multi-syllable word at the end of a line:

> While I was looking out the win-
> dow, I saw the crash.

Be sure that such word divisions come only between syllables, though, and never divide a single-syllable word. If you aren't sure where the syllable breaks are, check your dictionary.

Dash

Type a dash by using two unspaced hyphens (--). Use dashes to set off part of a sentence for special emphasis:

> He arrived at noon--a full three hours late--and expected to be paid for the whole workday.

Since you should use dashes only where you want special emphasis, use them sparingly.

Parentheses

Use parentheses to set off brief explanations:

> The Department of Romance Languages (Spanish, French, and Italian) is located in Brown Hall.

Quotation Marks

Use quotation marks to indicate the following:

- Direct quotation from written works:

> James Fallows says that *sodai gami* is "sometimes used to describe husbands who have retired" and are in the way around the house.

- Direct quotation of dialogue:

> "Please get ready now," she said.

- Titles of

> essays: "Back, but Not Home"
> short stories: "The Real Thing"
> poems: "The Canonization"
> songs: "St. Louis Blues"

See pages 300–1 and 322–24.

Italics (Underlining)

Use italics (or underlining) for the following purposes:

- To indicate the name of a

> book: *The Pelican Brief*

play: *Barefoot in the Park*

movie: *Schindler's List*

newspaper: *New York Times*

magazine: *People*

■ To refer to a word:

> The word *and* is a coordinating conjunction.

■ To indicate a foreign term: *sodai gami*

■ To give special emphasis:

> Compared to many of his fans, Tony Bennett is really *old*.

See page 324.

INDIVIDUAL ACTIVITY

In the following sentences, all from essays in this text, some marks of punctuation have been deleted. Add the necessary punctuation as specified at the end of each sentence.

1. In his studies of elementary school mathematics, Stevenson found that the highest scoring American school ranked below the lowest scoring Asian schools. (hyphens)

2. Every eight seconds of the school day, an American child drops out of school 552,000 in the 1987–88 school year. (parentheses)

3. About 60,000 teachers had only a high school education 6,000 schools closed because of a shortage of teachers. (semicolon)

4. I do not say to Cubans, It is time to lay aside the hurt and forgive and forget. (quotation marks)

5. Your attention wavers. You wonder about other things a football game, a dance, that cute new checker in the market. (colon)

6. He analyzed poems with us, had us reading sections from John Ciardis How Does a Poem Mean?—making a potentially difficult book accessible with his own explanations. (apostrophe, underlining)

7. We dont have people on our show to solve their problems, said Burt Dubrow, executive producer of the Sally Jessy Raphael show. (quotation marks, apostrophe, underlining)

8. Its not that we were fascinated by any of the stories or psychodramas that the guests on these shows were relating its more that we couldnt quite believe that people would actually go on television to discuss this stuff. (apostrophes, semicolon)

9. After American school, we picked up our cigar boxes, in which we had arranged books, brushes, and an inkbox neatly, and went to Chinese school, from 500 to 700 PM (colons, periods)

10. I made the attic where my mom kept her steamer trunk my personal domain I wouldnt even allow my sister to come up there with me. (semi-colon, apostrophe)

11. He got angry at me and told me that his father my stepfather had told him he didnt have to listen to me. (dashes, apostrophe)

12. If Raza Hussain, hospital groupie, is not at Baytown General, Hermann Hospital, Ben Taub General, St. Joseph Hospital, or M D Anderson, then he must be at home sleeping. (periods)

13. Iris Rotberg of the National Science Foundation not speaking for that agency, which does not support her views claims that the international assessments on which our students perform so poorly are invalid measures. (parentheses)

14. In a recent op-ed piece (US Schools: The Bad News Is Right), Diane Ravitch suggests that "the greatest obstacle to those who hope to reform American education is complacency." (periods, quotation marks)

15. Theres been a good deal of research and speculation suggesting the acknowledgment of school performance with extrinsic rewards smiling faces stars numbers grades diminishes the intrinsic satisfaction children experience by engaging in reading or writing or problem-solving. (apostrophe, dashes, commas)

SPELLING

English spelling is difficult because it so often seems unpredictable. There are silent letters (like the *n* at the end of *condemn*). And there are strange pronunciations. Just look at *ough:* it's pronounced "uff" in *tough,* but it's "owe" in *though,* "ow" in *plough,* and "oo" in *through.* Sometimes spelling makes strange shifts. We pronounce words, but we talk about their pron*u*nciation. What happened to that *o?* These oddities can all be explained by looking at the history of the English language and how it's changed over the years. But that isn't our purpose here. We simply want to give you a few tips to help you improve your spelling if you're having trouble.

Homonyms

Some of the most common mistakes aren't spelling errors at all; rather, they come from mistaking one word for another because the words sound alike even though they mean very different things. Like this:

> *They're* are *to weighs* to spell *sum* words.
> *Their* are *too weighs* to spell *some* words.
> *There* are *two weighs* to spell *some* words.
> *There* are *two ways* to spell *some* words.

All of those sentences are pronounced exactly the same, but only the last one has all of the words spelled correctly. (This is the kind of sentence that a computer spell-checker would completely ignore; the words are spelled correctly. You can't trust a computer to catch all of your spelling mistakes.)

Here's a list of words that sound the same (they're called *homonyms*) or very nearly the same and so are often confused for each other.

advice / advise (help that you get from someone else / to give advice)

accept / except (to take / to exclude)

ask / ax (to question / a tool to cut with)

brake / break (to stop / to destroy)

build / built (present tense: "I build houses for a living." / past tense: "Yesterday, I built a table.")

coarse / course (rough / class)

choose / chose (present tense: "I choose this." / past tense: "Yesterday, I chose that.")

clothes / cloths (things you wear / material clothes are made from)

conscious / conscience (awake and aware / makes you feel bad when you're wrong) *hear / here* (to listen / where you are right now)

hole / whole (gap, opening / complete)

its / it's (belonging to it / it is)

knew / new (past tense of *know* / opposite of *old*)

lead / led (a metal / guided, taken)

loose / lose (opposite of *tight* / opposite of *win*)

passed / past (gone, completed / a period of time that has passed)

piece /peace (portion, bit / opposite of *war*)

plain / plane (not fancy / aircraft)

right / write (correct / something you do with a pencil or computer)

spend / spent (present tense: "I spend money too quickly." / past tense: "I spent my entire salary yesterday.")

their / there / they're (belong to them / in that place / they are)

theirs / there's (belonging to them / there is)

threw / through (tossed / completed)

two / too / to (2 / also, overly / in the direction of)

your / you're (belonging to you / you are)

weak / week (opposite of *strong* / seven days)

whose / who's (belonging to whom / who is)

woman / women (one female person / two or more female persons)

If you can avoid confusing these words when you write, you'll probably eliminate many of your spelling errors.

Prefixes

Another common cause of spelling problems is misuse of prefixes. A prefix is a syllable or two added to the start of a word to change its meaning. (In *misuse,* the prefix *mis-* adds the meaning "improper" to the noun *use.*)

There are a great many prefixes in English, and knowing them will help you avoid some common misspellings. If you know the prefix *mis-*, for example, and you can spell *spell, inform,* or *use,* then you can also spell *misspell, misinform,* and *misuse.*

When you add a prefix to a word, add the whole prefix, even if the base word begins with the same letter the prefix ends with. The prefix *mis-* ends with *s* and the base word *spell* starts with *s,* so you have to keep both *s*'s: *misspelled.* The same thing would apply to *un-* and *natural: unnatural.*

Here are some common prefixes and some words that they can be used with.

dis-	service	agree
mis-	spelled	taken
over-	rated	looked
extra-	legal	ordinary
il-	legal	logical
im-	moral	possible
non-	entity	conformist
post-	game	traumatic
pre-	eminent	historic
hyper-	active	text
semi-	colon	literate
un-	natural	cooked
mal-	practice	nourished
sub-	standard	marine
trans-	pose	continental

Generally, you shouldn't use a hyphen between the prefix and the base word (for example, you should type *misuse,* not *mis-use*). The exceptions to this rule are words formed with the prefixes *all-, ex-,* and *self-.* They require the hyphen:

> He used to be an *all-around* good athlete, but now he's just an *ex-jock* with a poor *self-image.*

I before E

Finally, don't forget the old rhyme that can help you spell some words with the *ie* or *ei* combination:

> *I* before *e* except after *c*
> Or when sounded as *a,*
> As in *neighbor* or *weigh.*

But don't forget about those *weird* exceptions, like *either.*

INDIVIDUAL ACTIVITY

As you review your papers from this and other courses, note any misspelled words that your instructors or other student readers have pointed out. Use a part of your writer's notebook to keep a spelling log for these words, and refer to it every time you proofread a paper.

INDEX

ACKNOWLEDGMENTS

Cooke, Patrick, "TV Causes Violence? Says Who?" Copyright © 1993 by the New York Times Company. Reprinted by permission.

Dunn, Katherine, "Dallas Malloy: A Contender Regardless of Gender." Copyright © 1993 by *Interview* magazine. Reprinted by permission.

Fallows, James, "Land of Plenty." Copyright © 1989 by James Fallows, as first published in *The Atlantic Monthly*. Reprinted with permission of the author.

Fox, Nicols, "Gawk Shows," from *Lear's* magazine, 1991. Reprinted by permission of Frances Lear.

Giovanni, Nikki, "Shooting for the Moon: Mae Jemison" from *Racism 101* by Nikki Giovanni. Copyright © 1994 by Nikki Giovanni. By permission of William Morrow & Company, Inc.

Hoag, David, "Jim Bellanca," from "Mostly Likely to Succeed," reprinted with permission from *Los Angeles* magazine, June 1991, © *Los Angeles* magazine, all rights reserved. Reprinted with permission of the author.

Kingston, Maxine Hong, "Kindergarten," from *The Woman Warrior* by Maxine Hong Kingston. Copyright © 1975, 1976 by Maxine Hong Kingston. Reprinted by permission of Alfred A. Knopf, Inc.

Leinwand, Gerald, "A Priority for the Twenty-First Century," from *Public Education* by Gerald Leinwand. Copyright © 1992 by Gerald Leinwand and the Philip Leif Group. Reprinted with permission of Facts on File, Inc., New York.

Lowery, Stephen, "Television's Show-and-Tell." Reprinted with permission of the *Los Angeles Daily News*.

Malcolm X, "Learning to Read and Write," from *The Autobiography of Malcolm X,* with the assistance of Alex Haley. Copyright © 1964 by Alex Haley and Malcolm X and copyright © 1965 by Alex Haley and Betty Shabazz. Reprinted by permission of Random House, Inc.

Muniz, Maria, "Back, but Not Home." Copyright © 1979 by the New York Times Company. Reprinted by permission.

"Talk Shows," copyright © 1992 by *The New Yorker*. Reprinted by permission of *The New Yorker*.

Ravitch, Diane, "U.S. Schools: The Bad News is Right," © 1991 by the *Washington Post*. Reprinted with permission.

Rodriguez, Richard, "Aria: Memoir of a Bilingual Childhood," from *Hunger of Memory*. Reprinted by permission of David R. Godine, Publisher.

Rondinone, Peter, "Open Admissions and the Inward I." Reprinted by permission of the author.

Rose, Mike, "I Just Wanna Be Average," reprinted with the permission of The Free Press, an imprint of Simon & Schuster from *Lives on the Boundary: The Struggles and Achievements of America's Underprepared* by Mike Rose. Copyright © 1989 by Mike Rose.

Rotberg, Iris C., "What Test Scores Don't Measure," © 1991 by the *Washington Post*. Reprinted with permission.

Smith, Mark, "Student Protesters Want Their MTV." Reprinted with permission of the *Houston Chronicle*.

Vogt, Jenny. "The Arab Puzzle," reprinted by permission of Jenny Vogt and the *Palm Beach Post*.

Winfrey, Oprah, "When Should Teenagers Be Allowed To Date?" Reprinted by permission of *The Oprah Winfrey Show*.

Wingerson, Dick, "My Old Man," reprinted by permission of the author.